Fools Rush In

Fools Rush In

ANTHEA TURNER

LITTLE, BROWN AND COMPANY

A *Little, Brown* Book

First published in Great Britain in 2000
by Little, Brown and Company

Copyright © 2000 by Anthea Turner

The moral right of the author has been asserted

A CIP catalogue record for this book is
available from the British Library

ISBN 0 316 85499 9

Typeset in Garamond by M Rules
Printed and bound in Great Britain by
Clays Ltd, St Ives plc

Little, Brown and Company (UK)
Brettenham House
Lancaster Place
London WC2E 7EN

Contents

Acknowledgements		ix
Prologue		xi
1	Growing Pains	1
2	The Girl Next Door Grows Up	33
3	A Headless Chicken	58
4	A Bite of the Cake	83
5	A Little Blue Sailing Ship	110
6	The Big Girls' Game	132
7	The Danger Zone	166
8	The Show Must Go On	200
9	*Annus Horribilis*	234
	Epilogue	260

For Mum, Dad, Ruth, Wendy, Pete and Grant

Acknowledgements

There have been very many people who have been kind enough to help me along the way and who need to be acknowledged in this book. Most have already been mentioned in the text, but those who haven't include the following: Paul Chiani; Vivienne Parry and Paul Jackson; Jean-Ann Marnoch; David Young; Peter Salmon; Rob Warr; John Bishop; Marcus Plantain; Jane Moore, Alison McDougal; David Berdgi; Teresa and Paul Bovey; Peter's family – Margaret Powell, Paul, Ali, Sally and Kate Mindelsohn; Alison Astall; Darren Worsley; Julian Alexander and all at Lucas Alexander Whitley; Alan Samson and all at Little, Brown, and last, but by no means least, Wendy Holden. To those I have forgotten to mention, my apologies and thanks.

Prologue

June 1978, Norton, Staffordshire

The sun was high in the sky. Radio 1 was playing somewhere softly in the background, Kate Bush singing 'Wuthering Heights', I think. My sister Ruth was sitting alongside me, sunbathing in the back garden of my parents' bungalow on the outskirts of a small village not far from Stoke-on-Trent. Flicking absent-mindedly through the pages of my sister's *Jackie* magazine I spotted an article on *Grease*, the latest hit film starring John Travolta and Olivia Newton-John, which neither of us had seen yet.

'I'd really love to appear in something like that one day,' I told Ruth, dreamily. 'To dance and dress up and sing my way to stardom. Maybe David Cassidy could be my John Travolta.' Stretching lazily in the sunshine, I allowed myself a few delicious moments to enjoy my fantasy.

Mum had just come out on to the patio with a tray of cold drinks and she joined in with Ruth's laughter. 'I don't know what you're both laughing at,' I told them. 'I *will* meet David Cassidy one day. You see if I don't.' Flopping back on to the sun lounger, I closed my eyes and pretended to concentrate on my tan.

It was a few weeks after my eighteenth birthday. Ruth had just come home from her latest spell in hospital and Mum had suggested that we have a quiet day with our younger sister Wendy, who was somewhere inside playing at dressing up. We'd all spent many hours rummaging around in the big dressing-up suitcase, draping ourselves in cut-offs of lush furnishing fabrics from my father's shop, pretending to be the Liver Birds or the girls in *Man About the House*.

In return for a peaceful day at home, Mum had promised to take me into Hanley later in the week and buy me some material for a new halter-neck dress, which were all the rage. I secretly hoped for a pair of strappy, high-heeled platform shoes and some blue eyeshadow as well, but I knew my penny-wise mother would probably resist my pleas.

I opened my eyes again and reached for a glass of Tizer. Looking up, I noticed that Ruth looked sweaty and a little pale. As if reading my thoughts, she said softly: 'Mum, I don't think I feel terribly well.'

My mother put down her book, checked her temperature with the back of her hand, peered into her eyes and did the things she always did when Ruth was under the weather. 'Why don't you go inside and lie down for a while, darling?' she suggested gently. 'Perhaps you've had a little too much sun.'

She helped Ruth manoeuvre from the sun-lounger into her wheelchair, make her way up the ramp and in through the patio doors. I watched her disappear off into the spare bedroom, the closest and most convenient place for her to lie down. Mum, ever vigilant, followed to see that she was OK.

At times like this, I knew there was nothing much I could do to help. Mum and Dad had always tended to Ruth's every need, leaving Wendy and me largely to fend for ourselves. There was rarely any resentment – Ruth needed their attention and we didn't. Only once do I remember shouting petulantly: 'I wish I was an only child!' after spending an afternoon at the home of my friend Amanda, who had the luxury of her parents' undivided attention.

I lay back and closed my eyes once more. What on earth did I have to complain about? I was well and fit, with a loving family and a great bunch of friends. My passions were acting and dancing in a number of local amateur-dramatics groups, and whatever else was going wrong for me, the minute the footlights came up at the Queen's Theatre, Burslem, life felt good. A smile would creep across my face, there'd be a spring in my step and I could truly sparkle.

My plans for the future were well laid. I hoped to go to college to study performing arts as part of a fine-arts degree before going on to the stage full-time. But first I was toying with the idea of persuading the college to let me have a year out so that I could travel and earn some money.

Hearing a commotion inside the house, I opened my eyes. Jumping up, I pulled my T-shirt quickly over my bikini in case we had visitors. We did: the doctor from the surgery across the road. A few minutes later my dad suddenly appeared, breathless. He was never at home in the middle of the afternoon. I stood, frozen, and watched my mother talking to him urgently in the hallway. There was something about her expression that made my pulse race.

'What's the matter?' I called, but I think I already knew.

'It's Ruth,' Mum said, her voice tremulous. 'She's very poorly.'

She's very poorly.

My mind flashed back to the day Ruth was born – 5 June 1963. I was three years old and very much anticipating her arrival. Up until then, I'd had only Brian the Bear to play with. He was my most treas-ured companion, a present from Dad when he came back from a business trip to Germany. I loved Brian passionately and we went everywhere together, but he couldn't act and he wasn't much of a dancer. No, a baby brother or sister would be much more fun.

Clutching Brian, I'd allowed my father to lead me gingerly into my mother's bedroom. 'You've got a baby sister, Anthea,' he'd told me, 'but she's very poorly. She's going to have to go to hospital.'

The room was full of silent people, including my grandad and 'Daphne's Daddy', who was the local doctor. My mother had sunk back into her pillows, her face grey. There was a smell of disinfectant in the air. I wandered over to the cot just as the midwife, Nurse Carney, adjusted the blanket. There was the tiny baby I'd expected, but not as I'd imagined her, because in the middle of her back was a gaping hole full of blood and pus. Spina bifida meant nothing to me; I just knew that things weren't as they should be. I took a step back and my father ushered me silently from the room.

'Ruth's going to need some special love and attention,' Dad had told me gravely in the kitchen, making me my breakfast.

I nodded solemnly, trying to understand. 'I'll help you and Mummy look after her,' I said, looking up into my father's glistening eyes. He smiled but seemed unable to speak.

Now, almost exactly fifteen years later, Ruth was lying on the bed, pink and struggling for breath. 'I don't feel so good,' she said weakly, her eyes closed. 'I feel dizzy.' Dad sat beside her and patted her hand with that same pinched expression on his face.

When her breathing suddenly became even more laboured, she opened her eyes and stared up at him. 'Help me— Daddy—' she pleaded, taking her breath in great gulps and reaching out to the man who, with my mum, had looked after her every day of her life. 'Help me.'

That was the last thing she said. A few moments later, the gulping stopped and she let out a long, single sigh. Time seemed to stand still as we all stared down at the bed expectantly, waiting for Ruth to inhale. But she never did.

Dad was on his feet in an instant, leaning over her and pounding frantically at her chest. Those huge hands which had so carefully tended her were now vigorously trying to force her stalled heart to beat once more. Mum and I stood in the doorway, rigid, watching silently as Dad pinched Ruth's nose and tried to breathe life back into her while the young doctor did what he could. We were unable to fully take in what was happening, and powerless to help.

I can't remember what it was that finally stilled Dad's hands. I think the doctor must have touched his shoulder and whispered something in his ear. Slumping heavily on the bed, Dad turned to us and said: 'She's gone.'

My mother was beside herself. Her body folded and her mouth opened like that of a creature in pain. My father and I automatically moved towards her but faltered, unsure of what to do, both of us in shock.

Hearing my mother's wails, Wendy, then aged eleven, came running into the room and skidded to a halt. The look of horror and confusion on her face jerked my mother back to life. 'Get her away!' Mum screamed at me. 'Take her away!'

Grabbing Wendy's arm, I dragged her into the garden. We hurried to the far end and crouched side by side under the old apple tree next to the paddock. The ponies chewed the grass contentedly. Nothing had changed in their world.

Everything seemed to go into slow motion. I have no idea how long we stayed there. My knees ached. I told Wendy to stay put while I stood stiffly and cautiously approached the house. Through the patio doors, I could see that the lounge was now full of people, some of whom I didn't know, all of them pale with sadness. There were neighbours making cups of tea, relatives whispering in corridors, doctors and strangers everywhere, I remember thinking: 'Is this really happening?'

Through the lounge window, I saw my father collapse into an armchair, holding his head in his hands, and begin to sob. It was the first time I'd ever seen Dad cry and that shook me more than anything. You never think of your parents as anything other than invincible. Shattered, I scurried back to Wendy.

I didn't cry straight away. I couldn't. Even when I was led in from the garden by my father later that afternoon to kiss Ruth goodbye. She looked very peaceful by then; someone had closed her eyes and arranged her arms across her chest as if she were sleeping.

My mother was in a crumpled heap in a chair in the corner of the room, being comforted by a friend. Her eyes had a deranged look. Dad, his hands on my shoulders, pushed me forward silently and then let go, leaving me swaying at the edge of the bed, unsure of what to do or say.

'Goodbye, Ruth,' I said. My fingers lightly brushed her cheek.

I hurried from that room as quickly as I reasonably could and stood in the hall, leaning against the wall, feeling numb. Looking down, I realised I was dressed only in a bikini and T-shirt. I wondered if I should change.

1

Growing Pains

I loved the name Anthea when I was a child. It was my mum's idea: she named me after a favourite pupil of hers at school, an Anthea Brownrigg. A spirited young thing, by all accounts. I wonder where she is now? Mum chose Anthea because she thought it was a name that couldn't easily be shortened, but she was wrong. People often called me 'Anth', or, more commonly, 'AT'. My father calls me 'Lil' because when I was tiny I used to try to call myself 'little girl', but it used to come out as 'lil girl'.

It could have been a lot worse. My middle name is Millicent, after my maternal grandmother. Millicent Martin might have made it on to the stage, but I'm not sure Millicent Turner would have done.

I was born on 25 May 1960, at the very start of the Swinging Sixties. Harold Macmillan was prime minister, John. F. Kennedy had announced his intention to run for president of the United States and 'Cathy's Clown' by the Everly Brothers was Number 1 in the UK pop charts. I was a healthy baby, delivered after just thirty minutes of labour, except that my left leg went both ways, forwards and backwards, due to an unusual knee joint, which fortunately sorted itself out as I grew. I was also born with the 'Turner ear': the top of my right ear looks as if it has been sliced off. It is an hereditary trait I am proud to share with my Uncle Michael and a cousin. My father was at my mother's side throughout the home delivery and, once it was all over, he threw the afterbirth on to the rose garden to improve the soil quality. He always grew the best roses.

My parents, Jean and Brian, were both from the small rural village of Norton-in-the-Moors, Staffordshire. They'd first met properly on the school bus when they were teenagers, although, living in the same small community, they'd been aware of each other long before. 'I'd always liked the look of him,' my mother would say enigmatically. My father would simply smile.

They married when Mum was twenty-four and Dad twenty-one, having both gone on to higher education – each the first members of their respective families to gain a degree, my father in geology and mining engineering at Birmingham University and my mother in theology and teaching at Whitelands Ladies' College. Mum had been bolstered by her religious faith since childhood, and it had helped her enormously when her own mother died of lung cancer just after my parents married. An only child, Mum was very close to her mother and missed her tremendously – it still hurts her to talk of her death – but she found comfort in the Church.

As was the norm in our area in the 1950s, Dad went straight down the mines after college, starting his apprenticeship in the pits of the local Silverdale and Whitfield Collieries. As a graduate, he had every expectation of working his way up to management level and soon acquired his manager's certificate. He'd already started on that career path by the time I was born, travelling to Germany with the Coal Board to find out how mines were run in the Rühr Valley and bringing me back the best present I've ever had, Brian, the hump-backed teddy stuffed with straw.

At just twelve weeks old, I took to Brian the Bear instantly. He became my lifelong companion and the only male, apart from my father, never to let me down. From the day Brian came into my life we have never been parted. That poor creature has been squeezed and hugged, cried over and laughed with on countless occasions. His left ear is still stained with Ready Brek from a misguided childhood attempt to feed him.

The writing was already on the wall for the mining industry and the only jobs available were those filling dead men's shoes. So when my grandfather offered my father a job alongside his elder brother Michael in the family cabinet-making business, Dad decided to take him up on it and turn his back on the pits for good.

Turner & Sons began at the turn of the century by making coffins and loo seats. If they'd stayed in that line of business, they might still be around today, but after the Second World War there was an increasing demand for soft furnishings and fitted wardrobes, so the company diversified. It was a family business in the very old-fashioned sense, with my wonderfully unconventional grandmother, Doris, typing and keeping the books.

Doris was a remarkable woman, well known in the village, chiefly for her unusual dress sense. The lady I knew as 'Nana' was a vision in tulle and wore a different hat every day. One of her favourite outfits was a skirt made from a tablecloth I'd eaten off in my early life, on to which she'd sewn roses cut from some remnant of Turner & Sons curtain fabric. 'I applicked these on myself,' she'd announce proudly (she meant appliquéd). 'Do you like them, Anthea?' Nor did she confine her quirkiness to herself. All around the house were oversized dolls which she dressed extravagantly. When my father was a boy, she'd even dressed him as a girl in pretty smocking tops, because she desperately wanted a daughter and already had a son. She lived in a fantasy land where tea was always served on the best bone china and spent many happy hours writing a daily diary filled with the musings of a true eccentric. It was all a bit Miss Havisham.

My grandad, Vincent or 'Vin', was a long-suffering man who'd inherited the family business on his return from the First World War – he'd actually been too young to enlist, but like many young lads wanting to go off to war with the rest of the young men from his town of Burslem in the so-called 'Pals' Regiments', he'd lied about his age. Possessing a natural talent with wood, he took to his new responsibilities with enthusiasm, and under his gentle guidance the company flourished. He was a lovely old man who always called me 'my dear'. I sometimes wondered if he'd forgotten my name.

Grandad had always hoped that his two sons would follow him into the family firm. Michael, being painfully shy and slightly less academic than my father, jumped at the chance and joined straight after school. Dad, who'd developed an early fascination with rocks as an avid fell-walker and youth-hosteller, wanted to see a bit of the world first. He went to Woolstanton Grammar School and on to university to try to turn his hobby into a profession. Realising that there were not many career opportunities for geologists, he moved sideways into mining engineering, which is how he ended up at the rock face in Silverdale, chipping away for coal. By the time Grandad asked him to join Turner & Sons at their premises in Newcastle Street, Burslem in 1964, Dad knew in his heart of hearts that mining management wasn't for him. 'I'll give it a go for a few months,' he told my grandfather, embarking on a career that was to last until his retirement thirty years later.

I was born in the house where my mother was born, a brick-built, pebble-dashed 1920s bungalow called Clentville in the shadow of the Derbyshire moors. Clentville was on the other side of the Norton crossroads from two other bungalows: Morningside, where Dad had grown up, and Holly Fields, built by my Great Aunt Flossie and her husband Shad, to which we moved when I was sixteen, and where my parents still live. By the time I came into the world, Clentville was filled with lovely furniture made by my father and Uncle Michael, including a chest of drawers hand-tooled out of local oak, crafted by my father as a feature of my nursery. Generations of Turners have been cabinet-makers, and I've always been surrounded by quality furniture which has bound me to the history of my family.

In such simple but idyllic surroundings, and with wonderful parents, my childhood years were unerringly happy. My earliest memory is going on holiday to Rhyl to spend a week in a caravan owned by our neighbours, Fanny and Arthur. I must have been two and a half. I remember there were hens around and I was afraid to take my clothes off in case they pecked me. When I played on the beach, my mother tucked my dress into my knickers so that it wouldn't get wet. To me caravanning seemed so exciting, with the novelty of lighting fires and fetching fresh water in a can, but Mum vowed afterwards that she would never go again.

When Ruth arrived in our lives, nothing seemed to change at first, despite her illness and the trauma that must have accompanied it for my parents. I don't remember ever feeling jealous of all the attention she needed. My parents had been thrown in at the deep end and there was a steep learning curve to be negotiated. Spina bifida was certainly not something they had known anything about, but they soon became experts. It is a congenital defect, affecting some 2,500 babies a year in the sixties and seventies, in which one or more of the vertebrae in the spine fail to develop completely, leaving a portion of the spinal cord exposed and vulnerable to injury and causing various degrees of disability in the lower back and kidney area. Ruth was actually very lucky: in the year she was born a new operation was devised to prolong the lives of those with the condition.

From the waist up, she was a normal baby, happy and smiling, and didn't look remotely unusual. But from the waist down she was a severe case. She had no sensation at all, little use of her left leg and no real use of her right. She was also destined to be incontinent for life, trapped in a body that wouldn't work and which would require a series of operations. Her mind, however, was pin-sharp.

Some of my earliest memories are of taking my special 'hospital basket' full of crayons and paper and sitting on the floor drawing by her bed during the daily visiting ritual. I was too young to understand that Ruth was suffering or how terribly anxious my parents must have been about her. To me, it was just a reassuringly familiar routine, and I still find the smell of hospitals strangely comforting.

Once they were finally allowed to bring her home, Mum and Dad were adamant that Ruth should be treated no differently from any other member of the family. They refused to allow her to be sent away to a special school which, in those days, mixed mental and physical handicaps and were incredibly institutional. So instead of going back to work as a teacher after the birth, as she'd planned, my mother gave up her job at the local school and taught Ruth herself.

I don't think I even realised there was anything unusual about the newest member of our family until she grew older and showed no signs of leaving her pushchair. 'Why can't Ruth toddle like all the other children, Mummy?' I once asked.

'Because not everyone is blessed with two legs that work,' Mum said. 'Remember that.'

She might not have been able to walk, but Ruth was the fastest crawler on two arms I'd ever seen, and when she progressed to a wheelchair she became even more mobile. We fought like cat and dog over toys and territory, just like any sisters. 'She's *mine*,' I'd say, snatching my Sindy doll from her hands after she'd scuttled across the floor to grab it, 'and you can't play with her.' My mother, who'd longed for siblings as a child, would cry when we quarrelled and plead with us to get on with each other. Poor woman, she never understood that ours were just normal, everyday squabbles.

Disability wasn't well catered for in the 1960s and there were no special ramps or lifts for wheelchairs, so whenever we went anywhere as a family, we always seemed to end up using the service life or the back door. If we went to a restaurant, the waiting staff would look straight through Ruth and ask Mum: 'And what would *she* like?'

'Why don't you ask her yourself?' we'd say, indignant on Ruth's behalf.

My sister was physically handicapped, not in the slightest mentally impaired, as I was at pains to tell everyone who dared suggest other-wise. It was only later, when I began to go through a slightly self-conscious stage, that I felt uncomfortable about having her with us. I realised we were being treated differently because of Ruth. I wanted to be like all the other girls and I was sometimes very resent-ful of the wheelchair, wishing for my own selfish reasons that Ruth could walk.

When I was seven and Ruth was four, Mum became pregnant again. I was too young to appreciate how brave she was to risk having another child, for there was a fifty-fifty chance of it having spina bifida. All I knew was that I was very excited about the forthcoming birth and so was Ruth. We'd touch my mother's bulging stomach and try to talk to the baby through her clothes.

'You can name the baby when it arrives,' Mum told us one day. Thrilled by the prospect, Ruth and I scoured our children's books for inspiration. Reading *Peter Pan* together, we latched on to the perfect name if the baby turned out to be a little girl.

'Tinkerbell,' we announced proudly. 'We want you to call the baby Tinkerbell.'

My mother nearly fell off her chair. Clearly having second thoughts about the wisdom of her decision, she put down her sewing and called us over to her. 'And did you choose Tinkerbell after the fairy in *Peter Pan*?' she asked. When we nodded, she said gently: 'Well, Tinkerbell was rather naughty, wasn't she? Don't you think Wendy's a much nicer name?'

As soon as I heard the new baby cry a few months later, I was once again led into my parents' room by my father to meet our new little sister. 'This is Wendy,' he said, beaming. 'And she's perfect.'

Wendy was, indeed, the perfect little doll with her blonde hair and green eyes. Ruth and I helped look after her from an early age, taking delight in dressing her and bathing her, just as I had my Tiny Tears doll, and Wendy seemed to know that we adored her. At her christening in Longsdon village church, she screamed her lungs out, bawling and bawling while we stood at the font. Neither Mum nor her godmother could do a thing with her. 'Pass her down to Anthea,' my Mum whispered, handing the wriggling, white-robed bundle to my father. The screaming baby came down the line of relatives until she reached me. Taking her in my arms, rocking her gently and allowing her to suck on my little finger, I managed to quieten her down in a matter of seconds. She gurgled happily throughout the rest of the service.

With three young children and my mother no longer bringing home a wage, money was tight. My parents didn't smoke or drink, my mother made most of our clothes and we could afford only bucket-and-spade holidays. But Mum and Dad were never frugal. Our home was our castle, and everything went into it. There may have been few expensive Christmas presents or lavish birthday gifts, but we rarely felt hard done by because of the thought that went into what we did have. The best Christmas present I ever received was a little shop Dad built for me, complete with a till that rang a miniature bell. I was the envy of all my friends. I lived in a warm and welcoming house, with beautiful furniture, a big garden full of fruit trees and I went on holiday to a self-catering flat in Tenby on the

Pembrokeshire coast for a week each summer. What more could I want?

Tenby was always a delight. It took four and a half hours to get there in my Dad's Austin 1800, and the holiday really began when we stopped for a fish-and-chip lunch in Sennybridge, mid-Wales. I remember only wonderfully sunny weather, although it must have rained sometimes. We spent most days on the beach. Mum and Dad would lay blankets on the sand and set up a little stove to make tea. I loved clambering over the rocks and if there was anything else to climb, I'd be up it. Mum would have kittens over my escapades. 'Brian, Brian, make her come down, she'll only hurt herself,' she would call to my father.

Wendy, Ruth and I would spend hours building sandcastles and writing our names in the sand. We'd collect hundreds of shells to take home to decorate picture frames, lampshades and bottles. The flat we stayed in had bunk beds, and Wendy and I always fought over who had the top one. I usually won. During one of my worst arguments with Wendy, when I was being particularly beastly, I'm ashamed to say that I threatened to throw her over the balcony if she didn't shut up.

One year I spent my birthday in Tenby and was given a pair of roller skates. I remember hurtling down a hill on them, screaming at the top of my voice. The following year, Mum and Dad let me go for a walk on my own for the first time ever, because they thought it was probably safer in Tenby than at home. Carefully selecting my outfit for this solemn occasion from the dozens of clothes I'd packed and repacked a hundred times before the holiday, I chose a green Crimplene bell-bottom trouser suit Mum had made for me, slung a crocheted bag over my shoulder and set off, confident of how fabulous I looked. In the evenings, we'd stroll around the town, have fish and chips, maybe visit the amusement arcade, and then wander back to the flat for an evening of Monopoly or Snakes and Ladders. They were magical days.

Growing up in the same small village as my parents, grandparents, uncle and cousins gave me a tremendous sense of belonging. Uncle Michael was a quiet and thoughtful man, but always very kind. As a boy he'd been so shy he would climb out of the bedroom window and hide if anyone came to call. His wife, Eileen Winkle, was equally shy, but we'd still share Christmases and birthdays and family occasions. Their two children, Tim and Lindy, often played with us when we were young.

We were often entrusted to the care of our grandad while Mum and Dad went to hospital to see Ruth. My mother's father, widowed and living with us, was a retired engineering worker and Harold Wilson's number one fan. He kept hens and grew vegetables in his corner of the garden and I remember helping him collect the eggs. 'Come on, now,' he'd say to me. 'Pick them up gently.' He was heavily involved in union matters and would go off to meetings with his friends, a motley collection of men who nonetheless all looked the same in their coats, scarves, gloves and trilby hats. They smelled musty. I think he could be quite stubborn sometimes, and I'm sure there must have been tensions in the house between my parents and Grandad, though I don't recall any.

One morning when Grandad had taken an unusually long time in the bathroom, I heard Mum banging on the door to get him out.

'Dad? Dad? Are you in there?' she was calling as I was getting ready for school.

'What's the matter, Mum?' I asked, pulling on my coat.

'It's your Grandad,' she said, frowning. 'I can't get any reply. He's been in there ages.'

Fetching a vanity mirror from my bedroom and sliding it half in and half under the door, just like I'd seen people do on television, I tilted it to see what was happening inside. 'All I can make out is a sort of untidy pile of clothes on the floor,' I reported to my mother.

She told me not to worry and hurried me off to school. When I came home for lunch a few hours later, the house was full of people milling about. Finding Mum, I asked her: 'What's happened?'

She smiled sadly and brushed the hair from my face. 'Grandad's gone to see Jesus,' was all she said.

My grandparents on my father's side were in the rudest of health. Nana was still floating around Norton in her weird and wonderful outfits while Grandad continued to run Turner & Sons. We loved them: they were never too 'hands-on' with us or over-fussy. I remember my grandmother starting to knit a jumper for me when I was very young and by the time it was finished, it fitted Wendy. Nana would spend hours at her kitchen table, sewing, knitting or gluing something together; or just writing letters to people she didn't know – artists whose paintings she'd bought or authors whose books she'd read. She used to strike up quite a correspondence. Everything was always very flowery – she addressed everyone as 'my dearest darling'. She and Grandad had the most marvellous marriage and when she eventually died there was little reason for my grandfather to live.

One of my favourite childhood treats was to play in Nana's wardrobe, which was filled with all manner of delights for a child. She had dainty stiletto shoes with pieces of lace, roses or feathers she'd stitched or glued on to them, flamboyant scarves, gaily coloured gloves and her millions of outrageous hats. It was a veritable treasure trove. I'd sit on the floor, festooning myself with beads and layers of vividly patterned scarves and floral skirts, pretending to be Twiggy while singing my favourite song of the moment, 'Lily the Pink'. Flower Power had nothing on me and Nana.

Grandad preferred outdoor pursuits. He never took a driving test and was the most frightening driver I've ever known. He was completely fearless and showed little regard for other road-users. When we were small, he'd tie a rope to the back of his Mini, attach a spare wheel to it and tow us – hanging on for dear life – around the meadows near his bungalow. 'Only scream if you fall off,' he'd tell us, before sticking the car in first gear and zooming off. We adored him.

Norton was the centre of my universe. Its green-field boundaries were my horizons. I could never imagine leaving. On the rare occasions that we stepped outside its parish limits, I was always a little fearful. Even as an adult, I've never truly enjoyed long trips abroad. My father was the same. He'd even transferred his degree from Birmingham University to Stoke-on-Trent Technical College as a young man because he was homesick. Unlike him, I did eventually put Norton behind me, and long before it grew into a sprawling town of council houses and new homes with just a few pockets of farmland left. But because my parents still live there – on an oasis of green belt just on its periphery – and because I visit them often, it will always be home.

By the age of seven, I had started to show early promise as an enter-tainer. I'd always felt happiest performing. It was a wonderful antidote to my schoolwork, with which I was floundering dreadfully. I started taking ballet lessons, first locally in Norton and then in Hanley under a woman called Beryl Cooper, who taught me the Royal Academy syllabus. Beryl was tall, statuesque and dark with a great pair of legs. She chain-smoked and had been quite famous in her day as the founder of the Hanley Babes, a local dance troupe. She was the first teacher I'd ever had who wasn't lying when she said I was doing well.

'Come on now, everyone watch Anthea,' she'd say in her husky, smoke-stained voice. 'Plié and jeté, remember? One, two, three.' Her classes were held in the Methodist church hall at Birches Head, Hanley which – to our great excitement – was used to film part of the BBC's adaptation of Arnold Bennett's *Clayhanger*. Halfway through the filming, curiosity got the better of two of my fellow dance pupils and me, and we popped our heads up over a wall to take a closer look.

'Cut!' shouted the director angrily as our smiling faces spoiled the shot. 'Will someone please get those girls away?' It was the first, but not the last time Anthea Turner ended up on the cutting-room floor.

Like most little girls, I dreamed of being a prima ballerina like Margot Fonteyn and was never happier than when tying up the laces of my pink satin pumps. I truly felt that this was something I could one day make a career of. That or acting. From the earliest age I cajoled Ruth and Wendy into helping me put on little one-act plays for my parents at home or at Sunday school. The plots were all improvised from our favourite books: Enid Blyton's Mallory Towers series, *The Secret Garden*, *The Lion, the Witch and the Wardrobe* and *The Borrowers*. I was director, producer, prompt and, of course, star.

One of my greatest childhood moments was being chosen from the primary school to play a cherub in the junior school nativity play. I didn't have to say or do anything, I just had to do my best to look like a cherub, which I sort of did anyway with my big green eyes and my strawberry blonde kiss-curls. It was the first time in my life I'd worn theatrical make-up. I was given red lips and blue eyeshadow with black ticks at the side. The scent of Leichner make-up has never left me. I remember thinking, 'I like this,' and refusing to wash for days.

I developed a fascination for make-up. On a Friday afternoon Mum went off to the local hairdresser for a wash and set, and as soon as her car disappeared, I'd sneak into her bedroom and get out her make-up, jewellery, clothes and shoes. With my long, blonde hair parted to one side and plugged behind my big ears, I'd try on everything and parade around in front of the mirror, speaking lines I'd memorised from books or television shows I'd seen. *Andy Pandy* was a great childhood favourite and I loved playing Looby-Loo, or Little Weed in *Bill and Ben*. Wiping off all the rouge and powder with a tissue, I'd flush the evidence down the loo and carefully put everything back in its place again before Mum came home.

This went on for years, and part of the excitement was my belief that my mother never knew what I was up to, but of course she did. Dad would apparently watch me with great amusement through the bedroom window and report back to her on a weekly basis. But she never said a word. The smell of my Mum's Dior lipstick will always remind me of her. Whenever I'm homesick, I buy some just to sniff during weak moments.

Our huge dressing-up suitcase was almost as good as Nana's wardrobe, and we'd spend hours in costume in the spare room, or 'theatre', pretending to be queens and empresses, cowboys and Indians, sorcerers, wizards and witches. Pat, our scruffy mongrel dog, was enlisted in every production despite having the most terrible breath. His roles ranged from donkey to sheep, camel or horse, depending on the theme. We would parade around in crowns and cloaks. Wendy and Ruth usually had their own agendas, too. Wendy and I would fight tooth and nail over a little red cape Mum had made from a pair of old curtains as a Little Red Riding Hood costume. Wendy would usually win.

Ruth had a different dream. 'I want to be the fairy princess,' she'd say, never happier than when dressed in layers of shimmering tulle with a wand and glittering tiara. I'd almost always give in to her, because she looked so adorable in her costume, but she was never as enthusiastic when I cast her in other parts. I remember once getting terribly cross with her because she got a fit of the giggles halfway through a rehearsal of a weightier production – the birth of Jesus Christ.

'You're not taking your role seriously enough,' I scolded. 'You're meant to be the Archangel Gabriel, not Andy Pandy!' That only made her giggle even more, and before long Wendy and I were in hysterics on the floor next to her, laughing until our ribs hurt.

Birthdays were taken very seriously in our family and were something to look forward to. Ruth, Wendy and I always had a joint celebration, as our birthdays were only twelve days apart. There'd be balloons and party hats and special party frocks to wear. Trestle tables would be placed out in the garden, groaning under the weight of jellies and jams and cakes and sandwiches. Anything sweet would be covered in multicoloured hundreds and thousands and, in the turbo-charged gaps between scoffing as much as we could, we'd play treasure-hunt games in the garden, looking for tiny, silvery-coloured sticky stars which Mum had secreted everywhere, licking them and sticking them on to our forearms.

The first film I was ever taken to see, by Mum, was *Snow White and the Seven Dwarfs* at the Odeon in Hanley. I was immediately completely hooked. Mum brought me an ornate little antique mirror afterwards as a memento. 'This is something to look after and treasure,' she told me gravely. 'If it gets broken, you've only yourself to blame.' I carried it home like a baby, cradled in my arms. I still have it.

The next film that had any impact on me was *The Sound of Music* with Julie Andrews, which entranced me even more. I saw all those children running through the fields dressed in old curtains, just like some of the outfits Nana made, and I thought, 'That's it! That's me!'

From then on, I nurtured a secret ambition to play Liesl one day and sing: 'I am sixteen, going on seventeen . . .'

My first official theatrical engagements were at Norton Primary School, when I was old enough to take part in the school plays. I was eight when I was given my first major role as the Sandman in *Hansel and Gretel*. I wore a gold dress which Mum had made for me and which I still keep. I didn't have to speak, just dance, sprinkle fairy dust and put Hansel and Gretel to sleep in the woods. In the next production, I was promoted to moonbeam. Mum made an outfit in silver with circular moons and tulle around the bottom. After that, I was a nightingale in the Chinese story of the emperor and the nightingale, and had to perform a short ballet.

My first speaking part was as Sheherazade at the age of eleven. I had to say: 'Let me tell you a story,' and I delivered my speech with great deliberation. Some of the kids had teased me about my 'posh' accent, but I showed them. I still have the outfit I wore for that as well, again made by Mum: loose pantaloons with a bit of netting around them for a skirt; a matching top; a hat fashioned from a Blue Band margarine tub lid covered in a piece of elastic and netting, all in black and gold. It was very *Blue Peter*.

The school was famed for its middle-school production under the guidance of a woman called Marguerite Moss, a good friend of my mother's, who became my greatest artistic influence. People came from far and wide to see her shows, which were very ambitious for a small school and were staged for not one, but four consecutive nights. I loved taking part. Whenever I was on stage, I felt completely at ease. I'd think: 'This is OK; I can hold my own up here.' No one was going to ask me any questions or make me spell something and, for the duration of my turn, all eyes would be on me.

My schoolwork was a different matter entirely. My parents were always very encouraging, but even they could see that I wasn't academic. 'Never mind, Anthea,' Mum would say while I struggled with my homework, my brain feeling like an untidy filing cabinet. 'You might not make it to university, but everybody's good at something.' She knew I was better at dancing and acting, but, as a teacher herself, she also knew that I had to be nudged into achieving what I could at school. My parents did all they could to help me and at Norton Primary School, I couldn't have had a better environment in which to be educated.

Within walking distance from our bungalow (we always came home for a lunch of baked beans and home-made chips), the school was an extraordinary place. My teacher was a wonderful woman called Miss Sutton, who'd lost both her legs after slipping and falling under a train. She'd taught my mum at the same school many years before. Quite apart from always finding extra time for me, Miss Sutton kindly arranged for Ruth, who was very bright, to come into my class once a week and join in. Miss Sutton gave her every encouragement and enabled her to achieve the best she could academically. We also played the recorder together. '*Frère Jacques*' never sounded so bad. With both our teacher and my funny and capable sister in wheelchairs, every member of my class was brought up to appreciate my mother's maxim that not everyone is blessed with two legs that work.

Our headmaster was a lovely man called Alan Bales, who had been a Japanese prisoner of war during the Second World War, an event which had obviously affected him very deeply. Thereafter, he refused to practise any corporal punishment at all and adopted a truly marvellous way of running a school. He was a man of great kindness and intelligence and we all benefited under his tutelage.

But no matter how much they all motivated me, I still found it very difficult to get to grips with my work, English in particular. My reports spoke glowingly of my concentration and effort, but my written work always let me down. Some of the boys in my class teased me for my stupidity. They'd laugh out loud each time I made some howling mistake with a word. They'd even follow me home sometimes, throwing taunts and calling me 'Posh' (it was my nickname long before it was Victoria Beckham's). One day they threw clods of mud at me even as I walked up my own driveway. My friends rallied round me and told the bullies where to get off – I was never very good at standing up for myself.

I was growing more and more frustrated by my inability even to keep up with the rest of the class. My parents never made me feel that I hadn't matched up to their expectations, but I knew I'd fallen short of my own. Leaving Norton Primary School at the age of eleven was a terrifying prospect. At least there, I felt, the staff understood me. At Holden Lane Secondary School, a ten-minute drive away, nobody seemed to. I took an entrance exam which would decide which stream I was placed in but, through a combination of nerves and poor brainwork, I could provide only half the answers. At that time it was assumed that if you couldn't spell, you couldn't do anything else. Spelling was used as a barometer for your general intelligence. My spelling was awful so, without being given a second chance, I was classified as a dunce and dumped in the lowest stream. All my friends from Norton were in the higher CSE and O-Level streams, but I wasn't even being pushed towards O-Level standard. I felt utterly disposed of. Everything about that giant comprehensive was horrible. Even the way we lined up in the playground emphasised my place in the pecking order – 'cleverest' forms first and 'stupidest' last.

In such a negative atmosphere, I changed from a cheerful, ebullient girl into a quiet, miserable little thing with no confidence at all. My astute mother soon picked up on my unhappiness. She went to see the staff in an attempt to have me moved up to be with my friends, insisting that I would be able to keep up, but they wouldn't have it. 'I'm afraid Anthea simply isn't bright enough,' they told her. 'She'd only hold the others back.' I'd get home after school and lie on my bed, listening to my Donny Osmond records and sobbing my socks off.

In the winter of 1972, six months after starting at the new school, I fell off the slide in the playground and broke my wrist badly. I had to go to hospital for it to be reset, but because I was so depleted physically and mentally, I never recovered properly from the anaesthetic. A few days later, sitting on a wall outside during a bitterly cold PE lesson, unable to join in because of my wrist but dressed in my gym kit nonetheless, I asked my teacher if I could go inside and get warm. 'I'm not feeling too good, Miss,' I told her, shivering visibly. But she refused to let me leave the rest of the class. Within twenty-four hours I'd caught a bad cold, which turned into pneumonia.

I didn't mind being ill one little bit, because it meant I could be at home with Ruth and Mum, and didn't have to go to the school I'd come to detest. I lay in bed, reading magazines and listening to my records or to Radio 1 and wishing that I could stay there for ever. My convalescence took several weeks and I did all I could to delay the evil day when I'd have to return to school. 'I don't think I feel well enough to go back yet, Mum,' I'd moan, feigning illness.

After several days' procrastination, Dad finally sat down on the edge of my bed and said to me: 'Now, I think there's more to this than you're letting on, Lil. How are you getting on at school?' Depressed and afraid, willing myself not to get better, I burst into tears. The floodgates had opened, and over the next few days, Mum and Dad and I talked a lot about how miserable I really was and they began to fully appreciate how much I was dreading returning to the classroom.

They decided to make inquiries to see whether they could find another school for me. Their great friends Bert and Jean Foden re-commended St Dominic's High School, a Catholic grammar school in Hartshill, Stoke-on-Trent run by Dominican nuns, which their daughter Amanda, a friend of mine, attended. The problem was that it was a fee-paying school and my parents were hardly in a position to pay for my education. Nevertheless, they went to see the head-mistress, a kindly woman called Sister Mary Edwards, who told them enthusiastically: 'Our policy is to turn out happy, confident human beings.' They took to her instantly.

I was taken along for an interview. Sister Mary asked me lots of questions and was very kind. She told my mother afterwards: 'Anthea's not stupid by any means, but she does have a problem. If you do decide to bring her to us, I'm sure we'll find out what it is.' By this time, I'd almost resigned myself to the general consensus that I was thick, so I was as intrigued as my parents by what she had said.

Determined that I should be given the best chance, my parents scratched around to find the money for my fees and I was enrolled immediately. I was so relieved to be away from Holden Lane that I didn't mind about not knowing anyone in my year, or the fact that the school was several miles away. It was worth the bumpy trip in the back of Uncle Bert's old Land Rover or on the bus home, because the nuns took me under their wing completely. I felt like Maria newly accepted at the mountaintop convent in *The Sound of Music*.

Within a few weeks of my arrival, the nuns sent me to see an educational psychologist, who carried out all sorts of tests on my reading and sight before compiling his report. 'Anthea has an above-average IQ,' he wrote. 'There is no reason why she should not do well.' No one was more astonished than me. The word 'dyslexia' was mentioned, an uncommon one in the 1970s, but it labelled my problem for the first time. The educational psychologist explained that there was a physical fault in my brain which prevented me from dismantling and reconstructing a word to recognise it as a normal child would. 'Anthea has a good memory but she has word blindness. Nine times out of ten she simply guesses the words she's reading,' he told them. 'The only time she comes unstuck is when she tries to write it down again.' I was thirteen years old and intensely relieved to know that I wasn't stupid after all.

St Dominic's was a marvellous place and, with the nuns' help, I was able to rebuild my confidence. 'You'll never be Brain of Britain, Anthea,' Sister Mary Edwards would tell me with a smile, 'but we'll try and make the best of you.' They took away my fear of failure and taught me not to worry about writing things down. I was never stigmatised or punished for my lack of ability, just gently nudged in the right direction. I was reasonably good at sport, could play the piano and was congratulated warmly on anything I did do well. Drama, art, pottery, craft and design were my best subjects and I was allowed to concentrate on those.

I quickly made friends, the closest of whom was Jane Bradbury, with whom I've remained in touch, along with another girl called Angela Gallagher. I even became a school prefect. It was all that I'd hoped secondary school would be and more. The only thing I didn't like was having to stay for school lunches, which seemed to consist mainly of Spam and custard.

By this time, I had started to show an interest in boys. I remember one lad, Philip Leek, who lived across from our garden and was often in our house. I hear he's now a barrister. He was the first boy with whom I played doctors and nurses, so his was the first willy I ever saw. I giggled so much that the poor lad fled, red-faced. We had a lovely big garden, about an acre, with lots of nooks and crannies and blackberry bushes, pear and apple trees, all of which acted as a magnet to the local children. Mum's policy was deliberately open house. She actively encouraged us to have friends round, for our sakes as well as Ruth's, and she would get out the paints or let us dress up and play together with glee.

In the winter we'd hide in the front bushes of the garden and throw snowballs at passing cars before running back up our drive. Once I scored a direct hit, my snowball thumping satisfyingly into a car windscreen. The driver stopped and reversed to see where we'd gone. We ran off into the garden and hid as he marched up to the house in a rage, banged on the front door and berated my father. 'I could've been killed!' he yelled. 'Kindly keep your children under control!'

As soon as he'd driven off, Dad came and found us and gave us a roasting, but we couldn't take him very seriously because we could see he was trying hard not to laugh. When he'd finished his little speech, he added with a wink: 'And next time, run up someone else's drive, will you?'

My father was a very mild-mannered man. If he did get angry, you had cause to worry. He was brilliant with us. Even though he worked full-time at Turner & Sons, he was always home to tuck us in at night, got us up every morning and helped with the breakfast. He took on most of the practical aspects of Ruth's care as she grew older and bigger. He was the one who lifted and shifted and attended to her physical needs, while Mum concentrated on her educational requirements. I didn't know it at the time, but Dad and Uncle Michael were struggling to keep the business going in the face of cheap imports and high interest rates, a battle they eventually lost. But he never allowed his work stresses to interfere with his home life, and I remember him only as a cheerful and positive influence.

Weekends were the best fun because he was home and could play with us. We'd go out on our bikes and fish down at the little river for sticklebacks. And of course we went fossil-hunting whenever possible, rekindling Dad's passion for all things geological. I was given a geology hammer and a spy glass for one birthday instead of a toy. Day trips would be out into the Peak District, to visit the gardens at Chatsworth House, or maybe to a well-dressing in Buxton or a donkey ride at Alton Towers in the days when it was just the ruins of a house with lovely grounds. At home Mum would serve up a lovely Sunday roast with all the trimmings, the leftovers of which would be turned into something we called 'lobby' in the Potteries, all chopped up and put into a casserole. Delicious. Sunday roasts were to become a thing of the past in the Turner household by my mid-teens, when Mum and Dad became vegetarians. Wendy later went vegan, after hearing how calves for the veal industry were transported to France in horrific conditions, and I became the only meat-eater in the house.

Animals were an important part of my childhood. We had all manner of pets, from mice, parrots, tortoises and goldfish to cats, dogs, hamsters, gerbils and guinea pigs. We took in any waifs and strays, like the cat I found wandering the streets who stayed with us for fourteen years. Whenever we girls wanted a new pet, we simply clubbed together our pocket money and bought it for Mum for Mother's Day. How could she say no? Wendy was horse-mad and desperately wanted a pony of her own. I loved horses too, but was a little wary of them. Then Fella, a five-year-old grey Welsh mountain pony, came into our lives. Wendy especially adored him so, thinking I'd like one of my own, my parents bought me Pegasus, but there was something badly wrong with his hooves and he had to go back to where he had come from.

Later they scraped together enough money to buy me a far superior animal called Barabbas, whom I renamed Pepsi. He was sold to us as a broken-in four-year-old, but he turned out to be a two-year-old with attitude. He was gorgeous if you weren't on his back, but he must have had a previous bad encounter with a motorbike, because if ever he saw one, he just went for it, hooves flying. One day, as I was out riding in a country lane, a motorbike came up behind me unexpectedly. Pepsi reared and I fell off, almost straight into the path of an oncoming van. I rolled away into a ditch and it missed me by inches. My hard hat saved my life. Meanwhile, Pepsi went hell for leather after the motorbike, looking for all the world like some Thelwell cartoon pony. Another time, he shied from a jump for no particular reason and threw me. I fell heavily to the ground and dislocated my elbow.

'What did you do that for?' I shouted at him, looking up into his chestnut face and wincing with pain as people came running to help me. Chewing on his bit nonchalantly, Pepsi looked at me with complete disinterest. I knew now why he'd been called Barabbas.

Ruth was a part of most of our outings and activities, sitting in her chair and cheering us on during Pony Club meets or at our ballets and plays. We were never restricted in what we wanted to do by Ruth's limitations, and she was always given something else fun to do if she couldn't join us. She never once complained about her condition or made us feel guilty for doing things she couldn't do. Jealousy and self-pity were simply not features of her character. With my parents' guidance, it all seemed to even itself out and Mum and Dad were terribly careful to be fair. We were never put upon to look after Ruth and I was rarely aware of any favouritism.

We were also blissfully unencumbered by household chores, apart from a general rule that we were responsible for keeping our bedrooms tidy. Mum's attitude was 'you're only young for a short time, so enjoy it'. We were appalled to hear of friends who were expected to vacuum or do the dusting or put the rubbish out. It was an unknown concept to us. So much so that when I was once asked to supervise bathtime for my two younger sisters, I actually sent my father an invoice, charging him 2s 6d in the hope of adding to my pocket money. 'I should be grateful for an early settlement of this account as it is now overdue,' I wrote imperiously. I don't recall his response.

Thanks to my parents, Ruth was oblivious of an awful lot. She never even seemed to notice she was disabled. All her life, she'd been introduced to friends and acquaintances as if there was absolutely nothing wrong with her. 'This is my sister Ruth,' I'd say, offering no further explanation. If any of my schoolfriends took me to one side to ask me what was the matter with her, I'd shrug my shoulders and say: 'Nothing much, except that she tells terrible jokes.'

Nonetheless Ruth remained physically very fragile and she was in and out of North Staffordshire Hospital for much of her life. I suppose Mum and Dad protected us from most of the worry; in any event, they never appeared to be overly concerned. Whenever Ruth was in hospital, if I asked how she was doing, Mum would placate me with: 'Oh, don't worry, Anthea, the doctors will sort it all out. They always have in the past.' I honestly don't think Wendy and I gave her health very much more thought than that. She was just Ruth; she'd been poorly all her life and now she was poorly again. Situation normal.

Medicine was improving in the field of spina bifida and as each new development came about she seemed to benefit from it. The doctors loosened the ligaments in her leg, and with regular physiotherapy she soon grew strong enough to wheel herself around. Always smiling, she was good company as both a sister and a friend. She and I would watch *Top of the Pops* religiously every Thursday night after our bath, gazing awestruck at the black-and-white television screen. We'd spend hours in my room listening to records together, singing along to all our favourite songs in front of the mirror, using a hairbrush as a microphone, and fantasising about our favourite stars.

'Do you think Les McKeown will ever come to Stoke?' she'd sigh dreamily. The tartan teen sensation the Bay City Rollers had been her heart-throbs since she'd first seen them on *Top of the Pops* in 1971. Her room was plastered with posters of them and tartan scarves. The lead singer, Mr McKeown, was to Ruth what David Cassidy was to me.

'Not if he's got any sense,' I'd say, and she'd hurl a pillow at me.

Like most older sisters, I was often at loggerheads with my youngest sister, however, and the sibling rivalry for affection was acute. Once Wendy had grown up and her cuteness had worn off, she'd become a pest and a nuisance. She'd borrow my clothes, scratch my favourite records and pinch my make-up. If I had a friend or, worse still, a boyfriend over, she'd burst into the room unannounced and say something like: 'Do you want me to leave my bathwater in for you, Anthea?'

I would rise to the bait every time. Wendy and Ruth were closer; they shared a bedroom, while I had one all to myself after demanding privacy. Mum often had to use Ruth as a peacemaker, sitting her between Wendy and me in the back of the car on journeys out, events of such dangerously close proximity that they almost always sparked a fight.

To help make me feel special, Mum would take me to London once a year with Auntie Jean and Amanda for a big adventure. On our first visit, Mum made me a long-sleeved lavender dress with an embroidered bodice in which to 'see the Queen'. I remember being allowed to buy and wear my first-ever pair of American tan Pretty Polly tights and feeling like the bee's knees. We travelled down on the train and crammed all we could into a single day. We went to Madame Tussaud's, to Buckingham Palace to watch the changing of the guard and to the Tower of London to see the Crown Jewels. I can remember pushing my way right to the front of the glass case and peering in, open-mouthed at their beauty. In all my dressing-up dreams, I'd never imagined anything quite so fabulous. Mum and Auntie Jean would take us on to a show, a matinée performance of *A Chorus Line* or *Carousel* and, on one memorable occasion, to see Twiggy in *Cinderella*. 'She's so beautiful, Mum,' I gasped. 'Just like a real princess.'

We'd finish off by going to Selfridges. I'd never seen such a big store. The largest I knew were Huntbatches, or Bratt and Dykes in Hanley, places I'd spend hours in with my mum, flicking through pattern books and choosing materials for dresses. Selfridges was bewildering and in a league of its own. I'd come home on the train with my head spinning from all the wonders I'd seen.

By the time I was fourteen, I was developing nicely into a real Harry Enfield Kevin, a moody, precocious teenager. My personal heroine was Daphne, our babysitter, the doctor's daughter, who was six years older than me and a trainee hairdresser at the House of Courtney in Hanley. It was a real Elnett environment, with swirls of back-combing and hair lacquer. I wanted nothing more than to work there as a hairstylist. Even though Daphne's hands had been completely ruined by perming solution, I thought she was terribly sophisticated and when she branched out on her own and started up a mobile hairdressing service I was seriously impressed.

Not so with Wendy. I argued with her all the time, often screaming: 'I hate you!' and slamming my bedroom door behind me. I thought that nobody understood me. All I wanted to do was go out with my friends or stay alone in my room listening to records or reading magazines. My teenage bibles were *Fab 208* and *Jackie*. Through the pages of such girlhood publications I learned about everything from periods to spots. My walls were plastered with posters – David Cassidy chiefly, but other, similarly gorgeous icons of the day, including the dishiest Radio 1 DJ of them all, Peter Powell.

It was the era of the New Seekers, David Essex, Mud and Slade. Donny Osmond had once been a hot favourite of mine – I'd even practised signing my name 'Anthea Osmond' and planned my wedding outfit right down to the silver cowboy boots – but he had been usurped in my affections by the male lead in the American television series *The Partridge Family* after I failed to win a competition in *Fab 208* to meet the most attractive member of the Osmond clan. I had all the Partridge Family's albums and loads of memorabilia and spent many happy hours down at the local record shop, Mike Lloyd Music, with my girlfriends, drooling over David Cassidy's latest album cover. I particularly loved his hair, the way it was feathered and moved fluidly when he sang. I even tried to recreate the style myself.

I had a huge poster of him in pride of place at the bottom of my bed, so that I could see him night and day. 'Good night, David,' I'd whisper, blowing him a kiss just before I turned out the light, having made a quick round-up of the other young men adorning my walls. Each morning I'd sit up and check that David was still there, waiting for me.

My father didn't really understand young girls, having never had a sister, and was quietly bemused by the idol-worship going on in his daughters' bedrooms. It was with perverse delight that he read an article about my hero in the *Daily Telegraph* which claimed that David's make-up had melted during one of his concerts to reveal that his skin was blemished underneath. It was quite obviously a vicious attack by some highbrow journalist who didn't know what he was talking about, but my dad found it incredibly funny. While I was out he took a felt-tip pen and drew acne spots all over my beloved poster.

'What have you done?' I screamed when I first saw it. I was beside myself.

'Just added a touch of reality,' my father laughed, still highly amused.

I didn't see the funny side of it at all and, ripping the offending poster off the wall and tearing it in two, I locked myself in my room.

It was the second time my dad had upset and embarrassed me. A few months earlier, overhearing me complaining to Mum that all my friends wore bras now and I was the only girl who didn't, Dad decided to make me one. While I sat sulkily listening to Mum telling me that I didn't need a bra just yet, Dad had sneaked off to do his worst. He appeared, grinning from ear to ear, with his home-made product: two milk-bottle tops threaded on to a piece of string. He thought it was hilarious, but I was mortified.

Mum really laid into Dad over the bra incident and the David Cassidy prank, chiefly because she then had to buy me a bra, and go to the local record shop and plead for another poster to appease me. The replacement was duly reinstated on my wall and David resumed his position as my first true love. My fantasy affair with him ended in 1974, on the day he announced he was getting married. The 'other woman' was an actress called Kay Lens and I've never forgotten or forgiven her. That was it. Shortly before consigning him to the wastepaper bin for ever, I stood at the end of my bed and, in bright pink lipstick, scrawled the word 'Betrayal' across his smiling face.

My first proper boyfriend was Mark Stephenson. I was fourteen and he was fifteen. Mark lived a little bit further down Norton Lane and was very pretty to look at. I'd always rather fancied him. He went to Holden Lane School, and stuck out because he was the only one who actually bothered to wear his uniform. A schoolfriend, Deborah Corbett, found his number in the telephone book and rang him. 'My friend Anthea really fancies you,' she said, giggling, before slamming the phone down. After that he walked past our house every day to catch the bus, a detour from his normal route. I suddenly took an unusual interest in gardening in the hope of seeing him pass.

When he eventually plucked up the courage to come to the front door and ask if he could take me out, my father was indignant. 'You're far too young to have a boyfriend,' he told me, bristling. Mum calmed him down and invited Mark in for a cup of tea. Poor Dad, he had no previous experience of this and was on edge the whole time Mark was under our roof. We weren't allowed to leave the house so we had to sit in the front room playing records and stealing the occasional kiss. The kisses started out as pecks, lips clammed shut, and then developed into something more lingering. Mark's was the first tongue I ever tasted and I really wasn't sure. It all seemed a bit slobbery to me.

We stayed together for eighteen months, but we were never very serious, although he did come with us on our last family holiday together in Newquay, Cornwall, which was a big deal. My parents were in quite a dilemma when Mark and I eventually split up. Their experience in certain areas of life was very limited. They had really clicked with his mum by then, and I think they firmly believed that we would spend the rest of our lives together. In fact my parents and Mark's mum are still great friends. But I knew I was right to chuck him. We were never meant for each other.

Next I started dating a long-haired lad called David Wilcox. He went to the local St Joseph's Catholic School and was one of the few boys ever allowed into St Dominic's, to take the male lead in our the-atrical productions. David was very into music and guitars, and into the whole 'God Squad' thing. John Denver was his hero and he was for ever twanging away at his guitar and singing 'Annie's Song', which I thought was incredibly romantic. David had a driving licence and was occasionally allowed to borrow his parents' Ford Escort. There was a lot of furtive fumbling in the back seat in those days, but nothing more, I was far too frightened.

I had a major conscience about premarital sex; I knew it was wrong. My parents had only ever slept with each other and they instilled in me that it was something you did only with your hus-band. I must have been thirteen before I became aware that it could be pleasurable. Prior to that, I had a Reggie Perrin series of pictures in my mind of the kind of position you would have to get into to do it. It seemed sensible to me that sex would be something you did in the bathroom. I'd seen diagrams at school, but they only confused me. Our sex education was very Catholic: I was familiar with rodents, bunnies, rabbits and frogs, but not humans. Gray's Anatomy was the most well-thumbed book in the library.

After David, I went out with a lad called Gavin Spry, who was the reincarnation of Jesus Christ with his long, dark hair. Gavin played the guitar, too. He wore jeans and clogs and smelled permanently of patchouli oil. His parents were delightful. His father was the vicar of the Catholic church in Clayton, Stoke-on-Trent. I was very fond of Gavin, but our relationship came to an abrupt end after six months.

'I've met someone else,' he told me, halfway through a disco at St Joseph's, his mouth close to my ear to make sure I heard what he was saying above the thumping strains of 'Waterloo' by Abba. 'I'm sorry, Anthea, but we're finished.'

I was so upset I ran from the dancefloor. I had never been chucked and it was the first time my heart had been broken since I hadn't won the *Fab 208* competition to meet Donny Osmond. Fumbling for change in my suede patchwork handbag, I found a payphone and rang my parents. 'D-D-Dad,' I sobbed. 'It's me, Lil. Can you come and get me now? Gavin's finished with me.' I was normally embarrassed when Dad arrived anywhere to collect me in his Chrysler Sunbeam (though that attitude changed dramatically when he bought himself an MGB GT Jubilee edition with a gold flash down the side), but that night I ran to his car and threw myself into his arms.

'Oh, Daddy,' I wailed, soaking his shirt with my tears. 'I'm so unhappy.' On the way home I wept buckets. I thought my entire world had come to an end and I couldn't imagine how I was going to cope. Three days later I was over it.

I had my first and only dabble with drugs at about this stage in my life. Some of my friends started experimenting with cannabis and smoked the occasional joint. As with sex, I'd been instilled with fears of hell and damnation by my parents if I ever tried anything like that, so I always said no. When I eventually was persuaded into taking a few puffs, it did nothing for me, mainly because I was so scared it might that I didn't dare inhale. Everyone else thought it was brilliant and started to giggle, but all I wanted to do was go to sleep.

I think you either have an addictive personality or you don't, and I've never been addicted to anything. My parents rarely drink, so I never grew up with alcohol. A glass of Ribena or a Britvic orange was much more my scene. And because I was soon driving and borrowing my parents' car, I was too afraid of losing my licence to drink when I went out. There was also the question of money. I never had much, and would much rather spend my hard-earned cash on a new pair of shoes. I've always preferred tangible assets.

My sixteenth birthday party was held in the local village hall known as the Church Rooms. Mum and Dad organised and supervised the whole thing. There was a disco and a buffet for all my friends, plus a live band, a Status Quo lookalike group called Bullet. I really fancied the lead singer, a boy called Steve Bowers, who had long blond hair and looked just like Rick Parfitt. They even sang 'Down, Down' and 'Caroline'. After the gig, Steve and I went round the back of the village hall for a snog. Unfortunately my father found us and frogmarched me back inside. I didn't half get a dressing-down later.

A career on the stage was still my chief ambition in life and, to that end, I'd joined the North Staffordshire Amateur Operatic and Dramatic Society. One of the first productions they put on after I became a member was *The Sound of Music*. 'We'd like you to play Liesl, Anthea,' Gordon Allcock, the head of production, told me. Apparently, he'd seen me lined up in an audition for something else and told the producer: 'If she can sing and dance, she's my Liesl.' I thought my heart would burst. Standing on stage in a sailor suit, singing 'I Am Sixteen, Going On Seventeen' at the Queen's Theatre, Burslem was one of the happiest days of my life

By the time I was seventeen, I was having a blast with my friends, a big crowd of like-minded people. We'd regularly go out, sometimes to places like the New Bingley Hall in Stafford to see acts like David Bowie and Genesis. At this stage I was very rebellious, believing that my parents had been put on this earth just to ruin my life. I could not see that they were only thinking of my best interests. I wanted to be out all the time, and couldn't for the life of me understand why they insisted I always had to be collected from parties or was home before midnight. 'It's not fair!' I'd complain bitterly. 'All my friends' parents let them do exactly what they want.' That must be the most repeated phrase in history among parents and teenage children. Moody and hormonal, I bemoaned my lot constantly, and even Ruth's valiant attempts to cheer me up with a bad joke or a song were met with sulks and silence. My family were always there for me, Ruth particularly at that time, but I was far too busy socialising and coming to grips with being a teenager. I never spent any quality time with her, something I will regret for the rest of my life. I don't think I even bothered to go and visit her very often when she was in hospital. That would have been far too selfless.

She'd been ill with a serious kidney infection on and off for eighteen months and was in and out of hospital for dialysis. Her kidney function became a problem due to her incontinence. Because she couldn't feel anything below the waist, it was only when she started to look unwell or had a temperature that we'd know something was the matter.

I think I fully expected Ruth to live for ever. My parents certainly never gave us any indication that the life expectancy for those with spina bifida was greatly reduced. In fact Ruth was one of the longest surviving cases because of the pioneering operation she'd had as a child, but I never knew that then.

On the day she died, I felt as if someone had freeze-framed my life. For several hours, I was completely unable to feel anything or even to cry. Later that evening, a black van arrived outside our house. Four sombre-faced men in dark suits got out and walked silently into our home carrying a black coffin. The door to the spare bedroom was closed behind them and a few minutes later it reopened and they emerged, solemnly carrying the coffin out of the house. It was seeing the black box, knowing that Ruth was lying lifeless inside, that started the flood. Until then I think I imagined she was just asleep and was going to wake up any minute. But now these complete strangers were taking her away from us, the family she'd known and loved. It was more than I could bear.

I was a young woman on the brink of adult life experiencing death for the first time, and I wasn't in any way ready for it. My reactions weren't terribly grown up. I'd always been a late developer and was very immature for my age. I was still looking to my parents to sort everything out, and I never really understood the depths of their despair or how dreadful it must have been for them trying to keep themselves together for Wendy and me. But my parents were unable to hide their grief from us, and we felt it was no time for ours. They were completely shattered and went to hell and back, my mother particularly. Having relinquished the chance of becoming a headmistress to stay at home and care for Ruth, she had taken that task on cheerfully and unflinchingly. But now one of her chief reasons for living was gone, snuffed out in an instant. If it hadn't been for her religious faith, I think she might well have gone under.

The day of Ruth's funeral at St Chad's Church in Longsdon fell on the last day of school term and Mum decided that neither Wendy nor I should attend. 'It would be far too distressing,' she announced. I never knew if she meant for her or for us, but I was too bewildered in the face of her grief to argue. Wendy had, by then, gone into total denial and, if anyone asked how Ruth was, she'd tell them she was fine. As it was my responsibility to keep her amused and out of the way, it was arranged that she could come to St Dominic's with me so that I could look after her. Eleven years old and desperately pretending that her favourite sister was still alive, Wendy was highly excitable, chattering on about the novelty of being in the senior school and skipping along beside me while I held her hand. So on the day our dear Ruth was laid to rest in the grave at Longsdon village church next to my mum's parents, Wendy and I were at school as if nothing had happened.

But try as I might, I felt far from normal, of course. My head spun with images of Ruth as a child, play-acting with me in the attic, sitting with us and my parents on the beach at Caldey Island off Tenby, posing for the class photograph at Norton Primary School, moving with surprising agility from room to room on two arms when she became frustrated with her wheelchair. Laughing raucously at some silly joke of my father's.

For a long time after Ruth's death, I felt as if I were in limbo. I couldn't even bring myself to go to her grave afterwards. It simply wasn't somewhere I felt comfortable. In any event, I don't think I had the capacity to deal with much more. Once I'd got over the initial shock, my emotions steadied and I just sort of settled into a general sadness.

Being at home was like living in a library. Nobody spoke out loud. I'd taken Ruth for granted for much of her life, and now I found myself missing her incredibly, wanting to talk to her about the little things we'd always chatted about. I realised what a passive influence she'd always been, so calm and accepting of her fate. I felt guilty for the times I'd resented her wheelchair and blamed myself for every childhood spat we'd ever had.

I've never asked my parents exactly what Ruth died of, or why she should have suddenly gone like that. We've hardly spoken of that day since, although we do talk of her often to keep her memory alive. There was no post-mortem or inquest as far as I'm aware; no blame was apportioned or reasons given. It was just over; she was gone.

For a time after Ruth's death I remained an active member of the local church youth group, the Youth Fellowship, having always attended regularly. I think Mum thought it might help me to turn to God, as she had. But I wasn't religious – I just went along for the coffee and the social side. Some of the group were born-again Christians who claimed to have 'seen the light' and I remember sitting there waiting to feel the same and thinking maybe it would happen to me. It never did, even though I enthusiastically sang along with all the Jesus songs.

Not long after Ruth had died, we were at a prayer meeting at a friend's house, and Paul, the senior member in charge, suddenly stood up and said: 'Let's pray for Ruth Turner and her family.' Taken aback, I blushed crimson, but duly adopted the prayer position and bowed my head with the rest of them, staring intensely at the shag-pile carpet. Paul announced solemnly: 'We pray for them in their hour of need.' The silence was broken by a general murmur of 'Amen.'

Bolstered by this endorsement from the group and getting quite carried away, he went on: 'We pray for the Lord to give the Turner family peace in their bereavement and comfort in their sadness.' The amens came once again, rippling round the room. I wondered how much longer this farce was going to go on.

'Help the family to know that it was God's will,' Paul concluded softly. 'He wanted Ruth for his own. A flower in his kingdom.'

My head jerked up and I stared at the pious people all around me, my ears burning. I'd never heard such a load of old rubbish. It was the first time in my life I'd ever been really angry. Jumping up in the middle of this poor guy's living room, I was apoplectic.

'Fuck off!' I shouted. 'Just fuck off!'

They all looked at me in astonishment. But I could do nothing to stop myself. Trembling with rage, I yelled at Paul: 'What do you mean, it was God's will? What do you bloody well mean? Ruth had a perfectly contented family life. She was well loved and very happy. What sort of god would want to take her away from that and from us?'

I ran from the prayer meeting in tears, jumped into the car and drove home, where I fell on to my bed. Full of self-pity and remorse, I mourned Ruth's death that day more acutely than ever before. I was infuriated by the injustice of it. I decided there and then that Jesus and God weren't all they were cracked up to be. It is still an area of my life that I haven't fully worked out. If anything, I am inclined to side with my agnostic father, who believes in the ability of people and the human spirit above all else.

It was a very long time before Wendy or I were able to acknowledge the impact of our sister's death on us. It was not until we'd both grown up and moved away and were able to re-establish a friendship that we fully realised that someone was missing from our life. I certainly couldn't accept that I'd never see Ruth again. The idea of her soul simply disappearing upset me dreadfully. More than twenty years later, it still does. When I dream of my family, she's still a part of it. I'm haunted by the fact that I never got to know her properly as a woman.

Ruth would have been thirty-seven this year. I hope she would have been proud of us all. She's certainly still there for me. She was one of the most sensible, level-headed people I've ever known and thinking of her helps to keep my feet firmly on the ground. However crazy my life gets, however unreal it sometimes seems, I can feel Ruth pinching me hard every now and again and see that knowing grin on her face.

2

The Girl Next Door Grows Up

As I neared the end of my schooldays my dream was to go to drama school. I knew my parents couldn't afford the fees, so I applied for a grant from Staffordshire County Council, though without much hope of success. Then I heard about a course in the performing arts as part of a fine-arts degree at Lanchester College in Warwickshire. I was accepted provisionally for a place and expected to enrol in the autumn, but deep inside, something was bothering me. I'd hoped to feel a burning desire to launch myself into the next big phase of my life, but it wasn't there. I had no sense of a mission, just a vague feeling that when the right thing came along, I'd know. The trouble was I didn't know yet.

I left St Dominic's in the summer of 1978 with six O-Levels – in pottery, craft and design, RE, music, science, art and history (I had to drop French because I got left so far behind) – and two A-Levels, in drama and theatre arts and craft and design. My grades weren't anything to write home about, but it wasn't a bad result for someone who, according to my previous teachers, couldn't even take an exam. For my exams in craft and design, I'd made a beach out of clay with a shoreline of textured sand. I'd written a load of old claptrap claiming it represented 'the brink of life' and, astonishingly, the examiner believed me. I'd always been able to bluff my way through.

But with Ruth's death, everything changed. My zeal for drama left me and I felt as if the ground had been pulled from under my feet. I'd completely lost my way. Bereavement also had a powerful effect on my relationship with my family. It brought me closer to my parents than ever before, making me painfully aware of their vulnerability, although their grief seemed to me as if it was something apart from mine. The balance of power had shifted: I now felt responsible for them and for Wendy, and the idea of going away to college at such a crucial time bothered me.

'I don't think I want to go off to Lanchester straight away, Dad,' I told my father one Saturday afternoon while he was fiddling with his cine camera. 'I think I might take a year out, get a job and hang around for a while to see what comes up.' It had been an idea I'd toyed with before Ruth's death.

'OK, Lil,' Dad said, looking up and shrugging his shoulders. 'As long as you're happy. That's all that really matters.' There was a new sadness in his eyes which cut me to the core.

I took a job as a receptionist at a photographer's studio in Newcastle-under-Lyme. It was the late summer of 1978 and I planned to keep my head down for a while and allow my parents the time and space to grieve. I earned £30 a week. Turning up on my first day in a gingham shirt and flared jeans under a smelly old Afghan coat with my 1970s 'big' hair, all back-combed and shaggy like Olivia Newton-John's, I really thought I looked the part. But my boss, Neil Brightmore, disagreed.

Taking me to one side, he told me, as diplomatically as he could: 'I was rather hoping you might dress more, well, appropriately.' He couldn't take his eyes off my cowboy boots.

When I went home that night and told Mum what he'd said, she opened her handbag. 'Here,' she said, handing me some cash. 'Go and buy yourself something more suitable.' As I looked at her, amazed, she added: 'It's only a loan, mind, a sub on your wages. You'll have to pay me back when you get your first wage packet.' I gave my Afghan coat to Pat the dog for his bed – though it smelled so bad even he rejected it – and went out that weekend and bought a proper blouse, dark skirt and sensible shoes. Standing in front of the mirror that night, staring at my own reflection, I felt as if I'd suddenly grown up.

Neil Brightmore was a wedding and studio photographer in his late thirties, divorced and living with a woman called Vivienne. He was never happier than when in his studio surrounded by lights and cameras. I nicknamed him Nelly Brightlights. My role was 'front of house', taking calls and dealing with customers while he was in the studio or out at a function. The work was interesting inasmuch as it allowed me to meet the general public for the first time. Neil wasn't too bad to work for and the job at least gave me some cash of my own. Now all I needed was a boyfriend.

The last few I'd gone out with had left me feeling that there had to be something more. There was nothing wrong with them. It was me. One, a lovely young man called Martin Baker, who was in his twenties, was a class above me socially, and it showed. He taught me about some of the finer things in life like wine and antiques, but I was completely out of my depth. His parents were doctors with a large disposable income, and all his friends seemed more socially aware and sophisticated than me. I felt like a country hick. It was never going to work. Once we'd broken up, I was so disillusioned that I stayed single for a while, hanging out with friends in Newcastle-under-Lyme, going to the cinema (I saw *Saturday Night Fever* three times), to youth clubs, the odd pub or a pop concert, but never really finding anyone I wanted to be with.

All that changed when Andy Sims came into my life. He was the best thing to happen to me in ages. I met him at a party through a friend, Carol Barlow. Carol was the prettiest girl in school, could pass herself off as twenty-one and came second in the Miss Teenage International section of the Miss Universe beauty pageant. I never entered any of those competitions because I was far too gawky. Not only did Carol have a long-term boyfriend, but she'd had sex, which few of us had, least of all me. She dressed beautifully, was lovely to look at and I was hugely influenced by her. I felt I was moving up the scale just by being in her company.

I fell for Andy big-time. He was my first true love: all previous crushes, I now realised, were just that – crushes. Like all the men to

whom I've ever been attracted, he was gorgeous; best of all, Andy
was twenty and experienced – he'd done 'it'. I didn't know much,
but I did know it was better to be in expert hands when you're a
beginner. It was the end of summer, the Commodores were number
1 with 'Three Times a Lady' and I was in love. The only problem
was that Andy was a student at Surrey University in Guildford,
studying metallurgy and French, and was just about to take a year
out – on work placement in France. Surrey was far enough away,
but France was positively off the map. I missed him dreadfully,
although we wrote to each other constantly. I still have every letter
he sent me.

Whenever we were together, it was like all my birthdays rolled into
one. I've always carried a torch for Andy and he was a great comfort
to me at what was such a difficult time in my life. That Christmas
was to be my first without Ruth and I was dreading it. I couldn't
imagine helping Mum and Wendy decorate the tree and Ruth not
being there, directing us joyfully from her chair. My parents had
decided that we'd all go out for the day, to the Cock Inn at
Stableford, rather than stay at home as usual. But I knew that wherever we were it would feel terrible, the four of us sitting round the
table eating our meal, the place for Ruth's wheelchair empty.

Andy was coming home for Christmas, after six weeks of being
away, and I couldn't wait to see him. I knew that with him by my
side, I could face almost anything. Better still, his sister was getting
married on Christmas Eve (Nelly Brightlights was doing the photos),
so there was plenty to distract me from the pained atmosphere of our
house. Selfishly, I avoided being at home as much as I could, and no
sooner was the forced Christmas lunch over than I was off out to see
Andy again. Poor Wendy didn't have any such escape.

To my surprise, it turned out to be an amazing week. On New
Year's Eve, Andy and I were invited to five parties in one evening, so
we toured them all, before seeing in 1979 at the last and returning to
his parents' house in the early hours. We sneaked in as quietly as we
could so as not to wake anyone, and soon got cosy. 'Happy New
Year, Anthea,' he said, as he kissed me and pulled me to him.

'Happy New Year, Andy,' I replied, melting into his arms.

It was then, in the early hours of 1 January 1979, as 'Mary's Boy Child' by Boney M played somewhere on a radio, that we first made love. Andy was kind and gentle and I trusted him completely. It felt so right, somehow, with him, on that night. In his tender care Anthea Turner, at the ripe old age of eighteen and a half, finally lost her virginity. He brought out the woman in me and allowed me to feel that it was the start of another year; a time to look ahead, not back. I felt incredibly happy afterwards. I thought: 'That's it, girl. You've cracked it!' Getting dressed, I went into the bathroom and peered into the mirror to see if I looked any different. Needless to say I didn't, but I was sure I could detect a knowing look in my eyes.

Andy and I continued to practise our new-found activity every time we saw each other and had a gorgeous time. We'd lie on the floor in front of the television in his front room watching *The Old Grey Whistle Test* and making love. There was always music playing somewhere when I was with Andy; he was very into Neil Young and Caravan and the Eagles. Songs like 'Hotel California' and 'Heart of Gold' became the soundtracks to our courtship; Whispering Bob Harris provided our commentary.

I was so miserable each time Andy went back to France, and so happy when he was home. Our letters back and forth across the Channel catalogued our feelings for each other. One, written from his student digs on the outskirts of Paris, said: 'I miss you something awful . . . all I do is dream all day about being back in Stoke with you . . . Don't you think it was a real pity that my fairly short Christmas visit should have come to an end only a few hours after what I would call a significant step in our relationship? I don't know how you feel about what to me was a magical, out-of-the-ordinary New Year's Eve.' He always signed off by calling me 'babe' and sending his 'love, sunshine and kisses'. I lived for his letters and would watch every day for the postman, hoping for another.

Life at home was improving. Mum and Dad had emerged from the darkest months of their grief to face another year. It was only when there was an unexpected setback – like Pat the dog dying suddenly – that they'd slump again. 'No more dogs,' Dad announced, cross with himself for missing the smelly-mouthed mutt so badly.

But, having heard from the local vet about a stray litter of boxer puppies needing homes, I sprang a surprise on Mum.

'Your father'll go mad,' she told me as the tiny puppy licked her face and widdled all down her dress. Sure enough, when Dad came home from work that night, he was furious.

'No, no, NO,' he said, firmly. 'We're placing an advert in the *Sentinel* and we're finding him a good home. I said no more dogs, and I meant it.' Within an hour, the puppy had a name, Tom, and was curled up on Dad's knee, fast asleep. Tom didn't turn out quite as we'd expected. If he was a boxer, then I'm a Jack Russell. Regardless of what he looked like, though, that dog became a surrogate child to my parents; they adored him and when he died a few years ago we were all devastated. He is still sadly missed.

In January 1979, I changed jobs. I left the photographer's studio early that month after a tiff with Neil over money and found a position at Minton's pot bank in Stoke, packing china. The job was hardly demanding. An order would come in from a big department store like Harrods and I'd have to go to the stacks of china in the pot bank and pack the relevant pieces into crates. It was terminally boring, and my sanity was saved only by some of the truly fascinating characters I found myself working with.

Among them were three middle-aged women, all lovely, who introduced me to the joys of baked-bean sandwiches – lightly toasted white bread, buttered, stuffed full of hot baked beans so that they squelched out of the corners when you ate them. Delicious. They are still a comfort food for me if ever I'm below par. But even better than baked-bean sandwiches were their graphic sex stories.

'You'll never guess what the old man did to me last night,' one of them would begin, and then they'd be off. It was the best sex education I had. The nuns of St Dominic's would have been horrified. I learned about all sorts of things I'd never even dreamed about. My ears were like mini-radars as I picked up all the information I could and sifted it with the attention to detail of the truly studious. I discovered the world of sex aids and items like basques, stockings, suspenders, crotchless panties and all manner of other delights. It was the sort of thing one would expect in Soho, not in the back streets of Stoke.

I had extraordinary visions of these amply proportioned women dressed up in all these bizarre outfits doing things I could only snigger about. It was a revelation, I can tell you. I was paid £45 a week, but it would almost have been worth paying them for such a thorough sex education. Thank you, ladies, one and all.

Dozens of items of crockery were broken – apart from the ones I accidentally let slip from my hands while riveted to the conversations going on around me. There were some who shall remain nameless who enjoyed playing frisbee with plates to liven things up every now and again. I was personally responsible for quite a few breakages of Haddon Hall china. Minton still make it, and whenever I see its dark green edging in a china shop window, it takes me straight back to those days and I can't help but smile.

I stayed at Minton for five months, by which time I'd saved up enough money to do a bit of travelling. Andy was busy working at a metallurgy laboratory in France and couldn't have me with him, so the Far East beckoned. I knew exactly where I wanted to go: Singapore. My twenty-two-year-old second cousin Julia, the daughter of my mum's cousin June Russell, lived and worked out there for a bank and kindly invited me to visit her for a month. That July, with just £70 spending money in my pocket and my £444 ticket in my hand, I waved goodbye to Mum and Dad and caught a plane from Heathrow Airport, feeling as nervous as a kitten. This was my first big adventure out into the big wide world, and looking back now, I can't believe how naïve I was. Apart from one or two school trips abroad I'd hardly ever left Staffordshire and knew nothing.

On the plane a stranger approached me and started chatting me up. He was very good-looking and I was flattered by his attention. He told me he was a deep-sea diver. 'I first spotted you at the airport,' he said, pouring me another drink. 'I saw you struggling with this enormous suitcase and I thought, there's a girl who needs some help.' He smiled, his dazzling white teeth flashing at me.

I found him totally charming. 'Oh yes,' I blushed. 'My suitcase. My parents told me not to take so much, but I just couldn't leave anything out. I can hardly lift the blooming thing.'

Clinking his plastic cup against mine, the deep-sea diver grinned again. 'No problem, Anthea,' he said. 'I'll carry it for you.'

'What?' I said, taken aback.

'I'll carry your big suitcase for you,' he repeated, 'And you can carry mine. It's much smaller and more manageable. We'll meet outside the airport and swap them over.'

I was completely taken in. Without thinking, I agreed. What a nice chap, I thought as the plane came in to land. Then I went back to excitedly looking out of the window, and looking forward to seeing my cousin's smiling face.

When my giant case came round the carousel in the baggage hall, the diver lifted it off with the greatest of ease, and, pointing out his, waved at me before marching ahead through the customs and immigrations checks. To this day I do not know what was in the suitcase I carried through the various security gates and returned safely to my smiling 'Good Samaritan' on the other side. He kissed me goodbye and left long before I found Julia's face in the crowd. When I read of other young women who have been similarly duped into carrying drugs or contraband through customs and have ended up with a life sentence in a Far Eastern jail, I shiver. In that single, simple moment of stupidity, I could have ruined my entire life.

Singapore did nothing to disappoint. I was like a child in a sweet-shop and found it all humungously exciting. Julia took some time off from work and she and I took a trip to Penang in Malaysia; back in Singapore, we swanned from one five-star hotel to the next, using the swimming pools and bars and meeting all sorts of interesting people in the clubs of Boogie Street. Everyone seemed to be jumping into bed with everyone else and I'm ashamed to say that the lovely Andy, 6,000 miles away in France, was all but forgotten for a while. In such a climate of warmth and friendliness, I had a fling with a gorgeous steward from Qantas Airlines called David, and another (platonic) relationship with a Californian wine-distributor, who sent me a case of his finest wines. It was a real eye-opener to me. So this was what life was like outside Norton.

By the time I arrived home that summer, I knew that a return to full-time education wasn't going to be for me. I had an appointment at Lanchester College for a second interview but I kept it more out of duty than interest. The purpose of the interview was to give both sides the opportunity to reassess whether or not we still wanted to work together. I'd had a lot of growing up to do since I had last been there. Now, back in an environment where bells rang to signify the end of class and students scurried everywhere so as not to be late, my heart sank. An art professor tried to encourage me by showing off some hideously ugly creation by one of his students but I just sat looking at it, and him, and thought: 'I can't go through with this.' I went home and told Mum and Dad.

'Any idea what you want to do instead, Lil?' Dad asked.

I shook my head. My year out was up and, apart from a vague idea that one day I'd like to be on the stage, I hadn't a clue.

Andy was furious with me when I wrote and told him what I'd decided. 'You're crazy,' he wrote from France. 'You can't possibly imagine what three years at university will be like by just looking around it for one afternoon . . . you must know that by not furthering your education, you have chosen to limit yourself to brainless occupations. There are some well-paid, interesting brainless occupations, but they are few and far between. I hope you find one.'

It was already clear to me that Andy and I were drifting apart. Having moved to a new job in Provence from Paris, he was having a ball. He'd made loads of friends and was speaking French like a native, earning good money and enjoying his new life. I was a different person, too, much more worldly-wise after Singapore. Our letters to each other became less frequent and far shorter, and I could tell, without even seeing him, that the spark between us had gone.

I was busy in Stoke, having fun and still involved in dramatics. I even went to the Edinburgh Festival – my first and last visit – with the Stoke Original Theatre. We were there for two weeks and I played dizzy American dancer Shirley Taplow in a musical comedy called *Stagefright*, in between helping with the props, taking money on the door and sweeping up. The show came second in the family entertainment category. It was a wonderful experience for me, the first time I'd 'toured' with a show, and I was hooked. Among the cast was a talented and hilariously funny young actor called Neil

Morrissey, who lived with his foster parents in Newcastle. We slept on adjoining campbeds in the same room in Edinburgh and he lent me his jumper when I was cold.

When Andy eventually came back from France, he took up a position at British Aerospace in Welwyn Garden City, announcing, however, that his long-term plan was to live and work in South Africa. I think he fully expected us to pick up where we had left off; he might even have hoped that I would eventually go abroad with him, but I knew that I wouldn't. In the time we'd been apart, I'd created a whole new life for myself. I had a new group of friends, through people I'd met at Neil Brightmore's and Minton's pot bank, and somehow Andy just didn't fit into this. We agreed to split up, albeit with much sadness on both our parts.

'We can still keep in touch, can't we?' he asked on our final meeting as boyfriend and girlfriend.

'Of course we can,' I told him gently, unsure that I wasn't letting go of something special. There would always be a place in my heart for Andy, and for many years we kept in touch. He is married now, and living in Australia with his wife and two children. I'll always cherish the good times we had.

Having decided not to go to Lanchester College, I needed a job. I spotted an advertisement in the local newspaper for a vacancy at the Automobile Association as a member service operator (glorified telephonist), based in Hanley, Stoke-on-Trent. 'It would just be a stopgap, until I figure out exactly what I want to do,' I reassured my parents. It was a stopgap that was to last two and a half years.

'Hello, AA Breakdown and Information Services, how can I help you?' was now my best-rehearsed line. This was long before everything was computerised and centralised, and I had to acquire a smattering of information on everything from legal to general motoring, mapping and insurance. If I couldn't deal with a query, I had to find out what the answer was and ring the caller back. To help me through my dyslexia, I painstakingly copied out lists of towns, helpful phrases and abbreviations so that I'd never be caught out. But of course I was. I still wonder sometimes how I kept my job – I must have got people lost all around the country, or left them for hours on the roadside waiting for my call.

My wages enabled me to buy myself my first car, which I christened Champagne Charlie. It was a cream-coloured Mini, registration NVT 749W, which I loved and adored, and which I drove through every speed trap in Stoke-on-Trent. Driving to and from Hanley every day, listening to the latest Blondie hit on the radio, I began to enjoy a sense of freedom I'd never experienced before, a feeling of being young, free and single, with money in my pocket and a new focus to my life. My childhood dreams of fame and fortune had been shelved. I was twenty years old and had settled into a kind of comfortable routine. Still happy to be living at home, socialising at weekends with a terrific group of friends, I thought I had found myself at last.

Among the friends I'd made since I'd been working was a young man by the name of Bruno Brookes. I'd first met him through his father, Les, who was a friend of Neil Brightmore's. Les was a lovely, bubbly, very good-looking middle-aged man who ran a car-wash business in Stoke called Land of Soap and Glory. Bruno worked for his dad in the daytime, but in the evenings he was a disc jockey. Les was tremendously supportive of Bruno's other career and spent much of his time promoting his son. He'd even paid Neil to take some professional publicity shots of Bruno.

Les would often pop into the studio for a cup of coffee and a chat if he was passing, and I think he took a bit of a shine to me. 'You should meet Bruno,' he told me one day, holding up the latest pictures of the pretty young long-haired boy who bore more than a passing resemblance to David Cassidy. 'You'd really get on. He's a great DJ and he's determined to make it into the big league.'

I thought nothing of Les's suggestion at first. I was, after all, still technically going out with Andy at the time, but he was away for long periods, and I suppose I was a bit bored. So when, a few weeks later, Les invited me to a local nightclub called The Place where Bruno was a regular, I decided to go along. 'Come along and have some fun, Anthea,' said Les. 'Let your hair down. And, er, while you're there, you could meet Bruno.' Grinning from ear to ear, he gave me a cheeky wink.

The club was heaving. Les ushered us inside past the queues of people waiting to get in. 'Head for the bar,' he yelled above the Pretenders song 'Brass in Pocket' blaring out of the speakers. 'I'll look for Bruno.' Squeezing his way to the bar through the crush of people, Les spotted Bruno standing in the corner and pushed me towards him. He'd clearly been primed by Les. 'Hi, Anthea?' he said, introducing himself and holding out his hand. 'Bruno.'

I was surprised at how short he was, at least an inch shorter than my five feet six inches, but his eyes were very blue and he had a clean, fresh-faced look about him. I was less impressed to see that he was wearing jewellery, a lot of it – a gold ingot on a chain round his neck, a ring, a heavy bracelet and a flashy watch. I took his hand and shook it. His handshake was firm. He was obviously very sure of himself. 'Hello, Bruno,' I said, smiling.

'Can I get you a drink?' he asked, reaching into his pocket and pulling out a wallet stuffed with cash.

I was about to order my usual Britvic orange and lemonade, but instead I suddenly decided that it was time I went for something a little more sophisticated. Drawing myself up to my full height, and thinking of the Leonard Rossiter and Joan Collins adverts on the television, I said: 'Sweet Martini and lemonade, please. On the rocks.'

Over drinks, we started chatting. 'Les has told me a great deal about you,' I said.

'All bad, I hope,' Bruno replied, his eyes twinkling.

'Everything except why on earth he called you Bruno,' I smiled.

'Well, actually, he didn't,' he confided with a smile. 'Don't tell anyone, but my real name's Trevor.'

'*Trevor?*' I asked, incredulously, looking across at Les and laughing.

'I know, I know,' he said. 'What can I say? Bruno Brookes sounded like a better name for a DJ.'

'Trevor it is, then,' I said. It was the name I would use for him ever after.

Although I was still going out with Andy, Bruno was an attractive proposition to someone like me and I agreed to see him for the occasional date. As his father predicted, we did get on very well. I never fancied him in the way I'd fancied Andy, but he was certainly funny, bubbly and, in those days, good company. Bruno and I never even kissed, but there was always a frisson of excitement between us and the sense that something might happen if we let it.

Bruno was a year older than me, came from Stoke-on-Trent, and was, as Les had said, determined to make the big time. He'd started as a disc jockey in the era of *Saturday Night Fever* and *Grease* when discos, complete with mirrored balls and multicoloured lights, were in. Les sacrificed a lot to help his son achieve his ambitions, and they ran Bruno's Disco between them: Les drove the van, humped the gear and sat on the door at places like the King's Hall in Stoke to take the money. In between gigs, Bruno worked at BBC Radio Stoke as a weekend disc jockey.

At his request, I went to see one of his gigs at the King's Hall, a place I'd never been before. Lots of my friends were regulars but discos had never really been my scene. The place was packed, and Les was taking all the fifty-pence pieces at the door. On the stroke of eight o'clock, the taped music stopped and we were interrupted by the sound of Bruno's voice coming over a microphone.

'Well, hello there, Stoke!' he yelled. 'How are you?'

Everyone roared their approval as he took his position and started up the music. 'Here's a nice little number to get us all in the mood,' he began. '"Geno" by Dexy's Midnight Runners.' The thumping strains of the first number pounded through the speakers, the coloured lights flickered and flashed and swirled around the room. The disco had begun.

As I stood at the bar, sipping my drink, I was mesmerised by the attractive young man up at the turntables doing his stuff. Bruno was, without doubt, a very talented DJ. He was sparky, consumed with ambition and in his own way a little bit glamorous. There was definitely a certain cachet to be had from being his girlfriend and, after Andy, that is exactly what I became. When the lights dimmed and he took to his turntables, he performed as well as any actor I'd ever seen on stage. It was a slick act; he had all the jargon and he played great music. I was impressed.

There was a quieter side to Bruno, too. He loved fishing – his grandad had taught him when he was a boy – and he spent much of his spare time sitting at local gravel pits and lakes, quietly plotting his future as he waited for a fish to bite. He always enjoyed being in the country and had grand plans to own a big estate with his very own trout lake. 'I want it all, Anthea,' he'd tell me, 'and nothing's going to stand in my way.'

When he was in work mode, Bruno's world seemed so glamorous and vibrant compared to mine. Even in the early days, when it was just him and Les, Bruno had a swagger. He was going somewhere and his message was that if I tagged along, I just might get there too. I was still living at home with my parents and Wendy and had pretty much exhausted all that Stoke had to offer. Bruno was spontaneous, attentive and exciting, even though he sometimes missed the mark. On my nineteenth birthday, for example, he sent the Lady Mayoress of Stoke to my home to deliver a bouquet of flowers. I was hugely embarrassed and thought the gesture so old-fashioned.

It was only when the bottom started to fall out of the disco scene that Bruno began to concentrate more on his radio career. His aim then became to make it to Radio 1, at that time the biggest and best radio station in Europe. Its major rivals were pirate shows such as Luxembourg and Caroline. Bruno's Radio 1 heroes, the likes of Noel Edmonds, Tony Blackburn and Dave Lee Travis, commanded both the salaries and the adulation one would nowadays associate with pop stars. Bruno had even hired the gorgeous Peter Powell (then at Radio Luxembourg) to DJ at his eighteenth birthday party in the hope of picking up a few tips. I secretly admired Bruno's naked ambition and determination to find fame and fortune.

Bruno opened the door to a completely different way of life for me. It felt good to be the girl in the crowd to whom he'd dedicate a love song and I got a thrill listening to him on Radio Stoke and hearing my name mentioned. People treated me differently because I was with him and I relished my new 'celebrity' status. One day, he took me to Central Television in Birmingham to watch a recording of the children's programme *Tiswas*, presented by newcomers Sally James, Lenny Henry and Chris Tarrant. It was the first time I'd ever been inside a television studio and I was enthralled by all the lights and excitement and noise. I was amazed at how well the presenters kept everything together in what seemed like a totally chaotic but tremendously fun environment.

'If I could be anything in the world,' I told Bruno dreamily on the way home, 'I'd be a children's television presenter.'

I saw more and more of Bruno and started hanging around Radio Stoke just to be on the fringes of this exciting new life. When the AA invited me to read out the live road-traffic reports on Radio Stoke, I jumped at the chance. I already knew the layout and the drill, and the extra work would mean I could spend even more time with Bruno. 'This is Anthea Turner for AA Roadwatch, bringing you the traffic news on the hour every hour,' was my new line. This was my first brush with fame, and despite being terrified to begin with that my dyslexia would prevent me from reading my cue cards properly, I loved it. As long as I practised my set piece several times and took a few deep breaths beforehand, I was fine. The shift patterns I worked gave me even more time to 'anorak' at BBC Stoke, helping out with the roadshows and the behind-the-scenes stuff without getting paid for it.

Bruno's show was one of the most popular on the station. He mixed music with chat, competitions with interviews. He devoted a lot of time to the format, keeping it fun and funky, and arranging for interesting people to come on and talk. He had funny men and straight guys, cranks and weirdos, politicians and traffic wardens. Waiting at the studio for him to finish work, I met quite a few of them. I'll never forget one, a psychic, whom I was asked to escort out after her slot. Stopping in the corridor, she suddenly turned and asked me my name. I remember thinking, 'Well, surely you know?' and trying to suppress a smile. But I told her my name, and she said: 'Well, Anthea, all I can say is that you're not going to marry the man you think you're going to marry, but the man you will marry will be one of the great loves of your life.'

I didn't understand. How could the man I married be just one of the great loves of my life? Surely, he would be the only one? When I asked her to explain, she just smiled inscrutably and left.

The station manager at Stoke was Sandra Chalmers, the sister of television presenter Judith Chalmers, and when Sandra eventually left the station, Judith came along to her leaving party at the Leopard pub in Burslem. It was the first time I'd ever met anybody famous and I was more than a little tongue-tied. 'Hello, Judith,' I said nervously. 'I'm Anthea, Bruno's girlfriend. Nice to meet you.' I asked her for her autograph, and she was charming and friendly and all that I'd hoped she'd be. She was the presenter of a successful television holiday programme called *Wish You Were Here* and also co-presented something called *Good Afternoon* with Mary Parkinson. As I watched her mingling confidently at the party I was hugely impressed.

In the summer of 1983 a commercial franchise was awarded to a new local radio station in Stoke to be called Signal Radio. Keen to poach Bruno from the BBC, they made all the right moves. But when Radio Stoke got wind of it, they offered Bruno an even better package and a possible route to that elusive slot he was after on Radio 1. Bruno decided to stay. But I wondered whether Signal might have a job for me. I asked Bruno what he thought.

'Why not go and see Tony Hawkins?' he said. 'He's the programme director who's been after me. See if he's got anything for you – oh, and Anthea, tell him I sent you.'

So it was with Bruno's help that I applied for and was offered a position as Signal's new record librarian – my first proper job in radio. The salary was less than I was earning at the AA, but it was much more of a challenge: my brief was to collate a record library from scratch. I jumped at the chance, bluffing my way through the interview. I started work that July and was given three months to get the library together. I didn't know the first thing about it, but I had been a librarian at St Dominic's and I was a fast learner.

Tony Hawkins sent me over to his former colleagues at Piccadilly Radio in Manchester to find out how they'd got started. Steve Penk, an up-and-coming DJ there, gave me a few extra tips. 'Just go for it, girl,' he said. I got hold of the bible of the music business, a book that lists all the record companies, and figured that if I called them all up and sweet-talked their pluggers' departments into sending me their latest releases, I'd soon build up a good collection.

'Hello there,' I'd begin, in my most schmoozy telephone voice. 'My name's Anthea Turner and I work in the record library at Signal Radio, the exciting new commercial station in Stoke. I wonder if you could possibly help me. I'm after a copy of the latest songs by one of your artists, a band called the Police . . .'

The station went on air on 5 September 1983, and I'd just about managed to get enough records together to meet the demands of the disc jockeys' playlists. They needed all the very latest hits from bands like Kajagoogoo, Men at Work, UB40, Paul Young, Duran Duran, KC and the Sunshine Band and Culture Club. I even managed to get a reasonable quota of the back catalogue numbers, all the Beatles and Rolling Stones songs, for example, which were the hardest of all to wrestle from the record companies. Each record had to be catalogued and filed by hand. It was laborious work, but I got it all done in time. Tony Hawkins was pleased and I knew I'd done a good job. The trouble was that once the library was established and I'd got us on the pluggers' mailing lists, the record companies knew we existed (and that we were giving Radio Stoke a pasting to boot), so there wasn't anything very much left for me to do.

Having successfully set up the library, I was hungry for another challenge. Around this time commercial radio stations were realising that other forms of income were needed apart from straight advertising. Promotions departments were springing up all over the country, responsible for merchandising, PR and station events. After a certain amount of lobbying from me, Barry Machin, the station manager, put me on trial for the job. Thus it was that Anthea Turner, who five minutes before had been an AA telephonist, was put in charge of the rather grand-sounding promotions department of Signal Radio, which was actually the same old library I'd always worked in, piled to the rafters with records and now T-shirts.

I was given a trailer and went out with the disc jockeys when they did roadshows, handing out car stickers, pens, rubbers, mugs and T-shirts at every fête, gymkhana or agricultural show you could imagine. I organised a Miss Signal Radio competition and booked concerts for stars like Leo Sayer at the Theatre Royal, Hanley. It was hard work but great fun, and I was given the occasional assistance of students who came in for work experience.

The people I worked with were fantastic. We were like one big, happy family. My best supporters were Barry Machin, the accountant who ended up running the station, Donald Brooks, the managing director, and DJ Digby Taylor. For our first Christmas at Signal, I made them gifts, heating a pile of old singles individually in boiling water and moulding them into pen pots. Someone who visited the station recently said everyone still had them on their desks. I was amazed.

As part of my daily duties, I also began to present a short slot on the mid-morning show called 'What's On', for which I'd come on air to read out events listings for the next few days. It was nerve-wracking to start with, but I soon learned that if I wrote everything out in longhand and memorised much of it before I went on air, I wouldn't be tripped up by any difficult words.

Bruno and I were still dating, but the honeymoon period was definitely over. The busier he was, the more obsessed with the idea of making the big time, the more focused he became. Nothing was going to stand in the way of him or his ambition, and I quickly had to learn how to take second place. I found myself constantly checking what I said and how I looked, and worrying about what would happen if he ever did make it to London. As one of the brightest young DJs in the country, he knew that if he played his cards right, a job at the BBC in Portland Place would surely beckon. With hindsight, I don't think he ever doubted that he would succeed. It just wasn't in his make-up to accept failure.

'If you do get to go to Radio 1, Bruno, what do you think will happen to us?' I'd ask fearfully. In the two years we'd known each other, I'd become emotionally dependent on him.

'Well, we'll get married and you'll come to London with me, of course,' he'd say brusquely as I bit my lip, dreading the day I'd have to leave the security of Norton. He'd mentioned marriage before, always in the same vague way, as if it was the most inevitable thing in the world. I don't think it had even occurred to him that it might not happen.

Bruno was very busy at Radio Stoke, working five days a week broadcasting the popular drive-time programme. His evenings were spent out with his mates or in his studio thinking up new jingles and ideas for his shows. He'd bought a bungalow in the countryside at Baldwin's Gate, and he and I would meet up there on the evenings he was free. It was all rather perfunctory; so much so that I rarely stayed overnight, I'd almost always go home to Mum and Dad, however late.

In February 1985, Bruno was finally offered a job at Radio 1, initially taking over a slot from Steve Wright while he was on holiday, with a promise of regular work thereafter. He called me excitedly the afternoon he heard the news and I dropped everything and caught the first train down to London. We clubbed all night at Stringfellow's. I'd never seen him happier. To celebrate his good news, he bought me a ring with little diamonds in it. 'This isn't official or anything,' he said, sliding it on to my engagement finger. 'But you'll always be my girl, won't you?' I threw my arms around his neck and kissed him.

I wore that ring with such pride. It felt like a milestone after all the time I'd put in with him. Somewhere along the line, I'd completely lost my way and had allowed myself to revert to the timid little schoolgirl from Holden Lane when it came to handling Bruno. He was so confident, so sure of himself, that it made me question my own confidence and defer to him on everything. That is how dysfunctional relationships begin: the bullying side of one person brings out the victim in the other. Before long, the relationship is set and each side is equally to blame for allowing it to happen.

Mum and Dad were charitable enough to make all the right noises when we came home and showed them the ring. They'd never really taken to 'Trevor' but, as always, they stood by me and my decision and wished us both the very best. 'I hope you'll be very happy, Lil,' Dad told me, and I wondered at his emphasis on the word 'hope'. Lying in my own bed that night, twisting the ring round and round my finger, I couldn't sleep for thinking about what it would be like to be Mrs Bruno Brookes. I believed that without him I was nothing, and I began to accept that my only path now lay with him in London.

But there was no rush, Bruno assured me. 'Let me sort myself out for a few months and then we can start thinking about you joining me,' he said. 'I'll need some space for a while.' I knew that he was worried about his image: it might not look good for a new, young Radio 1 DJ to have a serious girlfriend, and he wanted to test the water. I remember going to one nightclub with him where he expressly forbade me from holding his hand in case it looked bad. Secretly I was relieved that I didn't have to make a decision about moving just yet. I wasn't in any great hurry to leave the bosom of my family. Wendy and I were still living at home, still in the same bed-rooms we'd had for years. She had followed me to St Dominic's and done rather better than me in her O-Levels, showing great promise as a writer. She, too, had started 'anoraking' at Signal Radio in her spare time and was planning a career as a journalist. We were still slightly strained in each other's company; we hadn't yet found a way of being friends as well as sisters and her circle of teenage chums was entirely separate from mine. But with the constant love and support of our parents and the happy home environment we'd always known, we lived together very companionably.

So for much of Bruno's first year at Radio 1, we saw each other only at weekends. He became a workaholic, always striving to make his show the best and to prove to his critics that he could stay the course. The atmosphere at Radio 1 was incredibly competitive. He was the new boy from the sticks and a lot of people treated him as such. He had a flat in Hampstead in north-west London, and lived alone apart from his cat, Harry. Initially he found living on his own in the capital very hard. He didn't know anybody and had few friends, so he became ever more and more dependent on me. Whenever I had a day off I'd go to London to see him or he'd come back up to Stoke.

'Please come down this weekend,' he'd plead on the telephone. 'I miss you.'

But as we both grew busier our weekends would be booked up with gigs or roadshows and we weren't able to see so much of each other. I was still in the promotions department and out most week-ends hitching up the trailer and going off to every Brownie jamboree and scouting event in the area. Away from his influence, I'd begun to develop a social life of my own and started to go out much more with the gang from work.

My happiness at Signal sustained me. The great bunch of friends I'd made there really helped to make me feel better about myself. They were terrific confidence-boosters. It was a far cry from the way Bruno was beginning to make me feel. In their company I felt as if I could do anything. Which was just as well, because one day, when Digby, the regular morning presenter, was taken ill, I was asked by John Evington, the new head of programming, if I would fill in for him. 'We need someone to take over the breakfast show at short notice, Anthea,' he said. 'Do you think you could give it a go?'

I didn't have enough time to think about it or to be nervous. I just went into the studio and was on air for three hours, playing records, chatting with listeners and hosting a phone-in. The Eurythmics were Number 1 with 'There Must Be An Angel (Playing with my Heart)' and I knew just what Annie Lennox meant. Once I got into my stride, I loved every minute of it. The slot went well, and so many people called in and kindly said they'd enjoyed listening to a local girl who knew the area presenting the show that I was allowed to do more. I hardly dared to hope, but I began to wonder whether I might have what it took to make a career in broadcasting.

Bruno was amazed when he heard what I'd done. He'd never had me down as a DJ. 'Now you know how hard it is,' he told me on the telephone. 'Maybe you'll be less impatient with me after this.'

The better my job was going, the more Bruno criticised me. Gaining power in London, I felt that he had lost touch with reality and become quite dictatorial. As the person closest to him, I was often the one who bore the brunt. I thought him jealous and possessive, and he chipped away at my confidence almost imperceptibly. He somehow managed to convince me that I owed him everything. 'Remember, if it wasn't for me,' he'd say over a meal out or in a nightclub, 'you'd never even be in that job that you love so much.' Drawing on a cigarette, he'd give me a knowing look.

Bruno had, by now, changed his mind about a girlfriend being bad for his image. He seemed to regard me as his personal property, to be used to his own advantage. It made him look good having a bubbly blonde on his arm, towering over him in her stilettos. It was all part of the persona. Once I was his, he no longer had to woo me and he didn't even try. In fact, he made me feel increasingly insecure about my looks and the way I dressed.

'What on earth are you wearing?' he'd say when I turned up to meet him somewhere. I'd look down at my trousers and my newest blouse with its shoulder pads and embroidered flowers and wonder what was wrong.

'It's hideous!' he'd exclaim, 'Go and change into something else, and for God's sake don't wear anything above the knee. Not with those legs.' I'd dutifully go off and change and come back in a tight-fitting top and a long skirt, hoping for a compliment. But the compliments never came. There were days and nights when I longed for the old Bruno, the pretty-faced boy who used to make me smile.

One Friday, not long after he'd moved to London, he rang to tell me he was coming home that night. He lived half an hour's drive from my parents and he asked me to meet him at his bungalow and stay over. I was sitting with my hair in a damp towel, fresh from the bath, having planned an early night. 'Oh, Bruno, no, I can't, I'm sorry,' I told him. 'I've got to be up at 6am tomorrow to get the trailer ready. I didn't expect you up this weekend.'

He was obviously miffed, and quite indignant that I wouldn't change my plans for him. 'Well, that's nice,' he spat. 'I'm coming all that way to see you and suddenly you're too busy.'

'Oh, come on, Bruno,' I argued. 'That's not fair. You know it's not like that. But you can't just pitch up here at nine o'clock and expect me to drop everything. I've got to work tomorrow.'

Knowing that I'd feel dreadful the next day if I didn't get an early night, I stuck to my guns and we ended the telephone conversation tersely. I went to bed, feeling incredibly guilty and worrying that I'd been too inflexible. After all, he was driving 200 miles to see me. So I decided to get up really early and drive over to the radio station to get everything ready ahead of schedule. Then I would have time to nip over to the bungalow and surprise him. I'd make him breakfast and serve it to him in bed before going off to work. That would make him smile.

The next morning I got everything done in good time and arrived at his house about 7am, letting myself in with my own key. Creeping in, I stepped across the hall and pushed open the door of his bedroom to check that he was still asleep and hadn't heard me.

The sight that met me was a complete shock. There was Bruno, the man I expected to marry and who I'd been dating for five years, lying in bed, stark naked, alongside a woman I'd never seen before in my life. I was so startled that I dropped my keys to the floor with a clatter and clasped my hands to my face. 'Bruno!' I exclaimed. 'How could you?'

The pair of them sat bolt upright and hastily tried to cover themselves. Bruno's face was a picture of contrition. Unable to look at him, I ran from the house, leaving the front door wide open. Outside, I just kept walking, hurrying through a gate and into a field opposite, where I stood trembling and watching the house. Within a few minutes, Bruno had come running out after me, half-dressed. 'I can explain,' he said, hopping barefoot towards me as he tried to pull up his trousers.

'Explain?' I asked incredulously, pointing back at his house. 'Explain how come you're in bed with another woman?'

'Don't worry, Anth,' he said. 'She's going.' Sure enough, moments later, the tall, blonde woman, now fully clothed and wearing white stilettos, emerged from the house. Bruno told me he was taking her home but that he'd be straight back.

I went back inside and rang the station manager. 'Something's happened,' I sobbed into the phone. 'It's personal, but I can't come in right now. I'm going to be late.' The manager was very kind. He told me not to worry and said he'd sort everything out.

Blowing my nose, I slumped into a chair in the lounge and waited for Bruno to come back. When he did, he paced around me cautiously and peered into my tear-stained face, doubtless wondering what to say. When he finally spoke, it was to cry: 'It's all your bloody fault!'

'What?' I said, astonished, twisting my tissue round and round in my hand.

'Yes, Anthea, your fault,' he said, rounding on me. 'If you'd come over when I asked you, this would never have happened.'

I was speechless. I couldn't even begin to argue with him. Within a matter of minutes, he had transformed himself from the offender into the hapless victim. With a persuasive speech worthy of the High Court, Bruno sold me the idea that I was entirely to blame, not him. 'You drove me to it, Anthea,' he said. 'I only succumbed to temptation because you refused to see me. I'm only flesh and blood, after all.' Battered and bemused, I didn't know any better than not to believe him. He had convinced me that I had little to offer anyone else and that without him I might well end up alone. I was so frightened of losing him, of giving up the dream that one day we'd be married and happy, that I forgave him. He was, after all, somebody and I was nobody. In spite of the destructive side to his nature, which affected both himself and those around him, he could also be very charming when he wanted to be. I learned to live for those moments.

Bruno went from strength to strength. He'd acquired a manager, Michael Cohen, and with Michael's help secured better and better slots on Radio 1. He became known as the compact disc jockey because of his size and within a year, he had manoeuvred himself into the hearts and minds of Radio 1 listeners. Bruno Brookes was here to stay.

Once he was established, there was no doubt in his mind that what he wanted most of all was me by his side. 'I need you down here, Anth,' he'd say with monotonous regularity. 'It's better if you're with me.' It wasn't that I wasn't enormously proud of him and what he had achieved – and of course there was great kudos in being a Radio 1 DJ's girlfriend – but moving to London had always seemed such a giant step to the girl from Norton I was afraid of being away from all that I knew. After a year of badgering me to leave my job, my home and my family to join him, however, he finally wore me down and I decided to take the plunge.

'What will you do in London?' my friends asked.

'Oh, I don't know,' I replied. 'Probably try to get a job working for one of the record companies.'

Signal Radio held a big leaving party for me at which I wept buckets. Their farewell card wished me all the best with 'Trevor'. Mum and Dad and Wendy were great. They helped me to pack my few belongings as I prepared to leave the nest for the first time in my life and to load up the Mini for the drive to London. I was twenty-five years old.

'Bye, sis,' said Wendy, now seventeen and gorgeous, squeezing me until it hurt. 'Ring me sometimes?'

I nodded.

'Goodbye, Anthea,' Mum added, embracing me warmly. 'And remember, you can always come back if things don't work out.'

I couldn't speak.

'Well, good luck, Lil,' Dad said, pulling me to him for a final hug. 'You will keep in touch now, won't you? Your mother will only worry.'

I promised I would and clung to him for far longer than I should have. Seeing them all standing in the driveway, waving to me as I pulled away, I swallowed hard and resisted the temptation to cry.

3

A Headless Chicken

London was as bewildering to me as it was exciting; bustling and vibrant, noisy, dirty, smelly, frightening and somehow quite wonderful. The wheels of the trucks trundling through it towered over my little Mini in the traffic queues. I spent most of my early days there trying to map-read while negotiating the roads. Everyone drove so fast, overtaking, undertaking, cutting me up. It was exhausting. Nothing in Norton-in-the-Moors had ever prepared me for the city's diversity and sheer scale. Although Hampstead had a village feel to it, with its red-brick Georgian houses and narrow streets set on a hill, the rest of the metropolis sprawled endlessly beyond its horizons, merging and melting into a vast, glimmering city of dreams.

But for me, the dreams seemed unattainable. Alone and friendless, with Bruno out at work every day and most weekends, I found myself wondering if I had been naïve to hope that moving south might mean that I either became his wife, or found myself some sort of career in broadcasting. 'It'll obviously take you a while to get to know people,' Bruno told me when I complained about being lonely. 'Nothing happens instantly. I was miserable to start with. I even thought about giving it all up and moving back to Stoke, but I stuck with it, and so must you. In the meantime, do you think that perhaps you could tidy this place up a bit and help me with some of my fan mail?'

Now that Bruno had made it, he clearly expected me to take a back seat and devote myself to being his right-hand woman. So, far from concentrating on my hopes of working for a record company or becoming a star of stage and screen, I spent my first year in London opening his mail, arranging all his personal appearances, charity shows and gigs, organising his diary, cooking his meals and washing his clothes. He eventually gave me the title of personal assistant and agreed to pay me £75 a week – a quarter of my salary at Signal – for working for him seven days a week.

'I don't want to be doing this for ever, Bruno,' I'd complain, having spent another day forging his signature on hundreds of publicity photographs. 'I'd like to get a proper job some time.'

'Don't be silly, Anth,' he'd say. 'You're brilliant at this and you know I couldn't possibly manage without you now. You're the one who keeps it all going. And anyway, where else could you work in a nice job, with a nice home, *and* get to sleep with the boss?'

To keep me company in the long hours when Bruno was away working, I had Harry, his black cat. It had been love at first sight between Harry and me at Baldwin's Gate. He was the son of Bruno's sealpoint Siamese, Pharaoh, who was later killed by a car. When, as a kitten, he kept leaping off the sofa we called him Harrier, after the jet, which then became shortened to Harry. Even Brian the Bear was jealous.

But Harry and Brian weren't enough company for me. I felt increasingly ill at ease about my decision to move to London and yet I was too ashamed to confide in my parents and Wendy that I wanted to come home. Bruno was, by now, presenting the live Sunday chart show to an audience of millions and had become a regular host of *Top of the Pops*. He wasn't just a radio personality, he was becoming a television celebrity as well. But the more he grew in public stature the more domineering I felt he became, making me completely dependent on him. He seemed increasingly controlling, criticising me constantly, twice throwing food I'd cooked at the wall, crushing any confidence I had in the possibility of a media career. Whenever he'd had enough of me, he'd disappear on a fishing expedition somewhere on his own, leaving me sitting at home, wondering what mood he'd be in when he came back. Anxious not to let my parents and friends know how unhappy I was, I didn't tell a soul. Even when I went home for Wendy's wedding in 1986 (she married a senior engineer from Signal Radio, having got a job there in commercial production), I held my tongue. Without Bruno, I had no home and no money and I was frightened of ending up penniless and lonely. Andy Sims had been right. Without an education, I'd wind up in a brainless occupation, and they didn't come much more brainless than this.

My chance to break the deadlock came at a dinner party given by Golly Gallagher, a record PR and friend of Bruno's, at his house in Surrey. The Radio 1 DJ David 'Kid' Jensen was there with his wife, Gudrun. It was a lovely evening and halfway through the meal, Golly turned to talk to me. 'Sky Trax are looking for a girl to be a video jockey for a new European music programme called *Here Comes the Weekend*,' he said. 'Kid's already signed up for it, along with Tony Blackburn, Gary Davies, Peter Powell and Pat Sharp. You should have a go, Anthea.'

Shaking my head and laughing, I told Golly: 'Oh no, I don't think so, I mean I haven't any experience of anything like that.'

Golly poured me some more wine and smiled. 'Everyone has to start somewhere,' he said.

The next day, home alone in Bruno's flat, I began to think about what Golly had said. He was right, everyone did have to start somewhere. I'd wandered aimlessly through life so far, going with the flow, taking what came along and trying to make the most of it. But deep inside, I think I'd always known I was different. I'd sometimes felt as if I was in a world of my own. I believed that one day a door would open and allow me to move forward and realise my full potential. There was something about what Golly had said that made me think that this might just be that door.

I picked up the telephone. 'Golly? It's Anthea. You know what you said last night about that vacancy at Sky? I wonder, do you have any more information?'

The director at Sky Trax was a lovely man called Ian Weiner and, when I spoke to him later that day, he suggested that I came along for an audition. I went for that screen test feeling quite ambivalent. 'I'll give it a go and if it doesn't work out, then I haven't lost anything,' I told my Mum on the phone the night before.

I'd never done a screen test before and the state-of-the-art equipment at the television production company's Tottenham Court Road studios looked intimidating. Wearing a pair of jeans and a pistachio green Benetton sweatshirt, I was led to a spot in front of the camera, my eyes dazzled by all the lights, and asked to read something from a rehearsed script. Squinting into the glare, flushed of face, struggling to differentiate the jumble of letters in my head, I must have presented a very sorry picture as I staccato-read my introductory lines.

'H-hello, um, this is *H-here Comes the W-weekend* and, er, my name is Anthea T-turner. Coming up, w-we've got – er – live competitions, special guests, romantic dedications, er, pop news and, um, party shows.'

I had to link three separate videos by Duran Duran, ABC and A-Ha. Technicians, producers and cameramen stood around watching me, along with Pat Sharp, then a very big name at Capital Radio. All eyes were on me. It was nothing like the days of the Queen's Theatre. I felt like a fish out of water, flapping around, gasping for oxygen. I went from being unable to speak to not being able to stop talking. In the end I was chattering on so much that they had to tell me to stop. I fled from the studios afterwards, chastising myself for ever thinking I could handle such a role. Bruno was right. I was crap.

No one was more surprised than me when Ian rang a few days later to tell me I'd got the job. 'Congratulations. You start in two weeks' time.' It was only part-time, a few hours four days a week on a year's contract, and when I told Bruno about it I sold it to him as something to keep me busy for a while.

He was clearly unhappy about it. His first reaction was to stop my wages, even though I still did just as much work for him.

I saw the Sky job almost as a hobby to give me some cash and fill the time when Bruno was working or away. I remember saying as much to Doreen Davies, the head of programming for Radio 1. She threw her head back and laughed out loud.

'Oh no, my dear,' she guffawed. 'You mark my words. Once you've had a bite of the cake, you'll want more.'

The one thing for which I will always thank Bruno was his insistence that before I signed the contract Sky sent me I sought some proper, professional advice. 'You can't be too careful with these things,' he said, speaking from experience. 'I'll make an appointment for you with James Grant, a new management company some of the lads at work have been talking about. It's been set up by Peter Powell and his business partner Russell Lindsay. Go and see them and listen to what they have to say.'

Peter Powell had shared my bedroom with me from the age of fourteen, when I'd first drooled over his picture in *Jackie* magazine, to sixteen. After David Cassidy, he had been my favourite teenage heart-throb and Radio Luxembourg and then Radio 1 DJ. By this time I had seen him in the flesh – and I'd made a complete fool of myself. It was not long after I'd joined Bruno in London when I'd arrived at Broadcasting House with a box of records and tapes for his next show.

Bruno had long regaled me with tales of rubbing shoulders with the likes of Paul Young, Boy George, Simon Le Bon and Wham! 'I saw Spandau Ballet in the corridor today,' he'd say casually. Or: 'Bryan Ferry was in the canteen this morning, having breakfast.' I'd stare at him in awe, wondering what life was really like on Planet Fame. Now there I was, standing by the lift in a pair of tight jeans and a drawstring T-shirt, suddenly aware of two people standing behind me, chatting. Turning, I almost dropped the box. A few feet behind me were Peter Powell and Steve Wright.

Peter was still, at thirty-five, the best-looking DJ around, with his floppy brown hair, twinkling eyes and boyish dimples. He, above all others, had played the soundtracks of my youth and had lived in an impossibly glamorous and distant world. Steve Wright was relatively new to the station, but had already gathered a loyal following of fans, refreshed and delighted by his wacky humour. Seeing the two of them together was almost as unreal as a fantasy encounter with David Cassidy.

Peter caught my eye, and I went so red in the face that I could have stopped traffic. Just as the lift arrived and the doors opened, I realised I couldn't possibly step into it with him, so I beat a hasty retreat. As I stumbled blindly for the stairwell, I glimpsed his rather bemused expression as he peered round the lift door. Unbeknown to me, he turned to Steve Wright and said: 'Who on earth was that?'

'Bruno Brooke's girlfriend,' Steve told him. 'They've been together for years.'

Pete leaned back against the lift wall. 'Wow!' was all he said.

Now here I was, a year later, sitting opposite him and his partner, Russ, at Pete's smart four-storey house in Chiswick, west London, overlooking the marina, soliciting their professional advice. I'd actually asked to see Russell, because I knew I'd be unable to face Peter without blushing. But when I got there, the two of them were waiting and of course I went blood-red the minute Peter looked at me with those piercing brown eyes. I was more than a bit gobsmacked and could hardly think of a single intelligent question to raise.

Russ tried to put me at my ease and talked me through what the Sky contract meant and what my obligations would be. He came across as incredibly efficient and competent. Peter was as enigmatic as I'd always imagined him to be. Chain-smoking, he sat silently watching me before saying finally: 'If you like, Rusty and I can represent you and help you deal with all this side of things in the future.'

I nodded enthusiastically. All I'd heard from Bruno was how astute it had been of Peter to set up James Grant Management while he was winding down his Radio 1 career, and I had no doubt, having met Russ, or 'Rusty', as well, that I'd be in very capable hands.

'Do you have any questions?' Pete asked, staring at me intensely.

'Um, yes,' I said. 'Why did you call your company James Grant?'

Relaxing, he grinned at me and I found myself automatically grinning back. 'James is my middle name and Grant is Rusty's,' he explained. 'Considering my age and the fact that I've already had one career, we thought James Grant sounded better than Rusty Pete.'

On my first day at Sky, I turned up for rehearsals in a sweatshirt, jeans and Farrah Fawcett hairstyle. I was twenty-six and full of beans but incredibly wet behind the ears. As one of the four presenters, it was my job to fill in between videos, introducing the next item and giving gossipy news about others, just like a disc jockey, really, but on television. The show was to be broadcast to 20,000 homes in the United Kingdom and many more across Europe, mainly in Holland.

The producers and directors at Sky were very kind. They told me where to sit and what to say and tried to put me at ease. It all felt very strange, though. I'd never been in the working part of a television studio before my audition and it showed. My links between videos were jerky and stiff; I was tongue-tied and wide-eyed. I was so nervous I'd miss something that I often looked completely terrified instead of laid-back and cool as I introduced the latest from Madonna, the Pet Shop Boys or Europe. I'm just so grateful that I made all my first mistakes on foreign television.

A few weeks into my contract, the people around me began to gently suggest that maybe I should loosen up a little bit, change my hairstyle, wear brighter clothes or alter the way I spoke. My accent was stronger than it is now, with much flatter vowels, and in those days conformity was the name of the game. I tried to round off my vowels, but I didn't really understand how to change my way of speaking. I might not have talked 'southern' but I knew that I was perfectly well understood. Gary Davy, the Australian producer, sent me to a renowned RADA coach in Alexandra Palace for elocution lessons, but when she heard me speak, she scowled and said: 'I don't know what the problem is.'

This conflicting advice served only to make me even more self-conscious and, with Bruno adding his tuppence-worth, for a while I didn't know which way to turn. Everyone else seemed trendy and chic. I tried to reinvent myself but I had no natural style at all – I didn't even know what the word meant. I rushed out and acquired a whole new wardrobe: leather trousers and jackets with huge shoulder pads which I wore with the sleeves rolled up. I added funky jewellery and generally tried to give myself a bit more street cred. The eighties were an ugly time for fashion and I'd embraced it all wholeheartedly. I looked horrific. When I went to a nightclub-opening in Holland with Tony Blackburn and Gary Davies, I actually wore the lavender moiré water taffeta bridesmaid dress I'd had for Wendy's wedding. It was sleeveless with a bodice, and entirely inappropriate. We were mobbed as we entered the new venue, a place called the Escape Club on the Rembrandtsplein, and I was hurriedly ushered inside by bouncers. I thought I looked so cool but behind my back people must have been whispering: 'What *does* she look like?' I truly hadn't a clue.

Bruno still didn't seem at all happy about my new job. He recognised that I had ambition, too, but everything he did seemed to undermine it. He'd always said that we made the perfect team, but I was a very long way from being his equal. He saw my hopes for a career as a threat to our cosy personal and professional relationship, but he dressed up this view as concern that I would be made a complete fool of. 'You're heading for a fall,' he'd say ominously. 'You'll only get hurt. It's a big, bad world out there.'

I listened to him and began to doubt myself. Whenever he was a complete pig, I always ended up thinking that it was probably no more than I deserved. I began to believe that in truth he wanted things to stay the way they were, because I was his personal serf and his walking, talking diary. If he needed to know where his next few gigs were as he toured the country with the Radio 1 Roadshow, he'd ask me. If he wanted a cup of coffee, I was expected to make it. If his vividly coloured jackets needed to be collected from the dry cleaner's, off I would trot.

It was the era of glam rock and Bruno was seen as the bright young thing of the airwaves, promoting the up-and-coming bands, so record companies and pluggers and all manner of people who wanted to speak to him were often channelled from his management company through me. I did it all unflinchingly, as well as my own job, and there were times when I enjoyed a great deal of it. Despite the fact that I was deeply unhappy with our relationship, working for him was undoubtedly an interesting time for a former photographer's receptionist from the Midlands. I guess I was hanging on to the comet's tail.

My greatest support in those early days was Peter Powell. Every time I came away from a meeting with him, I felt much better about myself. 'You've got so much going for you, AT,' he'd say. 'You're young and beautiful and enthusiastic and you've got bags of potential. Never forget that.' Pete has always laughed at my insecurities and claims he knew from the outset that I could make it to the big time. He's a fantastic motivator, a real inspiration to his clients, and it works. The more we talked, the more I liked him.

We'd come from remarkably similar backgrounds. Peter grew up in Stourbridge in the West Midlands, in a warm and supportive family atmosphere with a sister, Ally, and a loving mother, Margaret. His father, Monty, was a metallurgist by choice and a timber merchant by necessity. Pete was also marginally dyslexic, and had been weak at exams but strong on enthusiasm. Having listened to Radio 1 in his youth, he announced to his father that he wanted to be a DJ.

'Dear boy,' Monty had replied in all seriousness, 'why on earth do you want to be a dinner jacket?'

In between selling timber and even pig sheds, Peter managed a local band and secured himself a job at BBC Radio Birmingham. He was eighteen and their youngest DJ. Fired after nine months, he went to Radio Luxembourg to learn his craft before returning to the BBC for an eleven-year career with Radio 1.

Down-to-earth and still very close to all his old friends from Stourbridge, Peter shied away from the fame his celebrity status brought him. He was adored by his female fans and even had stalkers. It was all so unbalancing, he completely lost track of people's names, so he called everyone 'mate', a trademark which stuck. A free spirit, fiercely independent and someone who loved to be surrounded by lots of people, he developed a reputation for dumping girlfriends after a few months. His friends started to take bets on the near-certainty that he would never settle down.

Pete was at the height of his fame and success when he decided to move sideways into management. He was presenting the prestigious Radio 1 teatime show and had done everything anyone could wish to do in radio. He'd been the voicebox for the teenage generation and was hugely respected for the lead he had taken with the 'new romantic' era. But he was becoming more and more of a businessman and less of a DJ. With the blessing of Johnny Bealing, a controller of Radio 1, he set up his own management company because he felt that he had the greatest qualification of all: he had been there. Pete promised Johnny that he'd stay on and fulfil his contract, but that when the time came to go, he'd have to leave.

His first client was Phillip Schofield, a postboy at the BBC who liked to sit in on Pete's radio show. Pete told him: 'If ever you want a career in showbusiness, let me know and I'll help you.' When Phillip said he did, Pete knew it was time to move ahead. He had a series of very loyal friends and contacts who encouraged him, and before long he'd found Phillip a job in children's television. He went into partnership with Russ, who he'd known for years as a friend and former employee, and they added Mark Goodier and Simon Mayo to their books.

For three years Pete ran the two sides of his life in tandem, staying on at Radio 1 and running James Grant on the side. When I first met him, he was at the tail end of that period and about to go it alone. 'You've got to take chances in this life, AT,' he'd tell me. 'You learned that by applying for the job at Sky. I'm about to do the same. Hopefully, it'll work out fine for us both.'

I was at Sky for twelve months and, once I realised that I could actually do the job, I grew in confidence with every show and really began to enjoy it. I'd never been first off the mark in terms of go-getting but a little voice inside my head, supported by Pete's louder one, kept telling me: 'You can do it.' Ever since I was young, I'd kept scrapbooks of my theatrical reviews, cards and photographs and so on. Now I was proud to add to them the odd newspaper cutting about me as a video jockey and spent hours with scissors and glue snipping articles about Bruno, me or *Here Comes the Weekend* out of the newspapers. I worked hard at my job, swotting up on the music scene, reading all the teen magazines and rock papers so that when I had to interview people like Patsy Kensit, Boy George or Sam Fox, I'd have some clever things to say.

Shane MacGowan from the Pogues was my worst-ever inter-viewee. It was eleven in the morning when he came in and sat down, holding in his hand what looked like a large glass of Ribena. 'Hi, Shane, welcome to *Here Comes the Weekend*,' I said. 'Now tell me, what's been happening in your life?'

The answer I got was little more than a slur. Aghast, I realised that it wasn't Ribena he was drinking, it was neat port. He was off his face and this was a live show. Stumbling on through the interview, I couldn't get two words of sense out of him. I had to improvise until my allotted time was up and I floundered badly. I blamed myself entirely. 'This is terrible, awful television and it's all my fault,' I was thinking. Of course it wasn't, but I was so accustomed to taking the blame that I did it yet again. (I got my own back on Shane MacGowan years later, when I dressed up as him for a Hale and Pace spoof of *Stars in Their Eyes* and sang the lines: 'Ten years have I missed, I was permanently pissed, and my liver's the size of Dover.')

Apart from the odd glitch, though, the job was great fun and, amazingly, I was getting paid for it. With my first-ever cheque from Sky, for £2,000, I rushed out and traded in my Mini for a Suzuki jeep. It seemed like just the right car for the rough streets of London. At least I wouldn't be crushed by the truck wheels any more. Now I was really cooking with gas.

The people at Sky continued to help me through my first year in television. Pat Sharp was helpful and kind, Gary Davies was delightful and Tony Blackburn – what a survivor – ended up taking me on a tour of the red-light district of Amsterdam. Within the space of a few months, my life had turned round. I had a good job, a lovely car, I was living in London and I had money to burn. I never wanted it to end.

I wasn't in the right place at the right time, though. However much I'd improved my technique, I still didn't look hip enough and I had nothing pierced at all. So I wasn't altogether surprised when my contract ended and Gale Claydon, my producer, broke the news that I was to get the sack. 'I think you're a bit more *Blue Peter*, love,' she added, with great gravitas. She was right, of course. But I didn't realise that until much later.

'I told you so,' Bruno said when he heard I'd been dropped from Sky. 'I knew this would end in tears.' In the months that followed, I remained unemployed and began to believe him when he told me that I'd enjoyed my 'five minutes of fame' and should now consider becoming a secretary (as if I could be, with my spelling!).

Pete never stopped believing in me, however, and he and Russ found me a job as a co-presenter on *But First This* on Children's BBC for the 1987 school summer holidays. Along with my fellow presenters I'd fill in the gaps between programmes by reading out letters and birthday greetings and chatting to young viewers. There were three of us on the show, Tracy Brabin, who went on to work on *Coronation Street*, Simon Potter and Siobhan Mare. It was a great forum to show off what each of us was capable of, which, as far as I was concerned at that time, involved a lot of giggling and joking with my colleagues. Not that there weren't pitfalls to overcome first.

For the first time in my life, I had to learn how to use an earpiece, an essential piece of equipment for any television presenter. A hidden hearing device plugged into the ear, with wires trailing down the neck and under the clothing, the earpiece gives a link to the gallery, or studio control room. This enables the director and producer to prompt you on what's coming up and what you are meant to be doing next while you're still talking and on air.

'OK, Anthea, five seconds to the link to video, four, three, two, one . . .' The trouble is that when the device is on a facility called open talk, you can pick up every single sound in the gallery, from the production staff chatting to each other through instructions to other presenters to the secretary giggling in the background.

To get used to managing to think, move, talk and follow the autocue with this constant chattering in my ear, I asked a friend, Stephanie (now Phillip Schofield's wife), who worked at the BBC, to record some gallery noise on to a cassette for me. Then, for six weeks before *But First This* went on air, I walked everywhere, watched television, went to Waitrose and did my aerobics with my Walkman strapped to my side, its continuous and complicated instructions echoing in my ear. If anyone had been listening in, they'd have had me down as a complete fruitcake.

The hope of all three of us presenters was that one of us might be selected for the 'broom cupboard', the full-time link job on Children's BBC, but sadly, none of us was. When the summer holidays came to an end and the show finished, the work dried up again. Try as Pete and Russ might to put my name forward, no one snapped me up. My little pot of savings soon dwindled to nothing and I reluctantly went back to earning £75 a week from Bruno, supplementing my income by selling bric-a-brac, records and CDs at car-boot sales in Kent. I even agreed to dress up as a credit card once for a promotion on a garage forecourt in south-west London to earn a few extra pennies. It was humiliating and I felt a complete failure.

Bruno, on the other hand, was incredibly busy, working full-time and away a lot on gigs. He'd caught the tail end of the golden days of Radio 1 and was following in the footsteps of DLT, Annie Nightingale, Emperor Rosko and Mike Read. While I was feeling miserable and unwanted, he was earning great money both from Radio 1 and from a promotional contract with Sony and was really enjoying himself. He was doing so well that in 1987 he decided we should move from his three-bedroomed flat in Hampstead to a five-storey town house at the Wapping Pierhead in east London. The house, close to the Prospect of Whitby, dated back to 1811 and was a beautiful Regency property originally built by the Port of London Authority for their finest captains. Bruno paid a lot of money for it, but it needed a great deal of work.

In my capacity as domestic factotum to Bruno, it was my job to look after everything from the move itself to sorting out the builders in addition to doing all his household, secretarial and PR work. I threw myself into my new task, busying myself with getting everything straight and thinking that Bruno was almost certainly right: my moment of stardom had passed. That Christmas I went home to my parents, taking Harry the cat with me and feeling utterly down.

'How's everything going in London, Lil?' Dad asked as he served me some brussels sprouts.

'Fine,' I lied. 'My management company says something new should come in for me any day now.'

Dad emptied the spoon on my plate and gently kissed the top of my head.

For several months, I was busy being busy. The second-best thing Bruno ever did was to hire an interior designer for the house, a woman called Sue Van Der Ree. She and I hit it off straight away when we met at a dinner party at Jane and Jeff Chegwin's house (Jeff, the brother of Keith Chegwin, was in the music business and a friend of Bruno's) and Jane, Sue and I quickly became friends.

Under Bruno's specific and very detailed instructions, his ram-shackle house was transformed into a gin palace of mirrors and chandeliers, with silk flowers and plants everywhere. It looked like the Hanging Gardens of Babylon. Bruno installed a life-sized china Dalmatian dog, a chocolate vending machine, a sunken bath and huge ivory marble fireplace. He bought a bed from the Ideal Home Exhibition, which was all blue velvet and gold with a radio and con-trol panel in smoked glass, which he had draped with fabric so it looked like a bedouin tent. He'd arrive home in his Porsche, give the latest additions the once-over, pour himself a whisky, sign the neces-sary cheques and go out again. I often felt like little more than a caretaker.

Once again, it was Pete who came to the rescue with the chance of an audition for a job co-presenting *UP2U*, a lively Saturday-morning children's programme broadcast from Manchester, starting in May 1988. If I made it through the audition, I would be one of three pre-senters for the show, which was a summer version of the popular *Superstore*. The producer was Peter Hamilton and he and Ed Pugh, the head of children's television in Manchester, supervised the audi-tion. I was shaking like a leaf, but I'd learned the script they sent me off by heart so I hoped that I'd come across as a professional.

When I got there, the first thing Peter Hamilton said to me was: 'Oh, I don't know if anyone told you, Anthea, but we've changed the script. We won't be working from the one we sent you after all.' I nearly fainted. Instead they took me out to the BBC car park with a camera crew and told me: 'You've got two and a half minutes. Say anything that enters your head.' Panicking big-time, I swallowed hard and spun my head round searching for anything or anyone of interest. Suddenly spotting two builders in a nearby café, who were watching me with some amusement, I marched across to them, the camera in my wake, and started asking them ridiculous questions.

'What are you doing here?' was my first gem.

'Eating my breakfast,' came the stunning reply. I looked down at their plates of bacon and eggs and felt physically sick. I managed to fill half the time in the café, but when things became just too embarrassingly awkward, I hot-footed it back to the car park and prattled on about cars for the final minute and a half. God, it was awful.

To my great astonishment, however, the powers that be took me on, alongside Jenny Powell, a pretty, dark-haired girl, and a six-foot hunk called Tony Doherty. It was that show that really gave me my first break, although I have no doubt that I was ultimately employed for my hair colour as much as for what came out of my mouth. They had a brunette and a black guy and they needed a blonde. I was blonde, so I got the job.

Bruno wasn't happy, especially as this time I'd be away from home for at least three days a week in the middle of his major house-renovation project. But by now, thanks to Sue and Jane, who was a nurse, and who'd both given me a new perspective, it had begun to dawn on me that perhaps Bruno wasn't worth giving up a career for. I accepted the job and felt that I had something to look forward to at last.

UP2U was quite ahead of its time. We asked children to fax us with their requests (fax machines having only just become common household appliances), and the spontaneity was great, although I was always terrified of being caught on air unable to read something out. We had a diddly-squat budget, but we somehow managed to do outside broadcasts and all sorts of other gigs that really worked. The kids loved it, and so did I. I'd travel up north every Thursday and come back on Saturday afternoons.

Not that it was all plain sailing. I had one of my most embarrassing moments in television on *UP2U* with Hamish, the studio dog, a cairn terrier belonging to Peter Hamilton. Hamish, sitting on my knee while I was talking the viewers through a piece on fax machines, let rip the most disgusting fart I'd ever smelled in my life. Trying desperately to keep a straight face while those around me fled from the dreadful pong, I carried on valiantly until the piece was over. How I stopped myself from laughing, being sick or passing out, I'll never know.

I took my job terribly seriously and would spend hours in front of the television watching other presenters like Sarah Greene to see if I could pick up any tips. The worst children's television presenters wear bright clothes and shout a lot. I watched the good and the bad and learned my craft from them. I scrutinised everything and took as much advice as I could from people in the business.

'Give it up,' Bruno would tell me crossly, 'Go into PR, you're wasting your time.' But I knew he was wrong. In PR I'd have had to read reports and write up proposals and do all the things that my dyslexia made it difficult for me to do. At least in television, all I had to be was myself, and I always felt very comfortable with it. With *UP2U* going so well, I really felt as if I'd broken away from Bruno and was gaining in confidence again. My scrapbook was even filling up. Peter was helping me as much as he could, and had become a very important influence in my life. He was kind and gentle and wise and I was leaning on him more and more, both professionally and emotionally.

It was about this time that I first began to experience what it was like to be a 'celebrity'. Children would come up to me in the supermarket and ask for my autograph. 'Haven't I seen you on the telly?' mothers would ask, pointing at me just as I was about to reach for a packet of Tampax or something equally embarrassing. 'Yes,' I'd say, colouring up. I felt as if I'd finally found my niche.

The trouble was, the more fulfilled I was, the more resentful Bruno appeared to become. On one occasion, on the way to a night-club in London in his Porsche, I mentioned in passing that I'd been asked to present a show for Signal Radio at St Chad's Church, where Ruth is buried. 'I've said I'll do it, so I'll probably stay up there next weekend,' I told him. To my astonishment, he went into a rage, screaming and shouting at me. 'What on earth do you think you're playing at? he asked. 'Why are you doing that sort of rubbish and not even getting paid for it?' He nearly went off the road.

One of his most dramatic outbursts was witnessed by my sister Wendy, who was staying with us for a while. She'd asked me if she could use the telephone and I'd replied, without hesitation, 'Of course.' Bruno walked in while she was making her call and said angrily: 'Wendy's on the phone. Why didn't she ask me if she could use it?' There was a cold look in his eyes which by now I had come to recognise only too well. Backing away slightly, I explained quietly that she'd asked me and I'd told her it was fine. But clearly that wasn't good enough. He flew off the handle and went for me. 'It's *my* phone – *I* pay for it! You should have asked me,' he shrieked. Picking up the portable television, he hurled it to the floor, where it smashed into a hundred pieces.

All Bruno seemed to care about was himself. I never knew if he was proud of me, or if he felt for me when life wasn't going well. His only concern appeared to be that he had lost his full-time personal assistant. Because of the way he felt about me working, things became very unpleasant between us. There would be childish tantrums, often involving inanimate objects that got in his way after he'd drunk a few too many whiskies. I once watched in horror as he systematically destroyed his bedroom in a blind fury. When everything had been tipped upside down, ripped apart or hurled about, he stormed out and left me to clear up the mess.

It was through Wendy and my new-found friends that my eyes were opened and I started to see what was going on. My sister taught me a thing or two about life. It was she and Sue who first made me realise that Bruno had no right to treat me so badly. 'You know you can walk away from this any time you want,' Sue reminded me.

Scared as I was at the thought of life without Bruno as my anchor, they began to persuade me that such a prospect was not without its appeal. I'd known for some time that Bruno and I weren't the match made in heaven I'd always hoped we would be, but until people started to be brutally honest with me about him, I don't think I'd understood how much I was allowing myself to be used.

When I look back on this whole period of my life with Bruno it is all a bit of a fog. There is a great deal I have tried to erase from my memory and I still find some of it very disturbing. I rarely shared any of it with my friends and family. I was in the classic vicious circle of a woman in a dysfunctional relationship. It had started off with a loss of confidence on my part, which had served only to feed his sense of superiority. After the storms, he wouldn't be in the least bit contrite –

he'd just make me feel guilty for riling him. Like the time when I found him in bed with another woman, it would be all my fault, and because of my low self-esteem, I'd believe him. We were each in a downward spiral fuelled by the other. I decided that the time had come to do what I wanted to do, for me, and not to listen to him any more.

Bruno must have sensed my unhappiness because, completely out of the blue, he decided he ought to try to do something to salvage the relationship. We were downstairs together in Wapping, in the room with his mixer desk and his filing cabinets.

'I've decided that we should get married,' he said suddenly.

I turned to face him, shocked and stunned. There was no romance, no suggestion that he should even ask what I felt about the idea. Then, to put the icing on the cake, he handed me a brown envelope and told me: 'But first you'll have to sign this prenuptial agreement. It's nothing to worry about. It's all quite normal. Most people with money do it these days.' And with that he produced a complicated four-page document which he'd had drawn up by one of the best litigators in the country.

Speechless, I held the agreement in my hand and scanned through it. He was named as sole beneficial owner of the house I called home, and under the terms of the agreement, in the event of a divorce I would be entitled to an amount equivalent to only one-fifth of its net equity value in settlement. It effectively gave me a small share of his estate, but only from the moment we were married. It completely overlooked the years I'd spent with him before, helping him with his career. The only mention of that was a line that read: 'Bruno has paid to Anthea reasonable amounts of maintenance from time to time and wages for work undertaken by her upon his behalf.' He'd also added a clause which ran: 'Anthea undertakes and agrees that she will not discuss with, or make comment to, any third party (save in confidence with her legal advisers) about Bruno or her relationship with Bruno whether or not such information is in the public domain. Anthea further agrees to keep and maintain as confidential any and all information concerning Bruno, his personal and/or business affairs.'

Staring at the document, my heart was thumping in my chest. I couldn't believe it. Where was the trust? Where were the years of mutual respect? If I'd walked into Bruno's life after he'd become rich and famous, I might have understood him being a little wary. But I was someone who'd known him since he had a battered old Volkswagen Golf and a couple of turntables. I was someone who'd been part of his rise to success. I know that he would have made it without me – I'd never credit myself with that much influence on his career – but I'd been very much a part of it. For eight years I'd been the mainstay of his life and had smoothed his path. Hurt beyond words, I threw the papers to the floor. 'You know where you can stick that,' I finally told him before grabbing my coat and walking out.

After this episode the atmosphere between us deteriorated rapidly. I withdrew from him both emotionally and physically. On the advice of friends, I went to see a lawyer and had him look at the document. Letters flurried back and forth between the two sides, and my solicitor kept apologising for the way I was being treated. In the end, and on his advice, I simply refused to acknowledge or sign the agreement. 'It's not worth the paper it's written on,' I told Bruno, angry and hurt.

He was furious and said I was stupid. 'You'll live to regret not signing that,' he told me, 'once we're married, you'll live to regret it.' I didn't have the heart to tell him that he and I would never be walking down the aisle.

Work kept me busy and away from further pain. Peter knew that things weren't going well with Bruno and he tried to be as supportive as he could. He was always very straight with me, and although he only told me what anyone could have – that I needed to sort myself out – coming from him, this advice seemed to strike a chord. Increasingly, he'd been guiding me through. In the space of a few years he'd become a good friend as well as a brilliant manager. He was all the things to me Bruno hadn't been and I trusted him implicitly. Bit by bit, I realised that my feelings towards him were changing and that I was beginning to find myself attracted towards him as well. I'd been faithful to Bruno all along, and I knew that if I was feeling like this about Pete, then the writing really was on the wall.

Pete had by then taken the plunge and left Radio 1 to concentrate on his management career. It was a terrifying prospect for someone of his earning potential, but he knew he had to give it a shot. He'd taken on a new client, Caron Keating, the daughter of Gloria Hunniford. Caron, who was dating Phillip Schofield, was a presenter on *Blue Peter*. He asked me if I minded her joining the firm.

'Mind? Why should I mind?' I said.

'Well, you're the only girl on our books at the moment, and I thought you might worry that she could pick up jobs that you might have been in line for.'

'Don't be silly, Pete,' I told him, laughing. 'I'm way behind Caron. She's done really well. Of course you must sign her up.' Pete was hugely relieved. I knew he was under enormous pressure. He was desperate to make his new venture work, but at the same time he still had to give 100 per cent to those of us who'd been with him from the start. Just as he had sensed that I needed a friend, I understood that in him.

So when he and Russ invited me to a Whitney Houston concert at Wembley with a whole crowd of friends a few weeks later, I accepted without hesitation and we had a great night out. Whitney had real star quality and I was hugely impressed. When she sang the lines: 'Learning to love yourself is the greatest love of all,' I nearly cried, she was so spot-on.

I'd left my car at Pete's house and travelled to Wembley in his car, so when the concert was over, he and I drove back together, chatting animatedly all the way. 'Fancy a coffee?' he asked as we finally reached his front door shortly before midnight.

'Love one,' I replied, happy to spend a few more minutes with him. Anything but go home to an empty house. Bruno was away working.

He put the key in the door and we walked inside. The lights were off as we climbed the stairs and reached the landing, and he leaned across me to find the light switch. Suddenly, as our bodies collided in the dark, he grabbed hold of me firmly by the arms and kissed me on the lips. When he kissed me a second time, I found myself reciprocating, kissing his mouth as hungrily as he was kissing mine. Before

I knew it, he had scooped me up into his arms and, with my head resting on his shoulder, carried me into his bedroom.

I would never have made the first move, and if Pete hadn't, I don't think anything would ever have happened between us. But I was lonely and vulnerable. After eight years with Bruno, I was like a headless chicken, I didn't know which way to turn. The only person who ever gave me any positive input, who made me feel needed and protected and maybe even reasonably good at my job, was Pete. Without being aware of it I'd come to rely on him in every way. We were both adults, we knew what we were doing, but I think in retrospect that we were both very needy at that time, too.

What I hadn't banked on was how I'd feel afterwards. I'd always been drawn to Peter. He was someone I'd admired from afar, but once we'd been intimate, I very quickly fell in love. Lying next to him then, I knew that the thread was broken for ever with Bruno. My heart was lost. It was as if I'd come home at last.

But it wasn't that easy. It never is. Despite my secret happiness, I was also wracked with guilt and remorse. Reality was never far away. Being unfaithful to Bruno is not something I've ever been proud of. In an ideal world, I should have left him, made a clean break and then maybe started something up with Pete at a later date, but I didn't, chiefly because I was so terribly confused. By that time I was emotionally battered and bruised. I didn't honestly know if I was coming or going and Pete was the only one who made any sense of my life. Over the next few weeks I tried to pluck up the courage to tell Bruno about Pete, but somehow I never found the right moment.

I knew it wasn't right to see Pete behind his back. The two of them had never been close friends, but they were professional acquaintances and it was clear to me that this wasn't the best way to go about things. Bruno looked up to Pete; he was one of the reasons Bruno had wanted to become a Radio 1 DJ in the first place. I knew I was playing with fire and I wished it could've been different. I agonised over what my parents would say if they knew what I was doing and I often wondered how it would all end.

There were times when I remember thinking, 'What on earth am I playing at?' I knew it was the final straw for my relationship with

Bruno, but I was helplessly in love. Pete became my all-consuming passion. Thoughts of him crowded into my head and filled my heart. I felt released. I couldn't wait to see him again, to be in his arms. I felt as if I was walking on air, freed from the shackles of Bruno and the life I'd led before. But I had to stop my heart ruling my head. There was more to it all than just emotional considerations: Bruno and I shared a house, it was my home and had been for some years, even though I had no financial stake in it. Pete was my manager and friend, and if things turned sour between us, I wouldn't know who else to turn to. Whichever way I cut the cake, it was going to get very messy.

Bruno suspected nothing at first, but I have always been a poor liar. I'd flicked off a switch in my mind and could no longer pretend to be in love. I wouldn't sleep with him – it would have felt like betraying Pete somehow – so he realised quite quickly that something was up. In typical Bruno style, he didn't confront me about it but went off in a sulk to do a Radio 1 Roadshow. I watched him go and wished I could have been brave enough to tell him the truth before he left.

That night, I was alone at the house in Wapping when the telephone rang. It was Bruno. 'I think we should get married as soon as possible,' he said, apropos of nothing. I remained silent, holding my breath. 'You can forget all about the prenuptial agreement,' he added, thinking that this was the reason for my hesitation. 'It doesn't matter any more.'

I faltered. Finally, I took a deep breath and said: 'Listen, Bruno. Things haven't been right between us for a while. This really isn't a good time. If you want an answer right now, then it would have to be no.'

There was silence his end, while he digested my response. Then he said casually: 'You're seeing someone else.'

'No,' I replied, defensively, bristling. I was glad he couldn't see how the colour had drained from my face.

'I've hired a private detective. He's been watching you. It cost me £2,000. I know all about you and Peter Powell.'

I was staggered, although I shouldn't have been. That was Bruno through and through. I had been oblivious of it all, but apparently I'd been followed and had my photograph taken. Almost more surprising than this was how much money Bruno had been prepared to part with to arrange this surveillance. Something inside me made me want to laugh out loud and say: 'If you'd come to me first, I would have told you for a grand.'

But I didn't. Whatever he was to me now, Bruno was still the man with whom I'd shared my life and my bed for nearly eight years. He'd held my hand through the end of my teens, he'd been at my side through my first few jobs until I entered the world of television. In those early days, we'd had a lot of fun together and he had helped me to break away from my former life. He had his faults, chiefly that he had somehow made me feel guilty about every aspect of my life, but I suppose I was as much to blame for letting myself be so browbeaten. Guilt and uncertainty had kept me at his side for so long, and now he was making me feel more guilty than I'd ever thought possible. He made it crystal-clear that he deserved much better after all he'd done for me. There was no mention of the woman I'd found him in bed with, or the many other one-night stands I'd suspected him of indulging in over the years. Me and my heinous crime were the only topics on the agenda.

I knew he was going to be in Brighton that night for the roadshow the following day and I agreed to go down and see him so that we could talk things through. I replaced the receiver and stared at the telephone in shock and disbelief.

Picking it up again, I rang Pete straight away to tell him what had happened.

'Oh, fuck!' he said. I could tell from his voice that he didn't want this at all. He was backtracking big-time. Pete is the most non-confrontational person I know and he clearly wasn't prepared for a showdown. He was new to this – he hadn't even had that many serious girlfriends, and he'd always run a mile as soon as there had been a hint of commitment. Work he could handle, advice on your career and he was your man, but back him into a corner and ask him to tell you what he was really feeling or what his intentions were, and he was off. By the time we'd finished talking, I was beginning to wonder if I'd ever see him again.

Mum and Dad on their wedding day in 1955.

Me, aged three, sitting in Dad's MG pretending to drive.

Aged two and a half with kiss curls.

As the Virgin Mary in a school production. My sister Ruth is sitting on the
floor (far right).

As a teenager, all teeth and no confidence.

As a nightingale in another school production. I loved it when all eyes were on me.

A teenage dream, playing Liesl in *The Sound of Music*.

As a flapper girl on stage at the Queen's Theatre, Burslem.

OUR WORLD

BRUNO BROOKES & ANTHEA TURNER

He's a hit at spinning discs, but just for the record, home and girlfriend Anthea are number one with the Radio 1 DJ, as Ruby Millington discovered

When Radio 1 DJ Bruno Brookes finally moved into his elegant north London flat on Christmas Day two years ago, it was his fifth home in as many months. And if you've ever experienced the trials and traumas of a major house move, you'll sympathise with him! "I'm a typical Taurean," he reveals. "The sort whose home is his castle. I really need my roots, and when I move house I feel like my whole life has collapsed around me — I just can't think straight!"

Paradoxically, though, Bruno's one of those people who thrives on pressure — which is just as well when you consider that his hectic

With Bruno Brookes for an article in *Woman's World* magazine.

A publicity shot for Signal Radio.

In panto costume for Sky Trax with Tony Blackburn, Kid Jensen, Pat Sharp and colleagues.

An UP2U publicity shot with Jenny Powell and Tony Dortie.

Peter Powell in his days as a teenage heart-throb on Radio 1.

Frizzled like a grilled tomato after the accident at the Royal Tournament.

STUNT SENDS TV GIRL UP IN FLAMES

YOUNG viewers watched in horror yesterday as TV girl Anthea Turner was injured in a stunt that went wrong.

By ANNA FRANKLIN

Anthea, 26, was sitting on the back of a lorry when a motor bike burst out of it in a flash of smoke and flames.

She fell to the ground with her hair and yellow jacket in flames.

As the smoke cleared, the audience heard screams and a voice cry: "Are you all right, love?"

The horror happened as bubbly blonde Anthea was presenting the children's show UP2U from the Royal Tournament in London's Earls Court.

Last night she was being treated in hospital for burns to her face and hand.

Her manager, Peter Powell, said: "She could have been blinded. We're still waiting to see if she'll be scarred for life."

Tournament producer Major Michael Parker said: "There was a breakdown of communications. She should have been 10 yards away."

KIDS' favourite Anthea

ANTHEA chats to viewers before the accident

SECONDS later she falls to the ground in flames

How the *News of the World* reported the accident. JOHN FROST HISTORICAL NEWSPAPER SERVICE

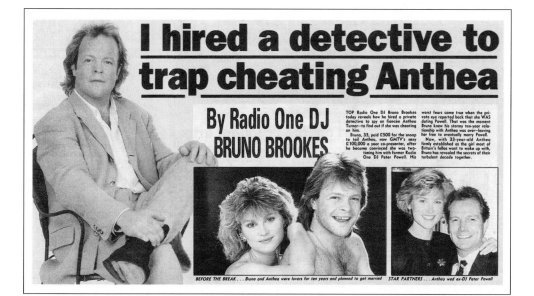

I hired a detective to trap cheating Anthea

By Radio One DJ BRUNO BROOKES

TOP Radio One DJ Bruno Brookes today reveals how he hired a private detective to spy on fiancée Anthea Turner—to find out if she was cheating on him.

Bruno, 33, paid £500 for the snoop to tail Anthea, now GMTV's sexy £100,000 a year co-presenter, after he become convinced she was two-timing him with former Radio One DJ Peter Powell. His worst fears come true when the private eye reported back that she WAS dating Powell. That was the moment Bruno knew his stormy ten-year relationship with Anthea was over—leaving her free to eventually marry Powell.

Now, with 33-year-old Anthea firmly established as the girl most of Britain's fellas want to wake up with, Bruno has revealed the secrets of their turbulent decade together.

BEFORE THE BREAK . . . Bruno and Anthea were lovers for ten years and planned to get married

STAR PARTNERS . . . Anthea wed ex-DJ Peter Powell

The *Sun* article in which Bruno Brookes spilled the beans about our relationship. JOHN FROST HISTORICAL NEWSPAPER SERVICE

Pete and me on our wedding day in February 1990.

As Cinders in panto at Winchester.

In pyjamas with Eamonn Holmes on *GMTV*. GMTV

Signing my *Blue Peter* contract at a wine bar over-looking the Thames in Chiswick with Pete and Penny Ewing.

In Christmas mood with *Blue Peter* co-presenters John Leslie and Diane-Louise Jordan.

With my Thunderbirds hat and a model of Tracy Island, I hit the headlines for *Blue Peter*. REX FEATURES

Ormonde House, the home Pete and I thought we'd share for ever.

Grant and me strolling by the River Thames, together at last. REX FEATURES

I took the train down to Brighton to see Bruno, agonising all the way about what I should do. I'd managed to make a complete mess of my life. I should have counted my blessings, I told myself. I lived in a palatial home. I had a famous boyfriend and the chance to develop a career in television. OK, so my relationship with Bruno wasn't exactly *Love Story*, but then, whose was?

Bruno didn't help matters one little bit. He was beside himself. He said he had come to his senses about me. He offered me the world to stay, even a car – a Golf GTi convertible – which he knew I'd dreamed of owning. He said he would tear up the prenuptial agreement and there would be nothing to stop me doing anything I chose. 'I've been a fool, Anthea,' he said, holding my hands in his. 'I know that now. Please, you owe it to me to give us another chance.' For a few fleeting seconds, he looked once more like the fresh-faced young man I'd first come to know in Stoke-on-Trent.

Foolishly or not, I decided to give it a second try. I had to admit that without him I would probably never have left Stoke and come to London and found my way into the television industry. He was right, I made myself believe. After all these years, I owed him another chance to patch things up between us. I was acting out of a sort of misguided loyalty and like the automaton I'd become when in his presence. But there was nothing between us any more. I tried desperately to regain the feelings I'd had for him but I was completely unable to do so.

Dealing with the maelstrom of emotions in my heart in those following months was scary. I felt as if I was jumping into an abyss. I'd been with Bruno so long I could barely imagine being without him; he'd ruled my life and my head for so long I didn't know if I was strong enough to make it on my own. Neither was I financially independent. I had very little money of my own although I'd worked hard for what I did have. In all but name I was Bruno's wife, but I knew if I walked away, I would have to leave with nothing but the clothes on my back. It simply wouldn't have been my style to fight him in court for anything more. Torn between my loyalty to Bruno and all that he had meant to me in the past, and my hopes for the possibility of a happier life with Pete, I felt as if I was being ripped in two.

The crunch came when, after three interminable months, I invited my parents to come and stay with me in London. Sitting them down in the kitchen, I took a deep breath and told them everything that had happened between Bruno and me. I also told them about Pete. My parents were fantastically supportive and as understanding as ever. It was my father who finally made me see sense. 'I love your mother now even more than the day we were married, Lil,' he said. 'If you don't feel that way about Bruno, then I think maybe you should get out while there's still time.'

My dad's words ringing in my ears, I told Bruno it was over. He had by then resigned himself to my departure anyway. He made sure he was away when I packed together my few belongings and closed the door, posting the key back through the letterbox. I was walking away from so much, so many memories and emotions; all the little things I'd bought or chosen for our home – kitchen utensils, pictures and knick-knacks. But I knew I just had to go and not look back. Hardest of all, I had to leave our beloved cat Harry behind, understanding that he'd be better off in the home he knew. I was twenty-eight, emotionally washed up and virtually broke.

4

A Bite of the Cake

I left Bruno Brookes to be on my own; I didn't leave him for Peter Powell, about whom I still felt very confused. Pete made it clear that he didn't need any of that complicated personal stuff and stopped our affair dead, leaving me believing that I had no one but myself to blame. I was a grown woman who'd never been alone before and I didn't like the overwhelming sense of insecurity it gave me.

Moving temporarily into Sue Van Der Ree's flat in Belsize Park, I had no choice but to take stock of my life. Having escaped from what had been such a controlling relationship, I realised that I was as much to blame as Bruno. I'd been weak. I'd allowed myself to be directed in every way. If I'd stood up to him in the beginning, he'd never have been able to exert so much power over me. Every time I caved in to him, I'd been sending him the signal that what he was doing was OK. Inadvertently, I'd been complicit in my own unhappiness. Now that I was away from his influence, I couldn't believe how frightened and timid I'd let myself become.

Work kept me occupied. Happily, after *UP2U* finished I had a fantastic break. Russ managed to get me a monthly slot presenting *Top of the Pops*, the longest-running and most successful music programme on British television. I was the first female non-Radio 1 disc jockey ever to present the show. It was the realisation of a teenage dream. Ruth and I had watched *Top of the Pops* religiously every Thursday night, singing along to songs like 'Bohemian Rhapsody' by Queen and 'Fernando' by Abba. I'd desperately wanted to be a member of the dance troupe Pan's People, and after the programme was over, Ruth and I would go to bed humming all the songs while I gyrated like Babs and Dee-Dee.

Now I could hardly believe I was introducing the programme. Dressed in extraordinary rhinestone outfits which make me cringe when I look back on them, I introduced turns like Kylie Minogue, Yaz and Tiffany and mingled backstage with the stars like an awestruck teenager. I was invariably petrified but I don't think it ever showed, although I did once introduce the band KLF as KLM, which is of course the Dutch national airline. I really wanted Scotty to beam me up then. I even got to meet Donny Osmond at last: he appeared on the show as part of his comeback tour. He was absolutely charming, had retained his good looks and was certainly not a disappointment after all those years. I wondered idly if I'd still look good in silver cowboy boots.

Determined to stand on my own two feet, I borrowed £3,000 as an advance on my earnings and rented a bedsit at 44 Minford Gardens, Shepherd's Bush. The entire living space would have fitted into my bathroom at Bruno's house in Wapping and the furniture was cheap and soulless. Moving in alone on a rainy winter's day, I sat on the floor, clutching Brian the Bear and my scrapbooks, and eating an entire packet of chocolate digestives in one go.

With no one to love or be loved by, missing my cat and the comfort of my former home, I sank into the depths of despair. There were times when I even considered going back to Bruno, who occasionally seemed a better option than a life of poverty and solitude. He wrote me a six-page letter apologising profusely for his years of bad behaviour and promising me a golden future at his side. He claimed there had always been a guardian spirit who brought out the tougher side in him and that he felt he'd had to prove to people that he wasn't going to end up as a waster married with three kids and living on a council estate. Nothing could stop his drive for success, he said.

He described me as his saviour and apologised for what he called 'this evil' that wouldn't allow him to give me what I deserved. He maintained that he had now broken free of it and was back in control. He said he was sorry for 'kicking me in the teeth' and pleaded with me to come home. A few days later, he dropped round with Harry to say how much they both missed me. But I resisted the temptation to run back to him and carried on alone. There were no crumbs of comfort from Pete, either. His shutters had come down completely after he'd told me we both needed some space. I lost a stone in weight and became very drawn and pale.

I can be dislodged with relative ease from my outwardly confident standpoint and I have always been very much in awe of people who fully believe in themselves. I was never the toughest kid on the block and, at this point in my life, I was as soft as putty. I felt incredibly lonely, emotionally. It was the sort of loneliness that even friends couldn't fill. I'd always been surrounded by friends and family, familiar possessions and a comfortable environment. I had, in effect, been spoiled rotten.

I didn't want to worry my parents, but I think they knew how low I was. Dad wrote me a lovely long letter, urging me to stay cheerful. 'Forgive me for mentioning Ruth, Lil,' he wrote, 'but she taught Mummy and me quite a lot – how to count your blessings and look on the bright side of life and to remain cheerful in all circumstances. Compared to her short life and disabilities, we should all be on top of the world, so go for it.' Mum wrote too, warning me not to be tempted to go back to 'Trevor', as they'd always known Bruno. 'I've never been spoken to in my whole life the way he speaks to you,' she reminded me.

I knew my situation was entirely of my own making and I had no one to blame but myself. My angst, too, was self-inflicted, but I had lost all confidence in my own ability. Not since Ruth's death had I felt so awful. After that dark time, I'd thrown myself into my relationship with Andy and then had been full on with Bruno ever since. I'd never allowed myself the time or the space to dwell on it. Now my sense of despair was total and tangible and I felt closer to the brink of serious depression than ever before. Worst of all, I had no idea how to shake myself out of it.

In an attempt to pep myself up, I raided Ikea and bought some brighter furniture for my new home. Dad came down from Stoke and laid a carpet for me and helped me get the bedsit straight. After we'd cleaned it all up and given it a facelift, it did look a lot better. 'There now,' Dad said, looking around proudly. 'Your very own little place.' I gazed around the sad little room and gave a half-hearted smile.

The only person who stopped me going out of my mind during that desperate time was Jonathan Morris, the star of the television programme *Bread*. We'd first met when I'd gone to interview the cast of the show for *UP2U*. We hit it off straight away, and during the interview I discovered that he came from Congleton, only a few miles away from Norton. We had spent the next hour reminiscing about the places we'd grown up: Trentham Park, Burslem, Newcastle-under-Lyme.

Jonathan was not only gorgeous, he was friendly, gregarious and funny. We swapped phone numbers, and promised to get together some time for a longer chat. But before we had a chance to call each other, we ended up as joint contestants on a children's television programme called *Physical Pursuits*, in which we had to undertake an obstacle course. Michaela Strachan, Timmy Mallet and Mike Read were the other contestants and the presenter was a young Irish lad called Eamonn Holmes. Jonathan and I got on very well again, and once more promised to keep in touch.

In November 1988, when I was at my lowest ebb and the first few bars of any Whitney Houston song would reduce me to floods, Jonathan was playing Jack in the pantomime *Jack and the Beanstalk* in Tunbridge Wells. He rang me and suggested we met for a drink at a café in Kensington. Just like before, we sat down and started talking and couldn't stop. He was just the boost I needed and, before too long, I was laughing until my stomach muscles ached.

We started to see each other more often and then gradually slipped into something a little more serious. It felt wonderful to be loved again, and I will always be grateful for the time we had. We stayed together for four months and are still very close to this day, but we were always better friends than lovers and it was never really going to work as a relationship. We both knew that I was still holding a candle for Pete. Having agreed that it wasn't working, we split entirely amicably, promising to remain friends. I missed his company and zany sense of humour but I knew it was for the best if I was going to try to sort my head out.

Work remained sporadic. During the filming of a corporate video I was presenting in Leicester for a train company, I had to dance with the multi-talented roller-skaters from *Starlight Express* and slipped and dislocated my elbow, injured first as a child and then again when I was living with Bruno. It hurt like hell and I had to go to Leicester Royal Infirmary where the doctors relocated it. They sent me home with a bottle of painkillers. I had to complete another two days' filming with my arm strategically placed and my face as white as a sheet.

Back home, unable to sleep because of my painful elbow and my constant worries about where the next cheque was coming from, I did what I often do when I am down: I completely forgot to eat. It's nothing but absent-mindedness on my part, but I often go for a whole day and then suddenly remember that nothing has passed my lips. It is quite easy to do when you're living alone. It makes me realise how important Meals on Wheels is for older people, because I can completely understand how easy it is to skip food. Anyway, the consequence was that I lost even more weight and became quite skeletal.

When Russ telephoned and asked me to attend a meeting about a prospective new Thames Television series called *Best of Magic*, for which my name had been put forward as a co-presenter with Simon Mayo and the Great Sorprendo (Geoffrey Durham, the magician husband of Victoria Wood), I was very excited. The format was that Simon and I were to be the stooges and Geoffrey would show us some amazing tricks.

'It'll be a good place for you to be seen,' Russ enthused.

'Thanks,' I said. 'It sounds great. 'You'll be at the meeting, won't you?'

There was a slight hesitation. 'Er, no,' he replied, clearly embarrassed. 'It's Pete's deal. He'll be there, not me.'

I hadn't seen Pete in weeks. He had clearly been avoiding me and
Russ had largely taken over my management to avoid any awkwardness. Putting my best foot forward, tidying up my hair and dressing
up, I drove myself to the restaurant in Hampton Court where we
were all meeting and stepped nervously inside.

Pete was waiting at the table and turned as I came in. Smiling, I
walked over to where he stood and held out my hand. 'Hiya,' I said,
trying to be as breezy as I could. But the expression on his face wasn't
what I'd expected at all. There was no hostility or embarrassment –
he just looked aghast. He couldn't take his eyes off me throughout
the meeting, and his gaze was less than flattering. I felt distinctly
uncomfortable.

As soon as it was over, he grabbed my arm, pulled me to one side
and spoke to me through gritted teeth. 'You look absolutely terrible!'
he said. 'What have you done to yourself? You're so thin! If you don't
sort yourself out, AT, you're going to blow everything. Nobody wants
to watch anyone on television who looks as ill as you do. You've got
to get your act together, and soon.' He suggested that I took a holiday to sort myself out. 'Just get away and have a long, hard think
about what you want,' he told me. 'Because if you want to carry on
in television, then this is certainly not the right way to go about it.'
He was very tough on me but, shocked as I was, when I looked in the
mirror later that night, I realised he was probably right.

So I followed Pete's advice and took myself off to Marbella for a
solo break which allowed me to distance myself from my problems.
I wasn't in the mood to go with friends, and Pete clearly wasn't offering to accompany me, so I packed a suitcase and went to the airport
on my own and took a flight to a place I didn't know. The Melia Don
Pepe Hotel was the perfect place to recharge my batteries. I arrived
looking pasty and thin and spent a week lying on the beach, explor-
ing the town and doing a great deal of thinking. Pete was right: it was
marvellous to get away. Distance was everything. I ate well and got a
suntan, I made an effort to talk to people and everyone was very nice
to me. I met a lovely old couple with whom I sometimes had supper.
It was just the tonic I needed, and far better than taking Valium.

I came back early in May 1989 looking a heck of a lot better than when I'd left. I'd gained half a stone and felt good. The sunshine had put colour into my cheeks, I had had my hair cut, put on make-up and bought myself some new clothes. I invited a friend round the day after I got home and she complimented me on how well I looked. I made some coffee and we were sitting on the floor having a chat, when the phone rang. It was Pete.

'Can you meet me in central London in an hour?' he asked. 'We need to catch up and chat about work.' His tone was businesslike.

Faltering, I agreed. Five minutes later, he rang back. 'Something's come up. Can you meet me tonight instead, at my house? Shall we say 7.30?'

I remember thinking: 'Oh, no. I can't do this,' but I said yes and put the phone down. Turning to my friend, I said: 'I can't believe I just said yes. I can't possibly go over to his house, I still have great feelings for the man. That's my problem.'

She told me not to be stupid. 'Of course you can go over and see him, Anthea,' she said. 'For heaven's sake, he's your manager.'

I duly arrived in Chiswick and Pete met me at the door and invited me in. The atmosphere between us was a little awkward at first. We sat, barely speaking, drinking a cup of tea on his L-shaped settee. We certainly didn't discuss work.

'How are you?' he asked after a while, his twinkly eyes peering into mine.

'Much better,' I told him. 'I've cleared out a lot of ghosts and gremlins.'

He smiled. 'Me too,' he said. 'For once, I took my own advice and went off on holiday by myself as well. I did a great deal of thinking while I was away.' He volunteered nothing more.

'The problems I had before are still there,' I added, choosing my words carefully. 'But now I think I know how to cope with them.'

He knew I was talking about him. 'Good,' he said, nodding. 'I'm very glad to hear that.' Putting his mug of tea down on the coffee table, he leaned forward and kissed me on the lips.

I froze for a moment, unable to respond, my eyes wide with confusion. Then Pete pulled me towards him and held me so tight I could hardly breathe. When he pulled away, he was smiling and stroking my face with his hands. 'Oh, Anthea, it's hopeless. I've missed you,' was all he said.

I kissed him gently on the lips and smiled back. 'Me too,' I said. Before long we were re-enacting what had happened in his house all those months before. The difference was that this time it was OK. He knew I'd needed to get away from Bruno, sort myself out and have some time alone. I think he'd deliberately pushed me away so that I could do that. He didn't want to be a crutch for me to lean on after Bruno. But now, within a day of flying home from our respective holidays, Pete and I had become lovers once again.

I felt as if a huge weight had been lifted from my shoulders. Relief and happiness washed over me in waves. All this time I'd been so miserable, it had been Pete who had been missing from my life. Now I was back in his arms once again everything fell into place. Better still, he seemed to feel the same way. Our 'meeting' finished at ten o'clock the following morning. It was a Friday, and the start of a Bank Holiday weekend. As I was leaving his house, hardly able to put him down, he asked me what I was doing for the next few days.

'Er, well, I've promised to go to Stoke to see my parents,' I said. 'It's also Bruno's father's fiftieth birthday party. I promised I'd be there. He's expecting me . . .' Inside I was screaming: 'Sod that, I'll cancel everything and spend the weekend with you,' but I remained very single-minded and cool and dutifully went north later that day, promising to ring Pete on my return. The weekend was fine, and Les had a great party, which I'm glad I didn't miss. He's such a lovely man and I wanted to be there for him, even though I was no longer his 'daughter-in-law-to-be'. Bruno was there, and we were perfectly civil to each other. I stayed with Mum and Dad in Norton and they were delighted to see me looking so well and happy after my break.

'You're back with Pete then?' Mum said knowingly, her eyes bright.

'Yes, Mum, I am,' I replied with a grin, 'and it feels great.'

I hurried back to London and to my new love and we started seeing each other regularly. We had a fantastic May and June before I started on a nationwide Cadbury's tour with *Top of the Pops* which Russ had arranged some months before. We visited nightclubs all around the UK, travelling around in a tour bus with a huge box of every Cadbury's product you could imagine in the back. I can't tell you how many times my little hand sneaked into that box to pull out another delight, and the weight I'd lost soon returned. I also stood in for Sarah Greene on BBC1's Saturday-morning show *Going Live* after she was injured in a helicopter crash, and a new series of *UP2U* was going out in July, which I was really looking forward to. Life seemed wonderful. I was flying and very, very happy. Pete was all I'd ever wanted, the great love of my life.

However, it was nearly all over before it began. On 15 July, the day of the first transmission of the new series of *UP2U*, I was compering from the Royal Tournament at Earl's Court as part of the 'Roving Eye' feature, watched by millions of young viewers. The smell of cordite filled the air and the sense of excitement and anticipation was extraordinary. I was preparing to introduce a high-speed motorcycle display by the Royal Air Force Motor Sports Association from the centre of the arena. The plan was that I would stand behind an apparently empty army truck waiting for my signal. My lines to camera were: 'I'm supposed to meet a motorcyclist here, but I think I'm being wound up.' Once I had moved a safe distance from the lorry, the 'mystery' motorcyclist, Vince Kearney, was to hurtle out behind me on his motorbike, crashing through a black sugar-paper screen. He would come to a halt beside me so that I could interview him about the display. He would then give me a lift to the other side of the stadium to interview the RAF dog-handlers. The only part of it that was rehearsed was me getting on and off the bike and making sure that I could put on the crash helmet and take it off again easily while talking.

At the last minute, the director, Tom Docherty, decided that it would look far more dramatic if the sequence began with me sitting on the tailgate of the lorry and then jumping to the ground and walking away. He gave me a leg-up on to the tailgate and I practised jumping down twice as everyone stood around watching. By the time we were ready and the bike was in place we were just a few minutes away from the live broadcast.

Tom had been very clear. There would be a manual (visual) countdown to my sequence – he would raise his arm and point at me –

and an additional soundcue through my earpiece given to me by my old friend Peter Hamilton, the studio director, from the gallery in Manchester. Once I'd had my signal and jumped down on cue, the director and the cameraman would then move away from me and the lorry, walking backwards, as I moved towards them talking to camera. At that point, Tom would give a signal to one of the motor-cycle display team members who would, in turn, give the motorcyclist his cue to set off.

Sitting there nervously waiting for the visual signal from Tom and the instruction in my earpiece that would be my cue to start talking and make the leap to the ground, I was almost choked by exhaust fumes as the rider of the motorbike, sitting astride it in his helmet a few feet behind me in the half-light, revved his engine to try to give himself enough momentum for when his own signal came. It was almost impossible to hear anything because of all the noise, and I was straining to listen for my instructions.

When my big moment approached, I heard the words 'Five, four, three, two, one – on air' in my ear. My eyes were locked on to Tom's for my directions. As agreed, I half rose to my feet, ready to leap to the ground, and, his hand raised above him, Tom gave me the visual cue. I can have spoken only two or three words before there was a tremendous roar behind me, and the next thing I knew, there was a huge bang as the motorbike lunged forward at speed. Its rider had mistakenly been given his signal to 'go, go, go!' at the same time as me.

The first thing I felt was the pain in my shoulder as the bike crashed into me. Flailing my arms and trying to maintain my bal-ance, I tumbled head-first off the back of the truck and into a pyrotechnics display which was, unbeknown to me, taking place to one side of the vehicle. The show's co-ordinator had thought that they'd make the bike's appearance even more dramatic. There was a huge explosion and an incredible noise in my head as, at that precise moment, the electrically operated 'bombs' I'd fallen into were trig-gered by the forward motion of the motorbike. The last thing I remember is falling face-first into what looked like a furnace, my clothes and hair on fire.

I had become a human torch. The flames licked at my face, searing off my eyelashes and eyebrows and setting my fringe alight. My jacket, jumper and microphone were all ablaze. My nostrils were full of the smell of burning hair. I fell to the ground and rolled in the dirt, desperately trying to put out the flames. My hands, clutching my face as I tried to save my eyes, were burning.

Watching me writhing live on television were millions of viewers – including my mum and dad and Pete and Bruno in their respective homes and offices – and the producers in Manchester, who had no choice but to cut the transmission. The screen went blank for a moment and then cut back to the studio, where the other presenters stood around looking shocked, not knowing what to say. Nothing was mentioned about whether I was alive or dead.

Back at Earl's Court, everything was a blur. Suddenly, I was surrounded by soldiers in uniform, all beating at the flames and covering me with their jackets. Picking me up like a rag doll, they manhandled me on to a stretcher and carried me into a medical Portakabin behind the scenes where an army field doctor could wash the soil away, which stung like crazy, and assess the damage. Someone was holding my hand.

I don't remember very much about the next few hours. I wasn't in any great pain to begin with – the flames had seared my nerve endings – but I was very shocked and dazed. I had first-degree flash burns to my face and to the back of my right hand. I looked like a grilled tomato with frizzy hair. I was able to call my parents and told them: 'I can see, I can hear and I'm alive. The rest doesn't matter.' They were very relieved to hear my voice; obviously they'd been at their wits' end after seeing the accident on television.

The next thing I knew, Pete and Bruno were both at my side. I thought I was hallucinating. They'd apparently arrived simultaneously, both equally anxious, and were vying with each other to be the one to accompany me to hospital. 'It's all right, AT, I'm here,' Pete told me, clasping my hand tightly.

The field doctor, who was far more accustomed to dealing with life-threatening battle injuries, decided that I was not in any immediate danger and told Pete to take me home. Pete and Bruno bundled me up and took me back to Pete's house in Chiswick. Waiting on the doorstep was Mark Stephens, Peter's solicitor and friend. He, too, had seen the accident on the television and had gone straight to Pete's to find out how I was. Taking one look at my fried features, he grimaced visibly. 'This isn't right,' he told Pete. 'Anthea should be in hospital.'

Burns are an unknown quantity at the best of times, yet here I was, a television presenter whose job depended on how I looked, with a bright red face and peeling and blistering skin, sent home with a tube of antiseptic cream.

Inside the phone was ringing. It was my friend Jane Chegwin, the nurse. 'I'll come right over and we'll take her to Ealing Hospital straight away,' she told Pete. She made sure that I was seen immediately. The doctors in casualty took one look at my now swelling face and declared that I was too serious a case to be dealt with by them. They made the necessary arrangements to transfer me to the specialist burns unit at Mount Vernon Hospital. Just as we were about to leave for north-west London, Jane took a phone call.

'You can't go out by the main entrance,' she told Pete, putting down the receiver.

'Why on earth not?' he asked, his only concern to get me to specialist care as quickly as possible.

'Because there are photographers waiting out there,' Jane explained. 'They saw it on the telly and want a picture of a char-grilled Anthea Turner.'

Throwing his hands up in despair, Pete cursed aloud. He'd never enjoyed publicity as a DJ and he certainly didn't welcome it now. Fortunately, Jane wasn't at all fazed. Taking me by the hand, she led us out through the hospital mortuary to a back door, where her car was waiting. The photographers knew my injuries were serious, but none of them had thought to check the morgue.

The staff at Mount Vernon were wonderful. They washed my face in saline solution to relieve the pain and put silicone over my face. My right hand was also placed into a plastic bag filled with silicone and I was told to have the dressings changed every day. Jane offered to do it for me at home. Obviously I couldn't go back to Minford

Gardens where I'd be on my own, so Pete offered to put me up in his spare bedroom and look after me. I was then put into the capable hands of a Harley Street specialist plastic surgeon by the name of Dev Bazra, a friend of Gloria Hunniford, Caron Keating's mum.

Dev was marvellous. It's largely thanks to him that my skin was saved. Within twenty-four hours my face had swollen up like a balloon and I couldn't eat, talk or sleep. A couple of days later I went back to the hospital to have my injuries checked and they gave me more silicone. Dev made sure that the dressings were changed regularly, that silicone was plastered on to my face, along with bandages, gauze and Retin A to reduce any scarring. I had to wear the plastic bag over my hand for two weeks, having silicone poured on to it constantly. My face then went yellow and cracked and peeled off like cornflakes. It was pink and raw underneath, sensitive to everything. I had given myself a free derma-peel, and it hurt like hell. I can't imagine why anyone would willingly want to undergo such agonising cosmetic surgery.

I couldn't bear to be touched for a while, everything was so sore and itchy. I couldn't smile or use my hand and, because of the bruising elsewhere on my body from the fall, I could move around only very slowly. I was placed on a course of antibiotics to stop any infection and was advised to wear false eyelashes and hypoallergenic make-up if I had to use any at all. Jane came in every day and Pete looked after me day and night. 'I look horrible and ugly,' I'd complain, staring at my scorched reflection in the mirror.

'You look beautiful, AT, and I love you just the way you are,' Pete would say, planting a kiss on the tip of my scalded nose. It was a funny way to start a relationship, but once I'd moved into his home, I never really moved out again.

In Pete's tender care, I fell more and more in love with the man who had now become my everything. He was so busy at work he could barely afford the time off, but he rushed home to me every day. 'How do you fancy going away somewhere to convalesce?' he asked. 'I think you deserve a holiday.' We both thought immediately of warmer climes and he suggested the Seychelles, but Dev banned me from going anywhere near sunshine for at least three months, so instead Pete took me (minus my eyebrows and eyelashes and with a rather peculiar fringe) to the Ring of Kerry in Ireland. It was cold and rainy but we were too much in love to even notice.

One night, over dinner in a lovely hotel, we had a heart-to-heart about a lot of things that had happened in our lives. Pete talked about his background and I told him more than I'd ever told anyone about Bruno. We really blew away some cobwebs. At the end of the meal Pete asked me if I'd consider moving in with him permanently. 'I'd like to look after you all the time,' he said. I thought long and hard before answering him. 'No, Pete, I don't think that'd be a good idea,' I said gently. 'I've been down that road before and I don't want to go there again.'

He looked crestfallen. In the weeks I'd been living in his spare room, slowly mending, he'd got used to having me around. 'Actually,' I added carefully, trying to keep my nerve, 'I've been thinking and I've decided that maybe the time has come for me to buy my own flat. Somewhere that's mine and no one else's. It would be a first for me, and not before time.'

Pete lit a cigarette and mused on this, blowing smoke rings into the air. 'Well, do you want to get engaged, then?' he asked, looking across at me hopefully.

'No, Pete,' I replied firmly, memories of my so-called 'engagement' to Bruno still raw in my mind. 'I've never really understood why people get engaged with no firm wedding plans. It seems to me that it means they'll never marry. Bruno bought me a ring and I wore it on my engagement finger for two years but it never meant anything at all.'

Peter listened to all I had to say and seemed to be taking it in. I'd never seen him more thoughtful. Nothing more was said that night, but the next morning on a lovely walk in the rain along the Owenmore River, he turned to me nervously. 'AT, would you marry me if I asked you to?' he began, his words spoken with great deliberation.

'Yes!' I said, and threw my arms around his neck. 'Yes, please.' I was over the moon. In my own way, I'd loved him since the days when his poster had adorned my bedroom wall. I wanted to be Mrs

Peter Powell more than anything else in the world. I'd hoped and prayed that my threat to move out and find a place of my own might nudge him in the right direction, and I was thrilled that my instincts had been right.

Having seen my delighted reaction, Pete knew there was no turning back. 'Oh, I think I just proposed,' he said, his face ashen. He maintains to this day that his original question had been more hypothetical, but that the minute he'd got the words out I was virtually ordering the dress. The thought of what it all meant gave him a bad dose of the jitters. Instead of scooping me up in his arms and doing something wildly romantic like kissing me, he clearly thought, 'Oh my God, what have I done?' Gaunt-faced, he lit a cigarette and hid behind a tree.

Once I had fully recovered, I was able to go back to *UP2U* and show my face to the world. Everyone thought it a good idea so that the children who had watched the accident could see that I was alive and well. I looked rather strange with my pencilled-in eyebrows, false eyelashes and new pink skin, plastered with a heavy layer of make-up to camouflage the discoloration. I brushed my hair forward over the worst bits and hoped no one would notice that I couldn't use my right hand, which was still bandaged and covered in permanent pigmentation marks underneath. But I was back, and I was able to carry on with the series to the end.

There came a point when blame had to be apportioned for what happened, and where the responsibility lay was a toss-up between the Ministry of Defence and the BBC. Each side said it was the other's fault and the matter ended up going to court. In the end the BBC lost and I had to claim from their insurance company. We eventually reached a settlement for my lost earnings and distress, but it took a very long time to sort out. There was also a criminal trial at Wells Street Magistrates' Court at which I had to give evidence against the director, Tom Docherty, which was a very painful reminder of an unhappy incident, not least because he was a very nice chap whose only crime had been a momentary lapse in concentration. He was given a twelve-month conditional discharge and ordered to pay

£1,000 costs for failing to take reasonable care of me under the Health and Safety Act. The video footage of me being roasted alive later became a key part of the BBC Interactive Safety Course, comprising four hours' film of avoidable disasters. Fame at last.

Having had to miss an episode of *The Best of Magic* because of my accident (Annabel Croft took over at short notice), I went back to finish the series with the help of a good make-up artist. I was also working on my first Y-plan fitness video, in between masterminding the preparations for my wedding. We didn't have that much money to splash around and Pete and I both wanted a simple country ceremony with a party for all our friends afterwards. Mum and I arranged everything. I fell in love with a £5,000 outfit in a shop window in Bond Street, and had my friend Teresa Correa, a designer for Thames Television, make a copy of it for me for £400. It was a little jacket over a cocktail dress with a removable skirt I could take off later for dancing. It was the most wonderful outfit I have ever worn. I loved it. I felt a million dollars. Very decadently, I had a pair of matching shoes made, too.

I decided to have my hair cut for the wedding and started to look around at different styles. Selina Scott, the television presenter, was doing *The Clothes Show* at the time and appeared on the front of the *Radio Times* with a smart new haircut, much shorter than before, and layered. It was credited to John Frieda. Trying to save money, I went along to Pete's barber in Euston and asked for a similar look.

'Sure,' he said and was soon snipping away.

I emerged from the barber's shop looking like a mushroom. My hair had been cut into a single-layer, Wendy Craig-style bob. It was tragic. I was due on *Top of the Pops* in a few days' time and was getting married in just over eight weeks. Panicking, I telephoned John Frieda's salon and virtually demanded an appointment. 'I don't care how much I have to pay or what time of day or night I have to see him, but I *must* see him soon,' I pleaded.

Having explained that John was abroad, the PR told me that while he had been credited with Selina's cut in the article, the stylist had actually been one of his new members of staff, a young unknown by the name of Nicky Clarke. Thinking she was trying to fob me off, I resisted making an appointment to see Nicky at first, but soon realised that I had little choice. Meeting him changed my life. Not only did he make the very best of a bad job, but he softened my eighties highlights and went on to craft and style my hair into what it is today.

My parents adored Pete. They'd taken to him from the start, and they were genuinely delighted for us both. 'Mum and I think the world of him, Lil,' Dad told me with great confidence the first time I brought him home to Norton.

Pete bought me a single emerald-cut diamond ring which I first wore in public on the Christmas edition of *Top of the Pops.* The BBC had paired up Bruno and me for the Christmas show, along with Mark Goodier. It was all a little awkward, but Bruno and I remained professional about it all and didn't let our personal feelings interfere with our work. Once we were off air, I told Bruno I was getting married and he didn't seem to mind about it. 'That's great, Anth,' he told me, kissing my cheek. 'I'm happy for you.' He had a new girlfriend by then, someone called Debbie Brooker. 'What's she like?' I asked. I've never forgotten his answer.

'She has no ambition and she goes my way,' he said, a state of affairs which clearly suited him far better.

That Christmas was the first and best for Pete and me. We spent it quietly at home together before heading north to see family and friends. On 28 December we were due to fly to Italy for a skiing holiday with a gang of twenty friends, which included Cathy and John Comerford (Cathy worked at James Grant and John was a *Blue Peter* producer); Gary Gordon, another old friend; Caron Keating and Russ (who were now an item); Caron's brother Michael and Mark Stephens, our solicitor and friend. It was my first time on skis. Mum thought I was mad to risk breaking a leg so close to the wedding. 'I can see you now, hobbling down the aisle on crutches,' she moaned.

'Mum, if you can't beat them you have to join them, and with Pete and skiing, I'm just going to have to take the plunge,' I argued. I think she understood. Pete promised he'd look after me, and off

we went. Pete loves skiing and adores big group holidays. He organised it all and the rest of us happily tagged along. Like all beginners
I was hopeless at first, spending most of my time on my bum in the
snow, but I soon picked up and by the end of the trip I could
actually go all the way downhill in an upright position without
falling over.

Peter was quite bewildered by the novelty of being engaged.
He'd never committed to anyone in his life before, not even his
fellow Radio 1 DJ Janice Long, with whom he'd had a six-month
relationship. By then in his late thirties, he'd pootled through life,
never devoting his energies and attention to just one person. He
threw himself into his work at 'Jimmy G's', which had moved out
of his home and into brand-new offices in Hammersmith. He now
had eighteen clients and was dishing out advice to hundreds more,
all the while trying not to think too much about the impending
nuptials.

He should have been more worried about the stag night. Phillip
Schofield, Russ and Mark Stephens, along with Gary Davies and
John Leslie (the *Blue Peter* presenter) and Paul Worsley from James
Grant masterminded it all: a pub crawl for forty of Pete's mates in
south-west London. I spent the night in alone and was tucked up in
bed by 11pm. I was fast asleep when the telephone rang some time
after midnight.

'Is that Miss Turner?' a man's voice asked. Yawning, I told him that
it was. 'This is Battersea Police here. We have a Mr Powell in one of
our cells and he's asked us to call you.'

I sat bolt upright in bed. 'Is this some sort of joke? Pete? In a cell?
Whatever for?'

There was an embarrassed silence before the sergeant answered: 'I
think it might be best if I let him tell you the story.'

The stag night had been riotous. The lads went go-karting before
going for a meal during which a food fight had ensued. The private
room above the Fulham pub where they'd had dinner had been the
scene of some pretty raucous celebrations. A Madame Lucy and her
girls had been employed to run a rather unique school for the night
and they got a little carried away, especially in the 'art class'. The boys

who took part in that one, including Pete, all had elephant faces painted on their private parts. I've always loved elephants.

Peter was so drunk by the end of the evening that, after the pub crawl in a fifty-two-seater coach, his so-called mates stripped him of his trousers, handcuffed him to a lamp post on the Albert Bridge, poured champagne over him and called the picture desks of every national tabloid newspaper. When the photographers had taken their fill of pictures, the fire brigade arrived to remove Peter's handcuffs and then the police arrested him for being drunk and indecent in a public place. They took him to Battersea to sober up, his coachload of mates following on, cheering.

The whole lot of them ended up back at our house at two in the morning, Pete sporting a white zip-up boiler suit the police had given him and an inane grin. I switched on every coffee machine in the house and made endless rounds of toast while the washing machine did its best with their food- and champagne-stained clothes. Most of them slept where they fell. In the morning they were a very sorry-looking bunch indeed.

Ten days later, on 31 January 1900, we were married at St Chad's Church, Longsdon, watched by most of the Albert Bridge mob along with other friends and family, among a hundred or so guests. I was twenty-nine, Pete was thirty-eight. It is every girl's dream to walk down the aisle on her father's arm in a beautiful dress and see the man of her dreams waiting for her, and that was how it was for me. And St Chad's, of course, was very special to me, as I'd been christened there, my mum had run the Sunday school there for twenty-five years and Ruth was buried in the graveyard.

A few days before the wedding, Piers Morgan, then a showbusiness reporter on the *Sun*, sent a colleague to Longsdon to snoop around and delve into my background. The reporter found out about Ruth, and Piers Morgan rang Peter to see if it was true that my sister had died. He then tried to contact my parents, wanting to run a story along the lines of 'on her wedding day, the bride's thoughts will be towards the grave of her dead sister'. He called me and asked if I would be thinking of Ruth on the day. I told him I wouldn't. I was very upset by his questions, and my fear was that all this would really hurt my parents. It was an intrusion for us all, but especially for them. They'd never had to deal with the adverse effects of fame.

In the end we were advised to speak to the *Sun* to make sure that at least they got the story straight. Reluctantly, I told the reporter who spoke to me that there would be no tears of sadness in my eyes. 'It's a joyous occasion, and Ruth, of all people, would be terribly happy for me,' I said. 'Please don't bother my mum and dad with this.' The article was published, giving me my first brush with the unattractive side of journalism. Needless to say, I didn't bother to cut that one out and stick it in my scrapbook.

But I was determined not to let it spoil our day, and it didn't. Wendy was my chief bridesmaid, along with Pete's lovely nieces Sally and Kate. They all wore moiré water taffeta dresses in peach. Russ was the best man and Dad, of course, gave me away. It started out as a dull day but then became beautifully bright. We had a vintage Silver Cloud Rolls–Royce to take us to the reception at the Olde Beams restaurant in Waterhouse. The cake cost £60 and was made by a lady who lived near Endon. The flowers – orchids and roses in flame and peach – were provided by a local florist. Even the brides-maids' dresses were made by a friend of my mum's.

There was a media scrum outside the church. It was long before the days of *Hello!* and *OK!* magazines signing up every celebrity wed-ding, and the press arrived in their droves. The Women's Institute took pity on them and set up a stall offering tea and cakes. I don't think the reporters had ever known such co-operation. Our smiling faces appeared in virtually every national newspaper the next day, alongside a snap of Steve Wright eating his headphones because he'd vowed to do so if Peter Powell ever got married.

Pete and I left the reception in his Porsche, which was covered in shaving foam and balloons, and honeymooned on the Caribbean island of Grenada. Neither of us had ever been so happy. We hired a Jeep and explored the island and all its little coves. 'Let's come back here for our tenth wedding anniversary,' Pete said, and, hugging him, I agreed immediately. I couldn't think of a nicer place to be with him in ten, twenty or even thirty years' time. I truly expected our marriage to last for ever. I loved him intensely, and I knew that he loved me. There was never the shadow of a doubt in my mind that he was the one for me, and me for him. And from that day to this, he has never given me cause to regret a single day of it.

We returned to married life and domesticity in Chiswick, and to a continuation of *The Best of Magic* and *Top of the Pops* for me. I was also offered a new television series for Anglia called *Anything Goes* about offbeat holidays and days out, co-presented by Paul Barnes. He and I travelled all over the country, showcasing the best attractions available. I had lions eating out of my hand at Windsor Safari Park, I toured Wales, walked the Peak District and played golf in Northern Ireland. Simon Mayo left *The Best of Magic* to pursue other interests, but Geoffrey and I stayed on for the new series, working with Arturo Brachette, a hilarious Frenchman famous for his quick-change routines.

I was very happy in my work. I woke up every morning in those early days and pinched myself, hardly able to believe that I was doing a job I loved so much and was being paid for it. I loved living with Pete and playing the supportive wife. When we got engaged he had offered to sell his 'bachelor pad' and buy somewhere new, but I liked the house and enjoyed living by the River Thames.

'I'll stay on one condition,' I told him.

'What's that?' he asked.

'That I can redecorate and throw some of this old stuff out,' I replied cheekily.

Pete looked terribly hurt. Casting his eye around the black-and-white lounge with its chrome furniture, jazzy carpets and gold discs all over the walls, he looked back at me in confusion. 'What's wrong with it?' he asked.

With the help of my old friend Sue Van Der Ree, I had that place stripped bare in no time. She ragrolled the walls and changed the carpets and curtains. We soon transformed the Peter Powell love den into a pretty, comfortable home. Pete loved it, thank goodness, and now it felt much more like our place than just his.

He was busier than ever, with new clients like Andi Peters, Zoe Ball and Jackie Brambles on his books. DJs and children's television

presenters were becoming the agency's speciality, and it had already
established a good reputation, but keeping it going at a time of reces-
sion and high interest rates was sometimes quite a struggle. Pete had
to plough a lot of his own money into the firm, and at first there was
little return. He had to work very long hours as he became more and
more tied up with his expanding company, giving his best to his
clients and trying to generate new business. 'It'll be better when I can
take on some more staff and delegate,' he promised. I'd sigh and hope
that happened soon.

Our first year of married life began to be characterised by notes left
for each other on the fridge door. 'Dinner in oven,' I'd write, having
lovingly prepared him his favourite meat and two veg. 'Back late,'
he'd write. 'Out with a client.' We were happy but busy, fulfilling our
work commitments and trying to see each other when we could. I
had a minor operation on my broken elbow to hoover out all the
little pieces of bone; Pete managed a few sailing holidays, resuming
his lifelong passion for boats; we squeezed in a ten-day break together
on the Amalfi coast in Italy, and that winter, a gang of us went skiing
in Colorado followed by a quick flip to Las Vegas. There were Pete
and myself, Paul Worsley, his girlfriend Liz, Russ and Caron and their
good friends Grant Bovey and his girlfriend Della. Russ and Grant
had met through work. Grant was in the video-rights business, and
had bought the house next door to Russ in Battersea, south-west
London. I didn't know him or Della terribly well – we'd met once or
twice before and only briefly – but they seemed nice enough.

For our first wedding anniversary that January, Pete took me away
for a weekend at the Lygon Arms in Broadway, Worcestershire, which
was magical. I couldn't believe a year had passed already and that we
had achieved so much. 'Thank you for making me so very happy,' I
told him in my anniversary card. 'Without you, I am nothing.' I
meant every word. A month later we were back at the same hotel for
Pete's fortieth birthday party, a celebratory weekend for twenty-two
friends. All the usual suspects were there, including Russ and Caron,
Phillip Schofield and Grant and Della. It was a fantastic weekend and
Pete, determined that his friends should have the time of their lives,
picked up the bill.

A few weeks after that, it was Grant's turn. He was ten years younger than Pete and his thirtieth-birthday bash was held in a private dining room at the smart new Conrad Hotel on Chelsea Harbour. Grant was by then running his own company, Watershed Pictures, and had given my sister Wendy a job as an assistant producer on his sports video titles. Pete and I had found Wendy a flat in Acton, not far from ours, and helped set her up there. Divorced and alone in London but for us, she was grateful that we also found her a flatmate – a talented young singer by the name of Darren Day.

The next few months passed without incident, apart from the fact that I caught German measles the day before my thirtieth birthday – just as I was due to appear live on *Richard and Judy* to promote fitness, of all things. I did the show, feeling lousy, and after that I was confined to bed, covered in spots. After plastering me with calamine lotion, Pete presented me with a gold Cartier ring to match a love bangle he'd already bought me. But I was miserable at not being able to go out and see my friends or have a party. Phillip Schofield came round with chocolates and balloons to cheer me up, but I wasn't impressed. The two of them just stood there laughing.

Russ and Caron were to be married at Hever Castle in Kent in June 1991. A month later, it was to be Grant and Della's turn. Caron invited me to a joint hen night with Della at Gloria Hunniford's house a few days before her wedding, and I went along and met all Della's friends, who'd come down in a coach from Derby. They were a lively bunch, arriving with a dustbin full of lucky-dip presents. I picked out a penis-shaped ice cream.

Pete was Russ's best man at the first celebrity wedding I'd ever attended. The happy couple looked gorgeous, as did Gloria, of whom I was becoming increasingly fond. The guest list read like *Who's Who*, with Emma Freud, Simon Mayo, Phillip Schofield, among those present. At the evening reception someone accidentally spilled coffee down my dress (made out of furnishing fabric by my mum), and the only clothes I had to change into were a pair of jeans and a T-shirt. Very stylish for a celebrity bash where everyone else was dressed up to the nines.

Grant and Della's wedding was in Derby and we travelled up in convoy with Russ and Caron, newly returned from their honeymoon in the Caribbean. As we watched them leave in the helicopter taking them to Gatwick for the start of their honeymoon, I marvelled at how so many of our close group of friends had got married in the space of a few months. I only hoped we'd all make it.

That Christmas I was offered a role in my first pantomime, *Cinderella* at the Theatre Royal, Winchester, another dream come true for someone who'd been so awestruck as a little girl by Twiggy in the role. Second only to playing Liesl, Cinders was wonderful.

Boy, did I take it seriously. I went to singing lessons and had learned all my words and all the songs before the first read-through. I thoroughly enjoyed myself, and the friends I made in the show are still pals to this day. I was the 'star turn' and my cast colleagues included the singer Rebecca Knight as Prince Charming, and Julie Spillers and Sarah Andrews, both dancers. We had a ball. John Spillers, Julie's dad, was the company owner. If ever you had an image of a panto promoter, John would be it: big winter overcoat, cigar, lived in Portugal much of the year and only came back to do a panto. I loved him.

Peter came to see me on my first night. I was shaking like a leaf. I hadn't sung in public for sixteen years and now I had to sing 'High Hopes', which wasn't the easiest of débuts. I worked especially hard on the acting: if I didn't make a few children in the front row cry during the scene where I found out I couldn't go to the ball, then I felt I hadn't done my job properly. One night a group of girlfriends came in and when I spoke the line 'But I've got nothing to wear!' there was a huge guffaw from their row, because I'm a well-known shopaholic.

The panto was not only hugely enjoyable, it was also very lucrative; so good, in fact, that I finally bought myself the navy blue golf GTi convertible I'd always wanted, and which Bruno had once promised to buy for me. I'd been looking at it in a car showroom in Chiswick for months and now it was mine. I loved that car, which I called Pumpkin. *Cinderella* also netted me some of the cuttings in my scrapbook of which I am most proud. There were photographs of me in my full Cinders ball costume, with layers of shimmering tulle, a wand and a glittering tiara, looking like the archetypal fairy princess. Ruth would have loved it.

With me in panto and Peter very stressed at work, we didn't have the best Christmas together that year. He worked so late that he was often still out when I got back from the evening performance. He has never been able to divorce himself from the company; he takes it all so personally. He is not dealing with a product, after all, he's dealing with people. It became a passion with him. If someone attacked one of his artists or the company, he might as well have attacked Peter himself. I missed him terribly over the Christmas period – we only got to spend one day, Christmas Day, together, along with our families – and I vowed never to do a panto again, however much fun it was, and whatever the financial reward, if it meant we had to spend such a special time apart.

After the panto, there was no work on the horizon. It was hoped the *The Best of Magic* would go into a third series, but nothing was certain. I filled my time home-making and catching up with friends. I started the ritual of a 'girly day': having all my girlfriends round for a day of indulgence once every three months with a hairdresser, masseur, colourist and beautician at their beck and call. Everyone had to bring a magazine, a video and something to eat. It lasted from 11am to 2.30am and there were up to twenty friends who would drop in at some point. The regular crowd included Julie Spillers, Sue Van Der Ree, Jane Chegwin, Jean-Anne Marnock (with whom I'd done some fitness videos), Stephanie Schofield and my sister Wendy. Della Bovey came once, heavily pregnant and still living with Grant in Battersea.

Despite such distractions, I sank into a minor depression about the lack of offers of work. I thought that maybe this was it – what I'd had was as good as it was going to get. I knew that the business was tough and I'd seen plenty of friends and colleagues fall by the wayside. The hit single 'Don't Let the Sun Go Down on Me' by George Michael and Elton John was played endlessly on the radio that winter, and it seemed particularly appropriate. If the sun had set for me, then I didn't know what I wanted to do next with my life. I wasn't qualified for anything else. I couldn't work in a job involving too much paper-work and I had little experience of anything outside television.

At that stage I didn't even consider starting a family with Pete. The maternal feelings I was waiting for had not so far happened, and I had no way of knowing whether they ever would. I had no over-whelming desire to replicate myself or Pete, and he felt the same. He was far too busy, anyway, with his own rebirth. He'd just finished one career and was starting a whole new one. Children were something we never discussed then. We had six goldfish instead.

By 1992 I was really worried. Things weren't looking at all rosy on the job front for me. On holiday together in Penang that March – my first return visit there since my crazy trip from Singapore with my cousin Julia – Pete delicately broached the subject Bruno had raised indelicately so often.

'AT,' he began over dinner one night, 'there's something I need to talk to you about. And, er, it's not easy for me.'

'OK,' I said, putting down my wineglass and studying his face carefully.

'Things haven't been going so well for you lately, work-wise, as you know, and, well, I think it may be time to start thinking about adding another string to your bow.'

I remained silent and looked at him suspiciously.

Pete carried on. 'Rusty and I have put you forward for quite a number of jobs,' he said, 'and I'm afraid you've been rejected for them all. You're considered too old for children's television and yet too inexperienced for 'grown-up' programmes. I'm afraid you're falling between two stools.'

It was quite a shock, hearing it from him, even though I had been filled with self-doubt for some time. I tried to take in what he was trying to tell me.

He reached across and squeezed my hand. 'Please don't get upset,' he said. 'Just think of all the fun you've had. A lot of people would give their right arm just to have had your chances. Now you've a whole new opportunity to try something completely different.'

It took a while, but in the end, I came to realise that maybe Pete was right; life in showbusiness was short, and there was nothing out there waiting for me, no one was biting any more. Hard as it was to accept his wisdom, I knew I had little choice.

On my return to London I thought long and hard about what I wanted to do and what people had been telling me for years. I was good with people, PR was my forte, they'd said, and I began to wonder if they were right. Taking the initiative, I contacted an old friend, Helen Parker, a producer for a video company, whom I'd first met doing my Y-plan fitness video. I knew she was at a crossroads in her career and thought she might be interested in joining forces with me. 'How do you fancy going into business together?' I asked her on the telephone. We agreed to meet up and discuss the proposition further. Helen was just the inspiration I needed. Positive, go-getting and dynamic, she filled me with enthusiasm for my fledgling idea. Having talked it all through, she finally agreed, but with one caveat. 'As long as you don't hog all the business lunches,' she said, laughing.

Our new company was to be called Parker/Turner PR and would utilise as many contacts as we had between us in the world of showbusiness. We spoke to various people about the possibility of doing some work for them and the responses were mostly positive. One of the best came from Grant Bovey, who agreed to use us to promote his video titles. He even offered us some office space in premises he had in Fulham. The video-producer and PR Gary Gordon, a friend of Pete's, also said he'd be interested in giving us some work, as did a company called Live Time Productions. The whole idea gathered momentum and we already had clients lined up, so we decided, using a combination of our own savings and a NatWest small-business loan, to take the plunge.

It was April 1992 and, with a slightly heavy heart, I packed away all my dreams of a showbiz career in an imaginary box. Anthea Turner was preparing to leave the world of television for good.

5

A Little Blue Sailing Ship

'Drop everything!' Pete told me on the mobile phone one afternoon a few weeks later. 'Come straight over. I've some wonderful news.'

I was sitting with Helen at her house in west London, drinking coffee and watching her fill in the NatWest loan application form for our big new venture. 'Sounds very mysterious,' I said, rising to my feet, but Pete wasn't joking. There was something in his tone which made me abandon my mug, still half full, jump into my car and head for his office in Hammersmith. Pete was standing on the doorstep.

'You've got it!' he cried, before I'd even had time to get my seatbelt off.

'Got what?'

'An audition for *Blue Peter*!' He was almost jumping up and down. 'It's yours.'

'What?' I wondered if the stress of running the business had finally got to him.

'You could be about to become the nineteenth presenter of *Blue Peter*, the flagship of children's television,' he announced. 'I've promised them you'll be perfect for it.'

Clasping my hands to my chest in amazement, I asked him what on earth he was talking about. Wasn't I about to leave television for ever? Hadn't he told me that PR was what I'd be best at? And now this?

Dragging me inside, he told me how, for the previous few weeks, he'd been secretly campaigning on my behalf for an audition for a forthcoming vacancy at *Blue Peter* created by the departure of Yvette Fielding after five years. 'I virtually begged them for it, I thought I'd give it one last shot,' he said, his eyes brighter than I'd seen them in a while. 'And Lewis Bronze has agreed you've got an audition next week.'

I felt faint. Lewis Bronze, the editor of *Blue Peter*, was going to give me a chance to have a go at the job I'd always thought I'd be happiest in and ideally suited to. It was light entertainment at its best, middle of the road and, aimed as it was at children, it would allow me to remain professional and in control and at the same time bring out the little girl in me who'd never really grown up. I'd been a *Blue Peter* fan since I was a kid; I'd even won a *Blue Peter* badge when I was eight by sending in little animals made of shells from Tenby beach which Ruth and Wendy had helped me to glue together. I'm sure the animals must have arrived in a hundred pieces, but the programme-makers sent me a kind letter, a badge and a picture of Petra, the *Blue Peter* dog, and I'd been a devotee ever since. Chris Trace, Valerie Singleton, John Noakes, Peter Purves – they had all been icons of my childhood and now I was being given an opportunity to join that illustrious hall of fame.

But I was also petrified. *Blue Peter* is known in the industry as the University of Television. It's live, it's unpredictable, it's varied, it's exciting and it's an immense responsibility. It is a television institution, and to have been a part of it, at any time, lends a person credibility and standing. I knew from friends like Caron (1986–90) that the audition was considered to be one of the toughest in the country. I feared I might be risking everything if I went for it and was then rejected. These things have a habit of coming out, and I was now a known face in television. 'What if I don't pass the audition?' I asked Pete fearfully. 'Won't that give me a big black mark?'

As always, he put me straight. 'You've nothing to lose, AT,' he reminded me. 'You were planning on getting out of the business anyway, remember?'

The audition certainly proved to be my hardest ever. Hoping that all those Blue Band margarine lids would stand me in good stead, and with my *Blue Peter* badge in my pocket as a lucky charm, I did a piece to camera about a conference on the Brazilian rainforests in Rio de Janeiro. Then I had to interview a bloke pretending to be Jonathon Porritt, of Friends of the Earth, about the Rio conference and other environmental issues, before talking about a spoof archaeological dig following the discovery by gas workers of some ancient Anglo-Saxon artefacts in Ealing (all of which were actually from John Lewis). 'Archaeologists believe that these precious treasures may come from the famous house of Kinnockus, headed by Neilus and his wife Glenys Maximus,' I reported as earnestly as I could.

My next task was to make a daffodil eggcup for Easter out of an egg carton and a paper plate in less than five minutes, my hands shaking like a leaf the whole time. Finally, I was asked to conduct an interview with a trampolinist while jumping up and down on a trampoline to prove that I could engage in a physical activity and hold a conversation simultaneously. It was the first time I'd ever been on a trampoline in my life, and it showed. I'd just got the hang of jumping up and down when I was asked to do twists and turns as well. It was a nightmare. Breathlessly, I wrapped up the show. It was like doing a decathlon. I felt that if I came out alive I'd have done well.

I did – just – only to be faced with some fairly tough questions about whether or not I'd ever had a gay relationship, whether I planned to have children and whether I'd ever posed for sexy photographs. 'The only time my clothes ever come off is when I go to bed or take a bath,' I told them. As the jewel in the crown of children's television, *Blue Peter* can't afford to have any scandal attached to it at all, which is why Richard Bacon, the presenter who recently admitted taking cocaine, had to go. There was a great hullabaloo, whereas if he had been on more or less any other programme it would probably all have blown over. You have to be squeaky clean for the little blue sailing ship.

There followed four days of complete agony which I spent analysing my every mistake and thinking that I'd been utterly useless.

I desperately wanted the job; more than anything in my whole life. I had no idea if I'd been any good or who I was up against, only that there were a terrifying 300 hopefuls going for that one vacancy. When Lewis Bronze eventually asked to see me, I went along expecting the worst.

I arrived at the East Tower at Television Centre with my knees knocking. I had to use the loo three times before I even checked in with the receptionist. Lewis came out to meet me and took me into the Beat Room, so called because it was where the legendary Biddy Baxter, *Blue Peter* editor for twenty-seven years, used to 'beat up' people if they were rubbish. As he sat down opposite me in this *Blue Peter* shrine he seemed businesslike and brusque. Dark-haired and middle-aged, he had a naturally dour expression which made it impossible for me to gauge what he thought of me. Without further ado, he played my audition tape, completely and utterly ripping me apart throughout. When he'd criticised just about every word I'd spoken, every gesture I'd made or face I'd pulled, he finally said, with a wry smile: 'For someone who's done one of the worst auditions I've ever seen, you'll be surprised to know that you've got the job.'

I jumped up, flung my arms round his neck and kissed him, much to his embarrassment. I wanted to scream and shout. I couldn't believe it. When he'd finally peeled my arms away, Lewis told me that although my age had gone against me from the outset – I was much older than the norm – the perception was that I was younger. Thank goodness for moisturiser and what Bruno had always called my crap voice.

That was truly the day everything changed for me. I can honestly say that from then on I have never looked back as far as my career is concerned. I was on the mobile phone straight away to Pete, and he was as thrilled as I was. He had desperately wanted me to get the job. Everything just fell into place: in the very same week, Helen Parker was headhunted for a fantastic new position with Polygram Records, so the fledgling company Parker/Turner PR was shelved indefinitely.

I wasn't allowed to tell a soul about *Blue Peter* for ages, in case the news was leaked to the press. Mum, Dad and Wendy knew, of

course, and were thrilled for me, but they were all sworn to secrecy.
(Wendy was by then back living with them in Stoke, having set up
her own production company to make corporate videos.) When
everything was finally agreed and the news was out, Pete hosted a
Sunday lunch on a balcony overlooking the Thames above a wine bar
in Chiswick. It was for me and his newest client, Darren Day, who
had just successfully auditioned for the lead role in the West End
show *Joseph and His Amazing Technicolor Dreamcoat* taking over from
Phillip Schofield. As the sun beat down, Pete popped the champagne corks and Darren and I signed our contracts simultaneously in
front of all our friends. I don't think I'd ever seen him more proud.

After a snatched week with Pete in Crete, I began two and a half of
my happiest years in television on 14 September 1992. On my first
Blue Peter appearance, I had to cycle in on Chris Boardman's award-
winning bike, which wasn't as easy as it sounds because he is a lot
taller than me, and it had no steering and no brakes. To stop, I had
to jump off and make sure that the bike didn't crash into anything in
the process. I didn't quite manage it, and John Leslie still has the scars
to prove it.

    Thinking, perhaps, that I'd be better off out of harm's way, the
producers dispatched me abroad. My first assignment was a two-
week stint in Hungary, during which I had to wade up to my waist
in icy water and prehistoric mud in a vast network of underground
caves and visited a camp for refugees from the Yugoslav civil war.
After this initiation into *Blue Peter* foreign assignments, I travelled
widely, to places like the Cook Islands, Romania, France for the
D-Day commemorations, the entire length of Argentina (where I got
terribly homesick after three weeks) and Phoenix, Arizona, where I
was looking for meteorite craters. I met wonderful people, learned
myriad new skills and had the time of my life.

    Back in Britain, I dressed as a Sumo wrestler, coxed the British
Olympic rowing crew, went rock-climbing, helped set the new world
conga-on-ice record and tickled a bat's stomach. I also tried high-
board diving with Chris Snode at Crystal Palace, the most
frightening thing I have ever had to do.

I got on famously with my co-presenters, John Leslie (who I already knew) and Diane-Louise Jordan, with whom I've remained very friendly. We were all in our thirties, and as a team rather older than was usual for *Blue Peter* presenters. I loved being allowed to dress up and bake cakes and be as childish as I liked. I'd grown up making Blue Peter-inspired objects from the famous sticky-backed plastic, cereal packets and loo rolls; now here I was, on the other side of the television screen, delivering the well-known and loved line 'Here's one I made earlier.' It was a strange feeling, living inside that box, peering out on to a world I'd once been a part of. The feeling that everything was inside out and upside down was only confirmed by the fact that every 'make' had to be performed upside down for the benefit of the overhead cameras. Diane, John and later Tim Vincent dreaded being asked to create something on air, but I loved it. So much so that Diane nicknamed me Pollyanna, a name she still uses. I'd volunteer for the 'makes' every time, even though it was sometimes like being asked to pat your head and rub your tummy simultaneously.

My biggest claim to fame was making Tracy Island, part of the Thunderbirds set, out of empty yoghurt pots, tin foil, tissue boxes, cheese tubs and pipe-cleaners. I dressed up as Lady Penelope for the part and spoke to Brains about the problem children had been having getting hold of the popular toy from shops. 'This sounds like a job for International Rescue,' I said. It was the most successful live 'make' in the history of *Blue Peter*, with in excess of 100,000 viewers writing in for details. The editor had to bring in extra staff (hordes of girl guides) to deal with the sackloads of mail asking for the so-called 'Brains Data Pack'. A photograph of me wearing a little Thunderbirds hat appeared all over the newspapers – definitely one for the scrapbook. Tracy Island was my grand slam. When I first attempted it in rehearsal it took me over an hour, especially making the little pipe-cleaner palm trees which parted to allow the Thunderbirds craft to take off. But by the time the programme went out, I had the 'make' down to twelve minutes flat.

I made rabbits out of socks, rockets out of washing-up-liquid bottles and cards for just about every occasion you can think of: Christmas, Easter, birthdays, Diwali, Rosh Hashanah. It was seat-of-the-pants television, not least because the programme always went out live, to keep its edge, and I had to be so careful what I said. How, for instance, should I introduce the idea of a Father's or Mother's Day card or present without upsetting a child from a broken home or one who'd lost a parent?

Even more trickily, I once had to make a chocolate tortoise cake with Mars bars for its feet and face and Smarties for its shell, but I wasn't allowed to mention the name of either product, so I ended up getting my tongue twisted around sentences like: 'You take your little coloured chocolate sweets and your chocolate-covered toffee bar . . .' There can never be a hiatus on the screen, so while you're juggling with the terminology and working upside down, you're also trying to keep the whole thing flowing. It was the most challenging work I'd done in my life.

There was a real family atmosphere about the place. Diane had apparently been thinking of leaving before I joined, to spend more time with her daughter, but we hit it off so well that she stayed on for a couple more years. Everyone, from the camera crew to the lighting staff, directors, producers, secretaries and props men, was a joy to work with.

Working for *Blue Peter* exposed me to a far wider audience than I'd ever known. Now I was recognised everywhere I went, not just by children but by their parents, by taxi-drivers, shop assistants, waiters, people in the street. It took me ages to get used to that and to stop myself from saying hello every time someone shouted: 'Hiya, Anthea!' It was weird having to get to grips with the idea that strangers thought they knew me.

It certainly wasn't all plain sailing, and I made my fair share of gaffes. One day I was handling Goldie, the *Blue Peter* hamster, during rehearsals and explaining the history of hamsters when it suddenly leaped from my hands, hitting the floor at great speed, and just lay there as if dead. I screamed, bent down and tweaked it to see if it was still alive. 'Oh, no, I've killed Goldie,' I said to camera, ashen-faced. But the little creature shook itself and got to its feet, allowing me to grab it seconds before Kari and Oki, the *Blue Peter* cats, had it for breakfast. I was so grateful it was only a rehearsal.

Indeed, rehearsals were vital, not only to enable us to run through the script and to practise our lines, but also so that we could get all innuendos and falling about out of our systems before we went out live. It didn't always work. One day, Tim, Diane and I were sitting on the banquette wrapping up the show, and Tim was telling people that Bonnie was going to be the star of a sponsored event somewhere. 'So, if anyone wants to see Bonnie,' he said, pointing down to her sitting at his feet, 'who's between my legs at the moment, then you can catch up with her at the Royal Orthopaedic Hospital.'

Without thinking, and out of camera view, I said: 'Ooh, that's a nice place to be, Bonnie,' before I realised quite how it would sound. As soon as the words left my lips, I thought 'Oh, no,' but it was too late. It was like being in church, where you are not supposed to laugh but you can't help yourself. Diane and I erupted into fits of barely concealed giggles while Tim valiantly tried to carry on. Within a few seconds the show was over. No sooner had the theme music cut in than Lewis Bronze flew down the metal stairs from the gallery and laid into Diane, thinking it was she who had made the unforgivable comment.

'What were you thinking of?' he yelled, eyes blazing.

Gulping hard, I had to stand up and admit that it wasn't Diane who was to blame but me, Little Miss Goody Two Shoes.

Lewis was furious. 'I can't imagine what made you say such a thing, Anthea,' he shouted, ticking me off in front of everyone. 'The switchboard will be jammed with irate calls, and rightly so. I may not be able to save you from this.'

Duly chastised, I waited for the tidal wave of opprobrium. On the duty log that night there were indeed several irate callers, including one mother who complained that we'd been 'peddling smut' to her children. And apparently the BBC link man hadn't been able to help sniggering as he was trying to announce the next show. The story made the papers, with headlines like '*Blue Peter* Anthea Gaffe', and 'Saucy Anthea's Slip of the Tongue', but, fortunately, in the end there wasn't too much of a brouhaha. Having promised Lewis that I'd learned my lesson and would never, ever make the same mistake again, I cut out the articles and stuck them in my scrapbook to remind myself to take care.

As a *Blue Peter* presenter I was inundated with other offers of work. Personal appearances became a large and important part of my schedule, many of them for charities with which I began to get involved, ranging from Action Research, the Association for Spina Bifida and Hydrocephalus, the Dyslexia Institute, the PDSA, Dogs for the Disabled, the Multiple Sclerosis Society, the Tidy Britain Group and the Elizabeth Trust for battered wives. I'd present cheques, give awards, judge competitions, switch on Christmas lights or simply turn up. My standing had increased enormously and suddenly I was in great demand for anything from *Children in Need* to appearing as a celebrity guest on *This is Your Life*.

Some of my best friendships came out of my new status. Invited to be a contributor to a Bobby Davro show called *Public Enemy Number One*, I met a relatively unknown young hopeful called Dale Winton. I found him funny, charming and talented, and we've been friends ever since. Others I met through the business are Esther Rantzen and her husband Desmond Wilcox, who both have the most amazing capacity to offer advice and support, and John Stapleton and his wife Lynn Faulds Wood, who were neighbours of ours in Chiswick.

By December 1992, I had presented a Christmas carol concert at the Royal Albert Hall and had become an occasional reporter for Radio 5 and for *The Good Health Show* on BBC1. In 1993 I introduced the Children's Royal Variety Performance in the presence of Princess Margaret. Later that year, I was selected by the BBC as one of three presenters to introduce the live opening of the Channel Tunnel. Nobody was more amazed than me that I'd got this far. There had always been people at school who were much brighter and cleverer than me, and better looking – Carol Barlow, for one. I'd always felt I had to work twice as hard just to keep up. Now, here I was, becoming famous, being paid well and doing a job I loved. I still had to pinch myself each morning.

My relationship with Pete, however, was becoming increasingly long-distance. With the crazy hours we were both working – I'd regularly have to be up at 4am for an 8am outside broadcast, and he wouldn't get to bed until 2am – we'd become the archetypal professional couple, ships passing in the night. We didn't argue or have any problems living together – we even managed to snatch a quick skiing holiday in Switzerland and thoroughly enjoyed what little time we could share – but we were just too busy to be together very often. Under such pressures, after a while the romance began to drift away.

The irony was that we still loved each other just as much as we always had. I was still his beloved 'AT' and he would always be my knight in shining armour, the heart-throb of my teenage years, the one who had rescued me from a life of misery. We were equally guilty of failing to find enough time for each other. We'd just grab five minutes here and there and end up having a fleeting conversation on a superficial level. 'When can I see you and talk about this properly?' I'd ask.

'Sorry,' Pete would say, flying out of the door with a half-eaten piece of toast in his hand. 'I'm absolutely chock-a-block this week.'

To try to have even one evening alone together we'd have to sit down with our diaries and pencil in a 'window' of opportunity. Invariably one or other of us would have to cancel because of work commitments. It was ridiculous.

Imperceptibly, at first, our relationship gradually became more and more professional and less light-hearted and intimate. Like all married couples, we settled into a domestic routine once the initial passion and spontaneity had worn off. When we did manage to get away for the odd break, perhaps for a weekend, or at most a week, Pete would spend much of the time on the telephone or answering faxes. At my cousin Jane's wedding that year, we stood side by side in the church and realised that this was the first time we'd seen each other properly in weeks. Listening to the vows and the sermon by the vicar on the importance of marriage, I chastised myself for not working harder at mine. For better for worse, for richer for poorer. We were definitely richer, but were we better people for it? I wasn't too sure sometimes.

Burdened by the heavy responsibility of his role as mentor and father figure to all his protégés, exhausted through overwork and stress, Pete had, somewhere along the line, developed a sort of messianic zeal for his work. I began to wonder if I would have to remind him that I was one of his clients to get his full attention. It wasn't just on an impersonal level, either; in our rare moments of intimacy, he felt increasingly unable to show me the physical affection I craved. I was as much to blame. We both knew this wasn't right and we both planned to do something about it, just as soon as we had the time. But with us both flying so high and no respite in sight, we simply carried on drifting further and further apart, each of us keen to capitalise on our success while we still could.

'You've got to run with the ball when you've got it,' he'd say. It became almost a mantra. But there were times when I didn't care a fig about the bloody ball.

In February 1994, Pete and Russ were at LWT with Darren Day, who was to star in the musical *Copacabana*, when Michael Metcalf, the senior director at GMTV, took Pete to one side. 'I need to talk to you about one of your artists,' he said. 'A position is likely to become available on *GMTV* when Lorraine Kelly leaves to have her baby, and I need someone to "do the settee" alongside Eamonn Holmes. I don't want to talk about it here, but can we arrange a lunch some time soon, away from the building?'

Pete nodded and asked Michael who it was he was interested in.

'I'd rather not say at this stage,' Michael replied. 'It's all rather sensitive.'

Pete left the meeting wracking his brains trying to work out which client it might be. He asked Russ if he had any ideas. 'Haven't a clue,' Russ replied in all honesty, knowing that no one on their books had the serious journalistic background required in most anchormen and women on breakfast television.

By the time the lunch was arranged, with Michael and Peter McHugh, the veteran director of programmes, Pete still couldn't for the life of him think who they could have in mind. Sitting down at a restaurant in west London, he told them: 'You're going to have to tell me who it is you want.' Smiling conspiratorially at each other, the two men uttered the name simultaneously. 'Anthea,' they said.

Pete nearly fell off his seat. 'Anthea?' he said, trying to remain calm and professional. 'My Anthea?'

'Why not?' said Michael Metcalf. 'I've seen her on *Blue Peter* and I like what I see. She's got a certain quality about her – a wholesome girl-next-door image that's just what we need on *GMTV*. I think she and Eamonn would work very well together.'

Gulping down a draught of water, Peter listened to what the two men had to say. He gave himself time for their proposal to sink in. Lighting a cigarette and blowing smoke into the air, he said finally: 'OK then, gentlemen. Let's discuss terms.'

My initial reaction was one of abject horror. 'No! No way,' I said when Pete first broke the news. *GMTV* was a programme I knew very well – I watched it most mornings while getting ready for work – and the thought of sitting there on the settee in a smart suit with my hair sprayed rigid terrified the living daylights out of me. I was far happier with my baggy jumpers, jeans and tousled locks on *Blue Peter*. I loved its family atmosphere and it was a job I never wanted to leave.

But Pete was nothing if not persistent. He told me I owed it to myself to pursue this offer. He made me realise that at least I had to consider it. 'There aren't that many *Blue Peter* presenters who leave and walk straight into another high-profile proper job in television,' he said. 'There are very few who make that leap and land on solid ground, and now here you are, aged thirty-four, being invited to be one of them. This is a lifeline, AT. You'd be crazy not to grab it.'

I sat blinking at him, trying to take in what he was telling me and wishing that there was some way I could cling on to *Blue Peter* for just a little longer. 'But I'm not ready, Pete,' I complained.

Taking my hand in his, and staring into my eyes, he reassured me as best he could. 'You can't stay in children's television for ever,' he said gently. 'Everyone has to leave Never-Never-Land some time.'

Throughout my life, I guess that if a door has opened for me, I've usually gone through it. I'm never sure exactly what will happen when I do, but I suppose the one thing I do have is the bottle to give it a go. That was what had happened at the AA when they asked me to present the traffic reports, and again when Golly Gallagher had told me about the video jockey job at Sky. Now yet another door was opening. People often say to me: 'Oh, you are so lucky, Anthea,' but it isn't a question of luck. A little of that goes into it, of course, but doors open in life all the time, and an awful lot of people choose not to go through them. Sometimes you have to make your own luck in this world, and you can only do that by taking a deep breath and walking into the unknown.

Still undecided, but knowing in my heart that I'd never go against Pete's advice, I went for a meeting with editor Liam Hamilton and Peter McHugh in Buchan's Restaurant, Battersea. I couldn't go to GMTV because it was all meant to be hush-hush and I couldn't be seen with them there. I was very nervous but they were both charming and friendly and put me at my ease. Over lunch they chatted to me about all the wonderful changes that would come about in my life if I accepted the job. Before long, I started to get carried away by their enthusiasm. Little by little, the men around me – Pete, Russ, Liam and Peter McHugh – were convincing me that this was a very big career step, and one that I had to take. I think what had held me back so much at first was a fear of the much greater responsibility I would be carrying, responsibility I wasn't sure if I could cope with. This was a big gig. A really big gig. And once I walked through this door, I knew I'd never be able to go back.

It took me three sleepless nights and four agonising days to come to a decision. After much deliberation, and having discussed it every which way with Pete, I agreed to accept the job offer. Then I had to face the difficult task of telling Lewis Bronze that I was leaving. As I started to speak, blurting out what I had to say, I had a tear in my eye and, to my amazement, so did he.

I cried even more the day I left *Blue Peter*, all on live television. I was so terribly sad to go. They put together a highlights video for me and, as part of the farewell show, allowed me to make a short film tracing the Turner family tree. It was a special tribute to my grandfather, Vin, by then ninety-six years old and recently widowed, and he helped me with it. Dressed in various period costumes, I told the story of my family after they came to Staffordshire around 1195. I followed them from their Norman farming roots through to the e0ighteenth century, when they were vicars of a parish church. Then, in the nineteenth century, the family turned their talents to cabinet-making in Burslem and the rest, as they say, is history.

Blue Peter was my home, the people who worked there were my family and it was like growing up and flying the nest. I was leaving children's television for good and was about to enter the big girls' game. The blessings of all my colleagues ringing in my ears, and clutching their farewell gift – a huge alarm clock to help get me up in the mornings – I moved onwards, but with the greatest trepidation.

I was right to be anxious. I started on *GMTV* at the end of July 1994, and although within a few months the figures were up to a healthy 2 million viewers, putting the show way ahead of its chief rival, *The Big Breakfast* with Chris Evans and Gaby Roslin, my early days there were a white-knuckle ride. It all began with the publicity. Headlines like: 'Anthea's £100,000 to front *GMTV*' and 'Anthea in breakfast challenge to Lorraine' didn't help. Neither did stories which claimed I'd been brought in to boost the station's share of younger audiences, or that I'd entered a 'cat-eat-cat' world.

I didn't catch so much as a glimpse of the famous settee for my first six weeks with *GMTV*. While Eamonn Holmes and Penny Smith kept it warm, I was dispatched to Torremolinos in Spain with Ross Kelly and Mr Motivator, *GMTV*'s keep fit man, to co-present their 'Fun in the Sun' roadshows for six weeks that summer, along with Sally Meen and Simon Biagi, the weather presenters. Our brief was to travel to various locations, filming reports to give a taste of Spain and presenting live links with the studio from the beaches of the Costa del Sol. I guess they thought it was a way of easing me in gently.

It's never easy being the new girl and trying to make friends and slot in; being in Spain made it doubly difficult because I had no time to get to know anybody before we were up and running, on air and talking live to Eamonn and his co-presenters back in the studio. The team spirit was great and no one was bitchy or unkind, but I didn't have any friends and there was nobody I could confide in. It was like arriving at a new school in the middle of the last term, when every-one else is great chums and you're all alone in the playground. I remembered my first few days at St Dominic's and shivered.

On my first day, I had the dazzlingly dressed Mr Motivator to compete with. 'Mote' as everyone called him (his real name is Derrick) was wonderful, and couldn't have been more friendly. 'Take no notice of anything anyone says and just go your own way,' was his advice, and it was to stand me in good stead. Ross Kelly was also very kind to me, which was just as well, because for the first two weeks I felt miserable, homesick and out of my depth; a fish out of water.

The working schedule was very fraught, a rollercoaster ride which started at 5am. Every time the cameras appeared on a beach or in a main street, a crowd of people would gather round us, sometimes heckling and almost always trying to do something outrageous or lewd. I saw more men's bottoms on that gig than I'd ever seen in my life. The bars and clubs belted out music day and night. I can never hear 'Love is All Around' by Wet Wet Wet without being trans-ported straight back to Spain. The satellite signal to London was often so bad that, with all the background noise, it was very difficult to hear the studio and the director in my earpiece, especially as there were three separate voices vying with each other. We were meant to be an all-singing, all-dancing show with four cameras but initially it was complete chaos. Many of the crew had never worked on such a demanding outside broadcast before. It was a learning curve for everybody, myself included, because I had been used to a very well-oiled and organised BBC environment. We just had to cope and we did, very well, in the circumstances.

By the second week everyone was tired out. There were technical problems right up until the last link on the Friday, which only added to the tensions. For some reason I can't now remember, I said some-thing in a different way from how Ross Kelly and I had rehearsed it and inadvertently gave him an awkward few seconds of grappling for an appropriate response. There was a brief but agonising pause during which no one knew what was going on or who was meant to be speaking. When the link finished and our bit was over, Ross rounded on me. 'Once we've agreed what you're going to say, Anthea,' he snapped, 'then kindly don't change it.'

I was feeling pretty low by that stage already and when Ross lost his temper with me so publicly, my self-esteem hit the floor. 'Excuse me,' I said, fleeing the beach. Speaking to Peter on the telephone later that day, I sobbed my socks off. 'They all hate me, I know they do,' I wailed.

'Don't be silly, AT,' he told me. 'You're just feeling insecure. I'm sure Ross didn't mean to bite your head off.'

Unable to face any of the crew, I took myself off and wandered around the town on my own that day, feeling awful. Spain was the last place on earth I wanted to be at that moment. Nothing about the place, not even the incessant sunshine, could cheer me up. Why had I ever left *Blue Peter*, I moaned inwardly. I had been so happy there. Turning a corner, I literally bumped into Ross Kelly, and my sunglasses fell off to reveal my red-rimmed eyes. He apologised immediately for shouting at me. 'I'm so sorry, Anthea,' he said. 'I was just very tense.'

Touched by his apology, I blurted out how homesick and miserable I was. He was very kind. Putting an arm around my shoulder, he took me to a bar and bought me a large sangria. 'Everyone's been very impressed so far, and London are more than happy, so buck up and start enjoying yourself,' he told me firmly. Ross and I have never had a cross word since. Whenever the chips are down, it is his letter or card that is always the first through the door.

He was right, of course. It was a wonderful job and a fantastic opportunity, and I should not have been feeling so sorry for myself. By the third week I was much more settled and everything was OK, especially after Pete flew out for the weekend. The daily slog continued, but it seemed far less of a chore and much more of an adventure as each day passed. We travelled all over Spain and saw some incredible sights. It is a beautiful country and yet ruined in some parts by the ugly face of tourism. Of all the places we visited, Benidorm was the biggest eye-opener for me. We'd go down to the beach first thing in the morning to film and there'd be crowds of young people who had literally just fallen out of the nightclubs. Couples would be openly having sex in the sand, cheered on by their friends. I was fascinated. This was a side of life I'd never seen before – the most public display of affection I'd ever witnessed in Norton was a couple snogging in a bus shelter – and it certainly wasn't remotely suitable for family television.

Before long, the crew and I had created a little family infrastructure for ourselves. We became very close – not just Ross, Mote and me, but people like Steve Wiseman, the technical operations manager, and Helen McMurray and Kate Fleming, both senior producers. It was the little things that meant a lot: the cards and notes congratulating one of us on a show well done, or the practical jokes we played on each other. As a presenter, I was allowed to stay in a hotel with laundry service, whereas some of the crew had to make do with self-catering accommodation. So I offered to collect their laundry and took it either to the launderette or back to my hotel, where I billed it to my room. I was often seen wandering up and down the seafront carrying someone else's washing. We'd fry together all day long – filming in sizzling heat isn't fun – and then cool down by meeting up for dinner every night. When we eventually got home, Ross said he found it difficult to eat with fewer than twenty people and without a menu with pictures on it.

Family and friends at home also helped to keep my spirits up with their jolly cards, letters and faxes, and I felt less isolated with each new message. By the time the six-week assignment neared its end, I was relaxed and happy and ready to face the rigours of the London studio. At least when I had some of the 'Fun in the Sun' crew around me in the studio I would be assured of the odd friendly face. The powers-that-be back in London seemed pleased with my performance in Spain and told me that the ratings were up, which was wonderful news so I returned to England tanned and triumphant. It was just as well, because the very next morning, 5 September 1994, I was due to hit the settee for the first time.

On my first day in the fourth-floor *GMTV* studio at the London Weekend Television Centre in south London, I turned up in a pink Whistles trouser suit. The minute I sat on the settee, facing what looked like a bank of Daleks rather than cameras, I regretted wearing it. The huge shoulder pads rode up when I sat down, making me look like a gangster. Fitted with a hidden microphone and earpiece, I looked like a rabbit caught in the headlights.

The make-up artist checked me over one last time, adding yet more powder to my sweaty top lip. I felt as if I was wearing a mask that would crack if I dared to smile. As the producer counted down the seconds to the start of the show, 'Five, four, three, two, one,' I stared into one of the enormous cameras, somehow managed to smile and announced: 'Hello, good morning, my name's Anthea Turner and you're watching *GMTV*.'

The rest of the show is a complete blur. Quite apart from the fact that I was fighting off a cold, had a raging sore throat and had to keep drinking Lemsip to ward off full-blown 'flu, I felt as if the whole thing was running away from me and I was sprinting breathlessly to keep up with it. My colleagues were serious journalists who had anchored news or discussion programmes and knew the correct jargon, but it was an entirely new discipline for me. There was a script of sorts on the autocue, the automatic prompt that scrolls up behind the camera, but it was very much up to me to ad lib. I had to change gear more times than a rally driver.

One moment I could be previewing the latest gossip from *Coronation Street*, next I'd have to do a smooth link to the fitness video and a few seconds later I might be reporting serious news from Westminster or interviewing someone with a tragic story to tell. It was very difficult to find the right level, especially for someone who'd never done news before.

I was completely in awe of Eamonn Holmes as a performer and spent much of the programme staring at him speechlessly. I considered it an honour to be working alongside such a professional and experienced anchorman. I knew I could learn a lot from him and I very much wanted us to be friends. Thankfully, he was kindness itself that first day. Every time the camera was on someone else, he reassured me, 'You're doing great,' and patted my hand. I was so grateful. But it must have been patently obvious to him and everyone else that I didn't have a clue what I was doing. On day two I arrived

in a little black pleated mini-skirt, a maroon jumper and knee-high
socks. Everyone else seemed so slick and professional and grown-up
in comparison. How did they manage it?

The trick, I was to discover, was to appear to be natural in the
most unnatural of circumstances. It isn't normal to be up, dressed up
to the nines and bright as a button at 7am, and when you have to
interview someone who patently feels groggier than you do, and
who is only there because their PR has told them to be, to promote
their new book, film or whatever, you have to help them through. I
had to ignore hangovers, body odour, bad breath, booze fumes, the
smell of cigarettes and general grumpiness. I had to learn how to flirt
with the camera, to forget that I was being watched by millions of
people and imagine that I was talking to just one friend. But it was
easier said than done.

I was at *GMTV* from June 1994 to December 1996, and I clocked
up some serious air miles in that time. The hours were long and hard
and played havoc with my social life. I would have to be in bed by
9.30pm every night (with my compulsory cup of hot chocolate and
a few biscuits) because I would be up at 3.45am the next day and off
to work half an hour later. I spent two hours in the studio, reading
through my script and preparing for the show while sorting out my
make-up and wardrobe. Then it was on set for 7am sharp, the smile,
and the 'Hello, good morning'.

It was a million miles from *Blue Peter*, the first time I'd ever
encountered the bitchy, backbiting side of television, and I was convinced everyone hated me. One female colleague who shall remain
nameless sauntered over to the settee one morning just as the show
was about to go on air, picked up the *Guardian* and asked sweetly:
'Did you want to read this, Anthea?'

Smiling up at her, I was just about to say 'No, thanks,' when her
expression changed.

'Oh, I'm sorry,' she said acidly, 'I forgot. You don't read the big
newspapers, do you?'

Wishing I didn't always blush quite so easily, I answered: 'No, I'm
a *Sun* girl through and through.' Seconds later I was on air.

Eamonn remained outwardly polite and friendly, although I was never sure what his real feelings were. I always felt that he thought I was just a tart from children's telly and not fit to sit next to a proper journalist like him. It took me a long time not to take the same view. Lorraine, with whom I shared a dressing room until she left, was sweetness itself and went out of her way to let me know she was there for me. 'I, of all people,' she told me, 'know how tough this gig can be.'

What really shocked me was the reaction of the press. If I'd ever been worthy of a mention previously, it had always been couched in a jovial, friendly 'we love Anthea' kind of tone. Now the papers made it perfectly clear that they hated me and I was devastated. Some reporters claimed that my 'bubble had burst' when I had only just begun. One unkind article held that me leaving *Blue Peter* for *GMTV* was 'a rare example of a presenter leaving a children's show and going intellectually downmarket'. Others claimed that Eamonn Holmes 'clearly detested' me. Lynda Lee-Potter called me 'a bulging-eyed, grinning pixie in a semi-waking nightmare'. I lost sleep for a week over that one.

What was my crime? I wasn't pretending to be anything I wasn't; I was simply doing my level best to help present a lightweight break-fast television programme. It was hardly *Newsnight*. I couldn't understand how people who had never met me and probably only rarely watched me on television could write such vitriolic things which they knew could have a direct and detrimental effect on my career. What is the mentality that drives such viciousness? How can someone sit down at a computer and even think like that? Despite my best intentions, to this day, I have never stopped being hurt by what people write about me.

There were times when I was consumed by the injustice of it all, helpless against the never-ending flood of criticism. I was all for offering to swap places with the journalists who were attacking me so they could see how easy they found my job. 'It isn't fair, Pete,' I'd rail. 'They don't even know me.'

Pete was as pragmatic as ever. 'Nobody ever said life was going to be fair, AT,' he reminded me.

I was still reeling from these pastings in the press, trying to gain some credibility and find my feet, when I was attacked from another and completely unexpected quarter. On 19 September, five days before Bruno Brookes was due to marry his new girlfriend a 'kiss-and-tell' article about me appeared in the *Sun*. It ran on the front page and was headlined: 'I Caught Anthea in Love Trap'. In his – very selective – exposé, Bruno revealed how he'd hired a private detective to 'snare his two-timing lover', and that when he had found out that I was seeing Peter Powell, he had ended our relationship. The article was billed as Bruno breaking his silence about his 'turbulent' affair with me. He said I drove him wild in bed and that we had 'romped' outside my parents' home while they slept inside. He claimed I'd asked him to marry me after a 'very rocky time' but that he'd turned me down. He admitted that he was 'no angel', that we'd had a lot of rows over 'the smallest things' and that he'd been 'driven' into the arms of other women. He conceded that he had been difficult and demanding to live with; that he had sometimes drunk a lot, which made him grumpy, and that he had been instrumental in driving me away. 'I was obsessed with ambition,' he said. 'It was all work, work, work.'

He maintained that I 'mothered' him when he was first working for Radio 1 but gave me credit for helping to run his organisation. He admitted that he'd been against me having a career in broadcasting and that he'd told me I should support him instead. He claimed I owed much of my success to him. 'When I watch her operate, there's so much of me in her,' he said. 'She learned a lot from me in the early days, like knowing how to survive.' He concluded by expressing his relief that we hadn't made the mistake of getting married.

I couldn't believe what I was reading. I knew that I had stuck my neck out by becoming a 'celebrity', and I was gradually growing accustomed to the professional diatribes against me, but I'd always believed my personal life was sacrosanct as far as my friends and family were concerned. It wounded me more than I can say and I have never been able to bring myself to speak to Bruno since.

Fortunately for me, I didn't have to say a word in my defence, because the press did it for me. They slaughtered him for his disloyalty. The *Guardian* ran an article describing Bruno as a 'risible figure'. Carole Malone, in a piece headed: 'You're a snivelling rat, Bruno', in the *Star*, called him 'Radio 1's resident dwarf' and a 'balding creep of a has-been', and accused 'this bucket of pigswill' of deliberately cashing in on my fame. I didn't know this woman from Adam, but I liked her immensely.

The Bruno article and others like it stung like hell, but Pete, as ever, said just the right thing at the right time to make me feel better. Ever the pro, he made me realise that I had to focus on the public, the only critics that mattered. 'Think of all the fan letters you receive from people telling you how much they enjoy watching you, and how you cheer them up every morning,' he said. 'Concentrate on all the positive responses you get from people on the streets, not on what someone like Bruno sold for thirty pieces of silver.' He was right, of course. He always was in his cool, calm way. But that didn't make it any less painful.

6

The Big Girls' Game

The television presenter Frank Bough once said: 'The day you know you're doing the job well on television is the day you make it all look so easy everybody thinks they could do it.' I was a long way off that day yet, and I needed all the help I could get. My learning curve was like the north face of the Eiger. It was a case of sink or swim. My transformation from bumbling novice to something akin to a reasonable news presenter only really began when the powers-that-be decided to take me in hand. I knew I had a lot of hard work to do and, with their help, I put myself through a crash course in television-presenting.

My tutors were Liam Hamilton, Michael Metcalf and the senior producer and friend from 'Fun in the Sun', Helen McMurray. They sat down with me after each show and, with infinite patience, went through the programme identifying difficult areas. 'Be careful when you cross your legs,' Helen told me. 'Apparently, you flashed your knickers at Camera 2 last week. Try to practise in the mirror at home.'

'I'd like you to take a little more care with your links,' Liam would say. 'See how others do it and try to learn from them. It needs to look a little more seamless.'

I listened carefully to it all and worked hard at improving myself, because I knew I wouldn't have very long to get it together. The life-expectancy of a television presenter can be incredibly short. I was still in the trial period of my contract, and if I didn't make the grade, they'd get rid of me in the time it took to say: 'Hello, good morning.'

GMTV hired a personal style adviser, an American television reporter turned image-maker called Gail Clevinger, who was instructed to help me find a more suitable look. She was fantastic; she went into everything from my fingernails to how I sat on the settee. With her by my side giving advice, I bought myself a plum-coloured trouser suit by Paul Smith and a grey jacket. I also bought an Edina Ronay suit. Gail taught me that power dressing works. With her assistance, and that of Hilary Simons, the wardrobe mistress who was detailed to buy me some designer clothes, I gradually began to find my way through this particular minefield.

The first thing Gail and Hilary bought me was a bright pink Yves Saint Laurent suit, which I hated. It was terribly smart and I didn't know how to hold myself in it. I felt as if I were dressed in somebody else's clothes. 'You'll grow into it,' Gail told me, and she was right. After wearing it just a few times I grew to like it and to feel comfortable in it. I learned that if you look right, you feel confident and you can do the job much better. Gloria Hunniford once told me that she wouldn't even consider doing her radio show without the right clothes.

'I've watched some of the other women in television news and they all seem to wear a sort of uniform of power suits and big shoulders,' I told Gail. 'I know I have to look smart, but can we please try to find me something a little less starchy?' She took me to my favourite store, Harvey Nichols, and, with the help of a personal shopper, introduced me to the concept of investment dressing. 'If you buy good-quality, classic clothes, you'll never grow out of them,' Gail said. Looking at my reflection in the mirror, clad from head to toe in a beautifully cut, chic designer outfit, I blushed with embarrassment at the thought of some of the extraordinarily naff clothes I'd worn on children's television: multicoloured waistcoats, striped trouser suits, floral leggings and gimmicky T-shirts. Pete was right. Anthea Turner had grown up. Never-Never-Land was receding fast.

Attention to such details as my appearance really paid off. Viewers began calling in to ask where I'd bought a particular outfit. People would come up to me in the supermarket and tell me how much they liked my clothes. One woman said to me: 'I always pop the television on to see what you're wearing in the morning and then I try to copy it from my own wardrobe.' Scary stuff. To my amazement, I was voted the Best Dressed Woman on Television by the Designers' Guild, an award which put me on the front cover of *Hello!* magazine, a first for me. The Designers' Guild gave me a beautiful little silver box to commemorate this honour, which is still one of my most treasured possessions. Best of all, my new title really opened doors for me in the fashion world. Designers began to offer me their clothes and people like Bruce Oldfield, Caroline Charles and the Whistles chain all give me discounts or kindly lend me outfits for special occasions.

If I thought I'd been inundated with invitations to all sorts of events and shows at *Blue Peter*, they now became a deluge. I was constantly asked to open everything from a new hospital wing to an airport shop, and my personal appearances became much more high-profile. The reasoning behind this was simple. If I was there, as the best-dressed woman on television, the organisers knew they'd get the press along and there would be good publicity for their event or product in the newspaper. In such situations I learned to appreciate how important it is to wear the right thing: a red Kenzo coat with black trim to turn on the Christmas lights, for example, or a chic pale pastel jacket and skirt to visit a hospital. My clothes quickly became the tools of my trade.

The only thing I rebelled against was altering my hair. Gail and Hilary suggested I had it cut into a far more manageable style, a sleek bob, to make it a bit tidier, but I didn't want to look just like everyone else. So I dug my heels in. Ever since I'd had all my long hair cropped off at the age of eighteen, shortly after Ruth's death, it had taken on a life of its own in a tousled, unruly sort of way, and I'd kind of got used to it. And to my astonishment, my Nicky Clarke-cut 'style' became so popular with viewers that it was known at hairdressers across the country as an 'Anthea' and I was voted Head of the Year by the Hairdressers' Federation.

I only wished the rest of my job was that simple. I might have looked all right, but most of the time I felt as if I was trudging through deep sand. It took me several months to gain confidence and, with it, the loyalty of the viewers. The press continued to slaughter me and my spirits plummeted regularly, but at the same time, virtually alongside the articles criticising me for being a 'brainless bimbo' who didn't know my arse from my elbow, there would be a huge photograph of me attending some function or other. It was a perfect example of the fickleness of the press.

Intense media scrutiny became part of my daily life. I was followed everywhere, photographed shopping, eating, coming out of the loo, having coffee with friends. For some considerable time I was tailed by a car driven by freelance photographers trying to find out if I had any skeletons in my closet. A controversial picture of me would have been worth upwards of £20,000 to someone like them. But I had to learn to accept that it was all part of my job. I was making a living out of being a celebrity, and so I was considered fair game. I would have been troubled by it if I'd been up to no good, or if they had seriously invaded my privacy or my property, but generally it was just lots of pictures and some light-hearted tittle tattle, and I wasn't too precious about it. My life is an open book and I have nothing to hide. In the end I learned to draw a veil over it in my mind. If someone wanted to follow me to Sainsbury's to watch me buying a tin of baked beans, it was up to them. One picture appeared of me in Chiswick High Road choosing a pumpkin for Hallowe'en. I mean, so what? A photographer even lay in wait outside my door at 3am to try to catch me looking half-asleep and dishevelled with curlers in my hair. I could see the caption already. 'Anthea Turner – best-dressed woman?' Fortunately, I looked half-decent that morning and my driver had tipped me off anyway, so I smiled, waved and ruined the picture completely.

I'm lucky that I am photogenic. My face is reasonably symmetrical, and I have learned how to be photographed to improve on that advantage. Many people realise far too late that you should never pull faces. If in doubt, present a blank canvas. You have to try to remember that when lenses are trained on you almost constantly you must keep your poise or they'll catch you out. And of course the only photograph that will appear will be the least flattering one. I have studied others religiously, taking note of their good and bad points. Princess Diana had it down to a fine art.

While I'd come to accept that the attention of the media was part of the gig, Pete absolutely hated it. He'd get unreasonably agitated if he knew there was a photographer waiting outside our house or at a party we were attending. 'What can they possibly get on the way out that they didn't get on the way in?' he'd ask angrily. He'd had a taste of life on Planet Fame as a Radio 1 DJ and had sometimes been followed home by photographers and female fans. He'd loathed it and believed he'd put all that behind him now. But suddenly he found himself back in the eye of the lens and it made him deeply uncomfortable. He started to balk at having to accompany me to events, and that served only to push him further into his work.

Gradually I found my feet at *GMTV* and began to feel comfortable in my own skin. I was still being punished by some of the papers, but my most severe critic by a long chalk was myself. Little by little I overcame my fear and realised that there was no great mystique about what I was doing at all. *GMTV* is tabloid telly, it has a 'feel good factor' for those watching first thing in the morning. Chris Evans was doing all sorts of mad antics on *The Big Breakfast*, the BBC offered serious news and *GMTV* fell somewhere in between. In many ways that made it a harder gig, because it meant that Eamonn and I had to be jacks-of-all-trades.

Television presentation became my thesis and I worked at it with the zeal of a model student. I'm a perfectionist and I put myself under a lot of pressure to get it right, but I knew I had to. There'd be no scuttling back to *Blue Peter* if I failed. I recorded everything I could on television and whenever I had a few days off, I'd sit down in front and watch myself on video, taking notes and picking up my weak points. My worst problem, I decided, was that I never looked like I was in control. I studied clips of just about everyone else working in television news to try to learn from them. Sue Lawley was my absolute heroine, so cool and calm and professional. Selina Scott was another great pro. Scrutinising people like them, rewinding and replaying their every little movement and gesture until I had them off pat, I slowly began to learn my craft.

I was particularly interested in how presenters linked the various parts of a show. It was like studying a knitting pattern to find out how to get from one point to another and on to the next row. I became addicted to *Richard and Judy*. It takes a lot of professionalism to keep the links flowing in a show as long as theirs and to maintain the pace at the same time. I have nothing but admiration for them. But while I was keen to learn from others, I didn't want to stray too far from who I was in the process. At *Blue Peter* my success had been put down to my wholesome girl-next-door appeal. I don't know about that, I was just being me – what you see is what you get – but I knew I had to hone some areas where I was letting myself down. I even became grateful for the attitude of some of those in the media who clearly detested me. But for them, I might easily have grown complacent.

My tenacity came to the forefront, and I'd return to work with renewed vision. I realised that to understand my job, I had to get under the skin of those I worked with, particularly the media. I had to find out what made them tick. I befriended some of the reporters and photographers who came to see me for interviews and photo shoots so that I could try to get inside their minds. To my astonishment, most of them were lovely people who often did not understand their newspapers' policies any more than I did, and several have remained friends. On their advice, I just carried on as best I could, and luckily, I didn't make too many major gaffes.

The biggest boost to my confidence came a few months after I joined *GMTV* when Mike Leggo, head of light entertainment at the BBC, called Pete and scheduled a meeting with him. 'I've got something I think Anthea might be interested in,' he told him over the phone. In typical Pete style, he didn't tell me anything about it until the next free evening we had together, a Wednesday – the night I'd invited Eamonn Holmes over for my version of Delia Smith's smoked-fish pie.

'I saw Mike Leggo yesterday,' Pete said almost casually, pouring me

a glass of wine while I prepared supper. 'He wants you to be one of
the co-presenters of the new National Lottery show.'

Dropping my spoon to the work surface with a clatter, I stared at
Pete, open-mouthed. 'You can't be serious,' I said.

'Yup,' said Pete, picking up the spoon and handing it back to me
with a grin. 'Never been more serious in my life.'

The new lottery show was one of the most sought-after jobs in
British television, although it was also certain to be a political hot
potato. It was one of those roles that could bomb terribly, or could be
the making of its presenter. My first concern was that I'd have to do
something mathematical with numbers like the gifted Carol
Vorderman on *Countdown*, and that my dyslexia might get in the
way. I'd retrained my brain to read autocues and scripts fairly quickly,
but I feared that I might somehow end up jumbling the numbers and
create chaos on a grand scale. Pete assured me I wouldn't have to have
anything to do with the little multicoloured balls.

I knew the lottery was going to be a success, but I was afraid that
I might be walking straight into the lions' den once again as far as the
press was concerned. Pete made me see the overwhelming benefits:
Saturday night, prime time, Mike Leggo (whom I liked), and the
blanket comfort of the BBC, where I'd always felt at home. 'If you
say no, I think you might live to regret it,' he told me.

Eamonn arrived for dinner a few minutes later and Pete showed
him in. I'd slaved over the stove for hours in an attempt to break the
ice between us, but I think it was well and truly broken when Pete
told him my news and asked his opinion. 'It's great,' Eamonn told
me, grinning. 'You've got to go for it, Anthea,'

I was already working five days a week at *GMTV*, and now I was
going to be driven off to some far-flung part of the country on Friday
nights or Saturday mornings to be ready to present the Saturday-
night show. On Sunday mornings, I'd be travelling back from filming
the previous night, and I'd still have to be up at 3.45am the following day. But it was only a six-month contract, I reasoned.

Of course there would be days when I'd feel like death, when I'd
have a stomach-ache or a headache or was just plain exhausted, and the
last thing I'd feel like doing would be dragging myself out of bed and

putting on the ritz. But I was young, healthy and fit, thanks to regular exercise, and I felt reasonably well able to cope. I knew I had to look after myself or I'd go under, so I watched my diet, got enough sleep and took regular vitamin supplements. It was the red-light syndrome – as long as the light was red, meaning 'on air,' I'd keep going. It was only when it went off that I'd go down with every virus known to man.

I knew the fact that I'd even been offered such a prestigious job was yet another testimony to Pete's ability and a vindication of his confidence in me, and I didn't want to let him down. He was still working all the hours God sent and was struggling to make a good life for us both. I still hoped for more time with him, and wished that we could stop the world sometimes so that we could spend a few days just being together and telling each other how we really felt. But now, more than ever, there was no time. Every minute of every day was jam-packed for both of us with meetings, studio dates, gigs, parties, dinners or travelling. Our idea of a date was to meet for a quick bite in the LWT canteen. It was all I could do to fit in the gym, hairdresser, clothes shopping, supermarket and things like appointments with the dentist or doctor. We allowed ourselves no room for manoeuvre when it came to our marriage.

The announcement of my new job as co-presenter of the *National Lottery Live* with Scottish comedian Gordon Kennedy, made nationwide news. 'Lady Luck smiles on Anthea in the fame game', 'Anthea is the big draw', 'National Anthea' and 'Anthea Wins the Lottery' ran the headlines. I almost needed a separate scrapbook for them all. The papers said that Gordon and I were set to become the most famous faces on British television, with 23 million viewers as well as a simultaneous broadcast on Radio 1.

Of course, there was the usual dissent. Anne Robinson wrote that she hoped there would be no words involved in reading out the winning numbers because I knew very few (being dyslexic, that hurt especially). Lynda Lee-Potter said: 'Anthea Turner is exceptionally pretty with glittering white teeth. She is also crashingly dull, with a well-honed instinct for uttering the banal, obvious and stomach-churning.' I tried to shrug it all off, but inside, it stung as acutely as ever.

Meanwhile, after two days of intensive rehearsals amid strict security, during which we were sworn to secrecy as to the show's content, the suspense-filled countdown to the lottery began at 7pm on 19 November 1994, and along with Gordon and Noel Edmonds (who made a special guest appearance), I became one of the first presenters of BBC1's *National Lottery Live* in an hour-long special programme with a £5.8 million jackpot. Noel drove a security van containing £3 million in cash into the Television Centre in London to show viewers what such a big win would look like.

I was broadcasting live from Nottingham's Victoria Shopping Centre, rushing around interviewing last-minute ticket-buyers and trying to find winners. As part of a promotion they were doing, the *Mirror* selected my outfit for me, taking me to Harvey Nichols the week before and helping me to choose a £4,000 plum-coloured trouser suit with brocade waistcoat and cravat, most of which were made by Alberta Ferretti and Paul Smith. I loved that outfit and certainly looked the part.

The show made television history and quickly became the BBC's highest-rated programme. Appearing regularly in what I called my 'Saturday job', I became the most-watched woman on British television screens. With the love and support of all those around me, and despite the fact that I really hadn't planned any of this, Anthea Turner had somehow arrived.

Once I got into my stride, even though I was permanently exhausted, work became enjoyable again, especially at *GMTV*, where I was allowed greater responsibility from the reassuring upholstery of the settee. It was still seat-of-the-pants television – only those who work in the industry know how hard it is to do that job – but I was getting better at it every day. I was beginning to control it rather than allowing it to control me. I also came to understand how lucky I was to be contributing to something that brought a little bit of light into people's lives. I even 'came out' about my dyslexia, hosting a series of programmes for *GMTV* for National Dyslexia Week with Dr Hilary Jones. The response from the public was overwhelming. People were inspired by the fact that someone who was once barely able to read and write could end up on national telly. It was Pete who taught me that I owed it to those people, the public, as much as to myself to shrug off my critics and carry on.

Clive James paid me the greatest compliment. Sitting next to me on the settee, having been interviewed, he watched as I cut to the next three items before being counted out to a commercial break. Turning to me with that cheeky smile of his as I reached under the cushion of the settee and pulled out a banana for an instant hit of energy, he shook his head in open admiration. 'I don't know how you do this job, Anthea,' he said. 'It's my idea of hell on earth.' I thought that was pretty good coming from him.

It wasn't hell on earth at all after a while. I never loved it as much as I'd loved *Blue Peter*, but it was very rewarding and fulfilling. Among the high spots was the chance to meet two of the greatest icons of my childhood. The first was Julie Andrews, who came into the studio to promote her latest role in *Sunset Boulevard* and was a complete star. She was beautiful to look at, had the most perfect diction and was charming. 'I'm so excited to meet you,' I stammered before the cameras started rolling. 'I saw *The Sound of Music* seven times and I once played Liesl at the Queen's Theatre, Burslem.'

She must have thought I was mad, but she didn't show it. Instead she squeezed my hand, leaned forward and said animatedly: 'I'm sure you were absolutely marvellous.' After the show I asked her for her autograph.

But meeting my next guest took my tendency to blush on to a whole new level. He was in a production of *Blood Brothers* in London and agreed to come in for an interview. I was scarlet from the moment he arrived in the studio until long after he'd left. 'I don't know what you're both laughing at,' I remembered telling Ruth and Mum the day Ruth died. 'I *will* meet David Cassidy one day. You see if I don't.'

I spent much of the interview embarrassingly tongue-tied, having been ribbed mercilessly about my crush by all the technicians and producers. David was well aware of my discomfort: egged on by my colleagues behind the scenes, he picked up my hand and held it in his while talking to me, leaving me completely speechless. A few evenings later, Peter and I went for a meal at the Caprice with David and his new wife, songwriter Sue Shifrin. It was one of the best nights of my life. I only wish Ruth could have been there.

Another highlight was meeting John McEnroe at the Wimbledon tennis championships. Despite his reputation, he was completely charming. When he offered to give me a tennis lesson, I was surprised. My tennis has never been good enough for public consumption, as John soon discovered. At the end of the piece, he turned to the camera and said, with mock indignation: 'Teach Anthea to play tennis? You cannot be serious!'

Sir Les Patterson (Dame Edna Everage's alter ego) tried to jump me, *Men Behaving Badly* stars Martin Clunes and Neil Morrissey made all sorts of lewd suggestions (until I shut Neil up by bringing out some old photos of us together in *Stagefright* at the Edinburgh Festival), and television's eccentric horse-racing presenter John McCririck had me in fits of giggles with his mad antics. Cliff Richard had me all of a dither, as did Robert Powell and Tony Curtis, but they were all very sweet. My trouble was that I was just as in awe of these celebrities as the average viewer, and it was perfectly obvious to everyone.

The National Lottery show was still going strong, and Gordon and I had a lot of fun doing it. He is a very lovable guy, a naturally hilarious man who had me in stitches much of the time. We were clearly good friends and I think the chemistry between us worked well on television. The night he dressed up as Queen Victoria particularly sticks in my memory for making me laugh, and several million people, as well, I hope.

There were some heart-stopping moments, too. Like the night I dangled, dressed in a blue sequinned leotard, from the wrists of an upturned acrobat as a dramatic opener to the show. Or the evening I had to perform a tap dance to 'We're in the Money' with Dame Edna Everage and a band of cheerleading dancers.

My worst night on the show – in fact probably my worst episode ever in television – was an outside broadcast in the Rhondda Valley in Wales when everything that could have gone wrong did. My earpiece was down, my autocue wasn't working and there was no monitor to show me what was happening. The moment came when

I had to announce the jackpot and I was the only person in the place who didn't know what it was. There was a full five-second falter before someone twisted a monitor round to show me the figures. I wanted to be transported to Planet Zog.

There were times off air, too, when I wished the ground would open up and swallow me, like the day I was walking in a London street when a taxi-driver who'd stopped at a red light recognised me. 'Hey, Anthea!' he yelled. Almost automatically, I turned to smile and wave. With the cheekiest of grins, the cabbie called out to me: 'Pull my balls out tonight, will you?' I could have died.

By the end of 1995, the *National Lottery Live* viewing figures had tailed off to about 15 million. The drop-off had always been expected – no one could keep pulling in 23 million viewers every week – and the audience was still high when you consider that nobody had to tune in to get the lottery numbers as soon as they were drawn: if people wanted to, they could just watch *Blind Date* on ITV and wait for them to pop up on the screen. Nonetheless the press was savage in its attacks.

With my exhaustion getting the better of me and my concerns about how little I was seeing of Pete increasing, I decided to give up my 'Saturday job' when my contract ran out in March 1996. I'd done the show for long enough, and I knew it was time to move on, especially since I had some exciting new job offers in the pipeline. I was still head of the domestic side of things at home. In between shows and early-morning starts, I had to fit in the weekly supermarket shop and the housework and try to see friends and family for lunch (never for dinner because that would go on way past my bedtime), as well as doing a workout in my gym every day. The crunch came one Sunday morning when I was putting out the rubbish and the bin-bag burst. It had been a long and frustrating week, I'd run myself into the ground and I hadn't seen Pete at all. The bin-bag was the final straw. Slumping into the scattered rubbish in the hall, I sobbed my heart out for what seemed like hours. I missed Pete, I wasn't eating or sleeping well, I hadn't worked out a proper system of coping with my hours and I knew that I had to turn my life round. I was painfully aware that television presenters have a limited shelf-life, which is why we're paid so much. The money has to last long after we've been forgotten. But working myself into an early grave just to keep 'running with the ball' couldn't be worth it. That just didn't make sense.

The headlines about my decision to leave the lottery programme were predictable. I knew that if ever there is a problem with a show, the presenters are usually blamed, and in my case there was always a risk of that from the outset. No one seems to take into consideration that television is a team game in which you can only be as good as your producers and the material they give you to work with. And with the best will in the world, it's difficult to make exciting television out of a programme whose highlight is the calling out of seven numbers. Alan Yentob, the BBC1 controller, admitted that *National Lottery Live* was having 'teething problems' and promised 'less banter and more excitement', but he defended my role and described the show's critics as snobs. I thought the media criticism unfair. By the time I did my last few programmes, it was a well-polished studio show produced by Richard Wolfe and directed by Stuart McDonald. And after I left, the viewing figures continued to drop.

What everyone failed to understand was that my decision to leave had very little to do with the flak the lottery programme was receiving and a great deal to do with what else was on offer – plus, of course, the hope that taking up a new deal might give me a little more free time to spend with my husband. We managed to get north that Christmas to see our families for a couple of days and have an ordinary celebration. It was just what we needed. It was the first time I'd seen Pete in nearly two weeks, and the photographs of us I have kept in my scrapbook reveal how tired and stressed we both were. Pete, particularly, looked pale and ill from overwork, and I had suitcases under my eyes.

That New Year's Eve, Pete and I flew to Scotland where I was presenting *National Lottery Live* from Edinburgh. Phillip Schofield was in town, playing Joseph, and my old friend John Leslie from *Blue Peter* was there too, playing Robin Hood in a panto, so we planned a big celebration after the show. We went for dinner at the Witchery, a fabulous restaurant in the lee of the castle, with Phil and Steph and ended up on the streets of Edinburgh at midnight, kissing people we'd never met before. 'Happy New Year, AT,' Pete told me, kissing me.

'Happy New Year, Pete,' I replied, hugging him tight.

The new year started with me opening the Forty-first International Boat Show at London's Earl's Court on 4 January. Once again it was time to wear the right clothes and to sparkle. I chose a navy blue Paul Smith suit, red coat and blue-and-white-striped top for a completely nautical look. The only consolation to that job was that Pete, boat-mad since he was a kid, came along to drool over all the speedboats.

In March we flew to Morocco for a week in an effort to escape from the madness, travelling to Casablanca and Marrakech. It was Pete's birthday and we had a lovely, relaxing time. 'Why can't we do this more often?' I complained as we lay by the pool. There was no answer. Pete was fast asleep.

A few weeks later, Littlewoods asked me to launch my own clothes collection for their catalogue. It was a terrific compliment: apparently I was following in the footsteps of Naomi Campbell, Linda Evangelista and Claudia Schiffer. Although when Littlewoods said they had chosen me precisely because my looks were the opposite of a supermodel's, I didn't know whether to be flattered or insulted. The job involved working closely with designers, showing them my wardrobe and what I liked, and helping them to come up with reasonably priced clothes that I'd be happy to wear myself. Then, when the collection was complete, I'd go on location with a photographer and crew and be photographed in each outfit for the catalogue. It was going to be great fun. But as usual, the press found a reason to snipe at me for this arrangement. Telephoning some disgruntled staff at Littlewoods, where there had recently been job cuts and lay-offs, they managed to get some of them to comment on how outraged they were that a lottery-show presenter had been chosen for the catalogue. 'If it wasn't for the lottery, some of our friends would still have jobs,' one said. 'I think it's disgusting.'

I carried on with my punishing *GMTV* schedule with hardly a break. I became an organisational monster: everything was filed neatly away into its place, from my underwear to my scrapbooks. Each time I was given a script for a new show or launch, I'd study it ten more times than anyone else, checking and rechecking names and spellings so that my dyslexia wouldn't trip me up. In the back of my mind I was still the thicko, waiting to be laughed at. I carried a personal organiser with me everywhere and was determined to keep on top of everything from my godchildren's birthdays to when my next hair appointment was. My friends used to laugh at me because I was the only person they knew who could tell them what I would be doing every minute of the day for weeks in advance. At night, tucked up in bed, I'd spend hours reading the newspapers and watching television and videos to prepare myself for whatever the next day was likely to throw at me. It was like endlessly revising for exams. I knew I had to improve my general knowledge and broaden my mind in order to silence those who still thought of me as a daffy blonde.

I appeared on the nation's television screens for ten hours and fifteen minutes a week, but those ten hours were often the product of up to ninety hours of preparation. People often think working at *GMTV* is a great job because it must all be over by 9am, but that was usually just the time when my day really started to get hectic. After a quick breakfast, I'd be involved in planning meetings for future shows. Then I'd devote at least an hour to answering viewers' letters and there'd always be a photo call or interview or film shoot to prepare for. Then there were the personal appearances, the charity gigs and letters; the fitness videos and my fashion work, not to mention phone calls, research and travelling. I ran myself like a business and even though I felt permanently jet-lagged, I had to keep bright and bubbly and looking like I'd never been happier.

That summer I returned to Spain with the team for another six weeks and my second 'Fun in the Sun' series. This time at least I knew what to expect. The crew celebrated my first anniversary at *GMTV* on air, giving me presents like a sombrero and a Spanish dress. Mote gave me an 'I've Been Motivated' T-shirt and the film crew sent me a lovely card wishing me well and congratulating me on a great year. That night we all went out for a meal at a beautiful restaurant on a hill overlooking the sea. It was a wonderful night and I only wished Pete could have been there to share it.

Somehow I managed to keep on top of my schedule, still succumbing to illness only on my days off. Something inside has always told me that if I go to bed I'm safe and no one can hurt me, so whenever I became too stressed out, I'd develop a headache or a backache or the sort of 'flu that would leave me horizontal for a week. 'It's nature's way of telling you to slow down,' Mum would scold. There were undoubtedly times when my work got in the way of my health and I allowed myself to lose more weight than I could afford. It was only to be expected, really. I'd rarely notice it myself – it always took someone else to point it out. I remember Mote taking me to one side early one morning at GMTV and saying: 'You're looking thin and pale, girl. What have you eaten in the last twenty-four hours?'

To my shame, I realised the answer was: not much. Coffee in copious quantities and the odd snack, but not a square meal. I'd been so busy I'd simply forgotten to eat again. The dietician to whom Mote sent me was equally horrified and told me that the combination of skipping meals and interfering with my body clock was a recipe for disaster. I'd dipped half a stone below my usual eight stone and I knew I couldn't afford to lose any more or I'd start to look lacklustre. With the dietician's help, I began to formulate a proper eating plan, making time for breakfast and snacking on seeds and bananas during the day to keep my energy levels up. I gave up coffee and developed a taste for herbal tea instead. Thank goodness for *Power Rangers*, the cartoon which gave us a break halfway through the show and me just enough time to eat some toast and honey.

I'd toyed with vegetarianism for some time, and for a while I embraced it wholeheartedly, following in the footsteps of my parents, who'd been vegetarians for twenty years, and my sister Wendy, who'd been a vegan for fifteen. I added vitamin and mineral supplements to my diet and enlisted for monthly acupuncture sessions to ease my stress levels. I gained weight and felt a lot healthier in a very short space of time. I might easily have been heading for some sort of physical collapse had I carried on the way I was going.

Emotional stresses and strains took their toll, too. It was all high-octane stuff and I loved the work I was doing – flying to France to interview Gary Barlow after Take That split up, for example – but it wasn't all glamour and glitz. Most days would see me hunched over my desk in the office going through my correspondence and researching for the next day. In among the piles of fan letters (from men and boys, mostly) I might find a really nasty one, a vicious poison-pen letter (almost always from a woman) telling me how much she hated me or my hair or my voice. 'Why don't you just get off our television screens for good?' it would scream. There'd be the usual quota of weirdos as well, the sickos who want to frighten you with their thin, spidery writing, but the bad letters were always very few and far between. Even so, as I always take the time to answer my mail personally, I'd read them and get quite upset by the vitriol that I sometimes seemed to inspire.

Whenever I had a really bad day I'd start spring-cleaning the minute I got home. Pete would walk in late at night and find me on my knees polishing like a woman possessed. He always knew when I was about to crack, because the place would be spotless. There would be mornings when the alarm would go off at 3.30am and I'd roll over with a groan and want nothing more than to go back to sleep. I was often so tired that I felt I could barely put one foot in front of the other. Pete was my mainstay, as ever, with his 'you can do it' routine. He was also the best in the world for making me a baked-bean butty, my favourite comfort food ever since the days at Minton's pottery.

Pete's management company was very much in the ascendant, and had become a name to be reckoned with in the industry. His latest clients included Toby Anstis and Emma Forbes. It was Russ who was Pete's rock, keeping it all together while trying to make time for Caron and their new baby and for a life beyond work. Somehow Russ succeeded in achieving this while Pete failed.

Pete and I were dubbed the hardest working couple in showbiz. By this stage we rarely sat down and ate a meal together or even saw each other. With Pete working equally long hours, often all weekend and sometimes through the night, when he did come home it would be way past my bedtime and he would be snoring when I left for work.

I'd taken to sleeping in the spare room to guarantee a good night's sleep, and gradually more and more of my clothes and toiletries and other bits and pieces moved in there with me, leaving his room full of his blokey stuff. We were effectively living apart.

For some reason which escapes me, during this, the busiest time of our lives, we decided to sell Pete's Chiswick house (to Darren Day), buy a plot of land in Twickenham and have a four-storey neo-Georgian mansion built for us, a place we were to call Ormonde House.

We'd been looking for a new home for a while, feeling that we'd both outgrown Pete's old house in Chiswick. We loved west London and wanted to stay there so I scoured the area for the right place. When a friend of ours told us about a building plot with planning permission in Twickenham, I knew it was just what we needed. 'We can't find what we want anywhere else, so let's build our own,' I told a sceptical Pete on one of our rare evenings together.

The land was in a conservation area. There was a lot of common ground around it, a view over the Thames and across into the deer park at Richmond. All that, and only twenty-seven minutes door-to-door from Harvey Nichols. Perfect. With the help of builders and the advice of my old friend Sue Van Der Ree, I knew we could build exactly what we wanted, stamping our own mark on to a home to be proud of, complete with gym, spa and sauna. Sue helped me organise everything from the curtains to the murals and furnishings, all to the highest standard. When Ormonde House was complete, we'd have six bedrooms, all with en-suite bathrooms, four reception rooms and a giant staircase descending through the heart of the house. Pete loved the idea of it, but left most of the planning of the interior to me and Sue.

For eight months we lived out of suitcases. It was a time in my life when all my possessions seemed to be scattered around the country – in Stoke, in store in Cambridge, at GMTV, at Pete's old garage in Ibis Lane and in the shell of Ormonde House. It was horrific. I actually had to go out and buy some new underwear one day because I couldn't find mine. We rented a house in Chiswick, but once again,

I moved into a separate bedroom because of my early starts. Everything was topsy-turvy for ages and, without a home base, I felt as if the ground was constantly shifting under my feet. Rising at 3.30 one morning in February and stumbling into the bathroom to splash my face with water, I turned on the light and was staggered to find the sink full of red roses. Pete had scrawled 'I Love You' on the mirror in one of my lipsticks. I hadn't even remembered it was Valentine's Day.

It wasn't that we didn't still love each other – that had never changed – but life always conspired to get in the way. If it wasn't work, it was the house and garden, which became all-consuming projects. We rarely argued and remained the best of friends whenever we were able to spend any time together. I can only remember ever having two arguments with Peter, both over trivial domestic matters.

Pete was still a great one for organising weekends away with friends and clients. He loved to be surrounded by people all the time. The further we drifted from each other, the more we became an archetypal case study on how young professional couples sacrifice on the altar of their careers and finances the one thing they need more than anything else: their passion. It was with a sad sense of irony that, in October 1995, I learned that I had been voted one of the world's sexiest women in a national poll, two slots down from Elle Macpherson and Sharon Stone, and just above Teri Hatcher, Pamela Anderson and Madonna. Pete and I hadn't made love in months.

The week of that poll, Pete was interviewed for a Midlands newspaper about being married to me and was quoted as saying: 'A manager is a father, a confidant, a strategist, an accountant and a lawyer all rolled into one.' Almost as an afterthought, he added, with a grin: 'Oh, and a husband.' That just about summed up our relationship.

My photograph was, by now, appearing in the newspapers almost daily in either fashion shoots or candid shots. In February 1996, I appeared on the cover of *Tatler* magazine, and topless inside (with my back to the camera, I hasten to add). The papers went wild. The *Sun* ran a whole page on the photographic spread under the headline 'Turning Hottery: Saucy Anthea Drops the Girly Look'.

Then I was voted Britain's Sexiest Voice in a national survey, in which one in four men questioned said they'd prefer to listen to me talking than a whole host of other famous people, including Ulrika Jonsson, Joanna Lumley and Princess Diana. A women's magazine poll that year which asked readers to nominate role models for women of the nineties placed Princess Diana first, Princess Anne second and me third. I won my place for being 'pretty, totally professional and scandal-free'. How boring.

I'd only just returned from Australia for a *GMTV* 'Down Under' series when I heard some news that really made my heart leap: I'd been voted BBC Personality of the Year by the television industry. It was a tremendous accolade and I felt so humbled. A month later I was awarded the prestigious Showbusiness Personality of the Year by the Variety Club of Great Britain at a glittering ceremony at the Hilton Hotel in Park Lane. Pete was there, beaming at me from ear to ear. I knew I'd made him proud of me. As I walked up to collect my prize, tears in my eyes, I only wished that I didn't feel quite so empty inside.

We moved into Ormonde House on Pete's birthday, 23 March 1996, having waited eighteen months for the builders to finish. We were moving from a modest three-bedroomed house in Chiswick with a small garden to 6,000 square feet and a huge garden. I loved it. The additional stress the project had put us under had been a high price to pay, but I felt terribly happy the day we moved in. 'We've both worked so hard for this, Pete,' I told him. 'Let's make this a new start.'

I don't know how we'd have managed the move if it hadn't been for my parents and Sue Van Der Ree. Pete and I had both been working flat out when the finishing touches were made and Mum and Dad came down from Stoke to supervise the moving in of most of our belongings. At the same time they were helping Wendy – who'd got a job on Live! TV – move into her own new flat in Docklands. Right up until the eleventh hour Dad was fitting cupboards and making shelves and Mum was sorting out my clothes. They should have been on the payroll. Of all the magazines which have featured me on their front covers – *Hello!*, *Tatler*, *You* – the one that really delights me came about because of Ormonde House. There I am, making toast, on the front cover of *Aga* magazine. Now that's what I call an accolade.

On 20 April, I presented my seventy-fifth and final *National Lottery Live* programme. On my departure Bob Monkhouse and Dale Winton were to take over on alternate weeks, and I was delighted to be handing it on to such a pair of professionals. Dale had already become a close friend and is a fantastic television host, while Bob Monkhouse is a national treasure. What a brain. People like him should be cherished. They might not be heavyweight presenters, but in the world of light entertainment they are kings.

The BBC were fantastic. For my last show they arranged for the opera-singer José Carreras to serenade me with a Spanish love song. The *Mirror* even presented me with a giant cake iced with the words 'Thanks a Lotto from the Mirror'. I was touched. It was a programme with which I'd been terribly proud to have been associated, and despite my desperate need to have my weekends back, I knew I'd miss it.

I'd loved nearly every minute of it. My biggest kicks, apart from working with Gordon, had come from meeting the ordinary winners: the mother of a baby with cerebral palsy who spent her £1,200 windfall on treatment which would enable him to see; the couple whose £1 million win meant they could give their twelve-year-old daughter, who was dyslexic and was being bullied at school, a new start (she was a little girl I especially took to my heart, for obvious reasons). I owed a great deal to those people, and to the forty-nine balls spinning in that lottery machine. I knew I might never shake them off – I'd probably always be the lottery girl – but I didn't care. That show, more than any other, made me famous. The name that had been borrowed from one of my Mum's former pupils became one of those, like 'Cilla' or 'Delia', that didn't need an identifying surname. Everyone knew who 'Anthea' was. The show had brought me fame and stardom beyond my wildest dreams.

In May Pete and I flew off for a two-week break in Montego Bay, Jamaica – our first proper holiday together since we'd married six

years earlier. The hotel was wonderful, the atmosphere perfect and I
spent a lot of time in my favourite pose: flat on my back on a sun-
lounger with a good book. Pete swam and slept and had massages in
between taking the usual round of phone calls and faxes. We took a
relaxing raft trip upriver, where we saw dozens of exotic wild birds
and heard animals chattering in the lush forests.

'Let's not go back,' I said to Pete one night over a candlelit dinner
on our private terrace. 'We could stay here for ever. Let's just set up
a beach bar and live here always, like this, like a normal husband and
wife.' It is the sort of pipe-dream everyone has when they fall in love
with a place on holiday. I know, but in my case it was more than that.
It was a cry from the heart. I never wanted to leave that magical
island where I could pretend that my marriage was as perfect as I'd
always wanted it to be. But even as Pete laughed affectionately at my
suggestion and tucked into dinner, I knew that responsibility was
beckoning.

Indeed, it wasn't long before we were jolted back to reality with a
vengeance. 'Mr Powell, there's a telephone call for you,' one of the
hotel staff told us at lunch the following day, bringing the telephone
to our table. 'A Mr Lindsay.' We knew Russ wouldn't have called
direct unless there was a problem.

'Russ?' Pete began. 'What's happened?' He sat opposite me, listening, nodding and not saying a word. Finally he said: 'OK, yes, I
understand. I'll tell her. 'Bye.'

Replacing the receiver, he lit a cigarette and inhaled deeply before
telling me anything. 'Russ says you're not to worry, it's not too
awful, but the *Sun* have printed a topless photo of you in this
morning's edition.'

'What?' I put down my fork and stared open-mouthed at him.

'There must have been a photographer out here somewhere who
caught you off guard. But he says it's quite tasteful and you're not to
get upset.'

'Not to get upset?' I cried, jumping to my feet and scanning the
bushes for any hidden lenses. For the benefit of any photographers
who might have been watching us, I yelled at the foliage: 'Leave us
alone. We're on bloody holiday, for God's sake!'

I was really shocked at the idea that I could be secretly photographed without my knowledge in such a tranquil place, and on a private beach at that. I hadn't even gone topless, so I knew the picture must have been captured in a second or two as I shifted position or rolled over, which meant that the lens must have been trained on me for hours on end. I was incensed. Sure enough, when I did eventually see the photograph, I realised exactly what had happened. Having been lying on my front to tan my back, in one misjudged moment I'd sat up. I'd quickly pulled my swimsuit up, but not before revealing my left boob for a split-second.

Stuart Higgins, the editor of the *Sun*, a man we knew quite well, sent us a letter which we found waiting for us on our return. He wrote: 'As you will be aware, we ran a sensational picture of Anthea topless which I bought from a freelance photographer. I sincerely hope the photograph did not offend either of you – it certainly was not designed to. As you are constantly aware, I am both personally and professionally supportive of you both. I firmly believe it was both tasteful and flattering – and fulfilled a personal fantasy. Hope to see you both soon, love Stuart.'

I had to laugh.

One of the first offers I took up after deciding to leave *National Lottery Live* was a show for Carlton, called *All You Need is Love*, a sort of *Jim'll Fix It* for lovers based on one of Europe's most successful television programmes which had originated in Holland. It was broadcast as a pilot at Easter. I was to play Cupid to singles hoping to get together or to couples wanting to add some spice to existing relationships by uniting them in the studio or on the 'Love Bus', which travelled the country collecting moving tales of passion and intrigue. The pilot pulled in an audience of 7.2 million, not bad for a one-off show. But it was a dangerous format, and people would either love it or hate it. The critics panned it as too syrupy and pronounced it a flop. DJ Chris Evans called it 'the biggest pile of defecation that's ever been on British television' and said he'd like to kick me in the mouth.

There was a new development in my life that helped to keep my spirits up, however. My sister Wendy, by now a television presenter herself, fronting *Absolutely Animals* on Channel 4 and *Video Box* and *Revelations* on Live! TV after establishing a successful career as a free-lance feature writer, had unexpectedly become my best friend. From our inauspicious start, when we were always at each other's throats and Ruth had to act as peacemaker between us, we'd learned to like each other enormously and spent a lot of our spare time together.

We'd become particularly close since her divorce, and now, at this difficult time in my life, having her around me helped me enor-mously. We weren't yet so intimate that I felt I could confide in her about my own marriage problems, and I think I was in any case scared to voice my fears. But we were drawn to each other in a way we hadn't been before. Because we were sisters, there was a bond between us that was quite different from that between close friends, and it made us both realise how different our lives would have been if Ruth had still been alive and we'd all been together as we had been as children. We even talked about Ruth's death for the first time.

'I never cried,' Wendy said guiltily. 'I couldn't.'

'Neither did I, not really,' I confided. 'It's only now that the thought of her can reduce me to tears.' Hugging each other, we wept together at last for the sister we'd lost.

Wendy and I are very close today. We don't ring each other every day, but we do whenever there is any kind of crisis, which is when sis-ters really come into their own. We even produced a children's book together, called *Underneath the Underground*, about a group of mice who live in the London tube system. We first got the idea after seeing mice scuttling around the rails while we were waiting for a train at Hammersmith. Watching people throwing bread to them, we won-dered what sort of life they led. As a result we came up with two resourceful families of mice, the Bells and the Knights. The newspa-per they read was called the *Daily Tail*. The redoubtable parents of one of the families were called Doris and Vincent, after our paternal grandparents. Another character, who lived at Baker Street, was called Charlotte Holmes, and then there was Martha, who made shirts out of discarded handkerchiefs. Another mouse built a Zimmer frame out of old matchsticks. I came up with most of the storylines, Wendy wrote it all and Mum checked our copy for spelling mistakes. Ever the teacher, she awarded us marks: happily, an A-plus. The book sold well and more were to follow. A donation from the sale of each copy was made to the Humane Research Trust, which raises money to develop alternative methods to the use of animals in medical research.

That summer, I went on another *GMTV* roadshow and ended up in Blackpool at the same time as Darren Day, who was about to open in the hit show *Summer Holiday*. It poured with rain and we were soaked to the skin, but loads of people turned up anyway and there was a great party atmosphere, with everyone singing their heads off to songs like 'Wannabe' from the hottest new band around, five lively young women who called themselves the Spice Girls.

Pete and Russ had organised a big launch party to celebrate Darren's new role, and invited nearly everyone they knew from London to see the show. There were lots of old friends there, people I hadn't caught up with in ages. Among them was Grant Bovey, Russ's mate, who'd come up from London specially. Pete and I were both pleased to see him; he had three small children by then and seemed happy to have 'had his pass signed', as he put it.

Pete was busy mingling, so Grant and I spent much of the evening laughing and joking together. When Pete returned to my side and told me that he wanted to introduce me to some people, I couldn't help but notice that Grant spent the rest of the night enjoying himself and flirting a little with another guest. I'd already decided in my mind that if anyone was likely to be unfaithful, it would be Grant Bovey – an absolute charmer.

As for me, my public persona continued to be that of a happy, bubbly young woman with a perfect marriage and a brilliant career. But deep inside, I knew there was something missing. I ached for love and the sensation of being cherished. I'd had such wild, romantic notions of what being married would be like – having a soulmate, sitting quietly by a fire together, reading companionably side by side, sharing a bottle of wine and feeling contented and adored all at once – but my marriage wasn't like that. It was all hastily scrawled notes, bolted meals, rushed conversations and loveless nights; it was all work, work, work, and no play. Pete still loved me – I never doubted that for a second – but the flame had all but gone out, leaving me feeling cold and bereft. The tabloids ran headlines like 'Anthea's Jackpot' and dubbed me 'Anthea Earner' – apparently I'd become the second-highest-paid woman in television after Cilla Black. I'd have given up every penny in an instant for a return to the way Pete and I had felt on honeymoon in Grenada.

Articles also began to appear about my supposed 'effect' on the nation's women. The *Daily Mail*, in an article headlined 'The Cloning of Anthea', claimed that everyone from Princess Diana to Julia Carling, Sophie Rhys-Jones, Helena Bonham-Carter and Emma Forbes had copied my hairstyle. What nonsense. And just in case I might be getting big-headed, my usual band of dissenters dusted off their poison pens and laid into me once again. I guess they thought I was getting too much of the cake. Lynda Lee-Porter wrote that my 'constant vivacity' was 'draining'; the reason I was popular, she added, was because I looked 'as unthreatening as a suburban hairdresser'. Allison Pearson observed of me on the *GMTV* settee: 'She has two expressions: her worried expression, when she suspects giggling may be out of the question (road crashes, cancer, ladders in Claudia Schiffer's tights) and the chipmunk grin she uses for everything else.' I was also held up as a prime example of the Great British Bimbo. Looking up the exact definition of 'bimbo' in the dictionary, I read: 'an attractive person, especially a woman, who is naïve or of limited intelligence'. So bimbo it is, then.

But the good press outweighed the insults, and the accolades I was beginning to accumulate seemed to coincide with a sea change in Eamonn Holmes attitude towards me at *GMTV*. I felt he'd long been prone to picking up on my every mistake, but what I saw as his on-air sniping now started to become a matter of general concern. It wasn't the first time there had been problems. When Eamonn had worked with Lorraine Kelly before I arrived on the scene it had hardly been a match made in heaven. Lorraine is a feisty Scot who held her own at *GMTV*. She is actually one of the nicest people in the business, a journalist who's been around a long time, and she wasn't going to take any nonsense. Because Lorraine had given Eamonn a run for his money, and had fought for every interview, I think he probably saw me as a walkover to start with, someone who would be happy to pick up his leftovers. Obviously I didn't have nearly as many miles on the clock as he did and was meekly going to say, 'Yes, Eamonn, no, Eamonn.' And indeed that was pretty much what I did to start with, not least because of my enormous respect for him.

But once I'd started to establish myself in my own right, gaining confidence and taking on some of the bigger interviews, he wasn't quite as nice. I thought he was quite snappy with me some mornings and I felt sure people would begin to notice. For example, if I was working with Ross Kelly or another presenter, we'd often work out what we were going to say beforehand. When I suggested to Eamonn that we did the same, he'd say: 'I'm not telling you what I'm going to say.' Then when the moment came, he'd throw me a line which would catch me off guard and make me look stupid. It seemed as if it was almost a sport with him.

One morning, while we were off air during a news break, I was reading through a piece I was due to announce about the stars of *The X Files*. I looked down at my sheet of paper and saw the name David Duchovny. I wasn't an *X Files* fan and didn't know the actor. I looked at the name again and my word blindness suddenly dazzled me. Squinting at the page, I struggled to sort the letters out in my mind. Turning to Eamonn, I asked: 'How *do* you pronounce that name?'

'Which name would that be?' he inquired. 'David Du-shove-knee?'

'Ah yes,' I said, repeating Eamonn's deliberate mistake, 'Du-shove-knee.' I didn't realise the pronunciation was wrong until someone behind the cameras started tittering. I'd never felt more ashamed of my dyslexia in my life.

Thereafter Eamonn seemed to enjoy the moments when I couldn't pronounce a tricky word or name. The more he teased me, in the give-and-take banter exchanged by all presenters, the more unnerved I'd become, and suddenly the entire page of my script or the words on the autocue would turn into complete gobbledegook.

It wasn't the easiest of relationships, but I would simply go on and do the best I could. By and large there were more good days than bad, chiefly because I was surrounded by some lovely people who had become firm allies and who helped me through. That was the irony of *GMTV*: nearly everyone was supportive and kind and delightful to work with. Some of my closest friends in the business are from those days – Ross, Lorraine, Sally Meen, and too many people to mention behind the scenes.

Fortunately, the rest of the industry seemed to like me. I had no shortage of job offers and I had already signed a contract for a new show called *Pet Power*, in which I'd interview pet-owners and recount stories of animals involved in unusual, humorous or dramatic incidents. I'd been asked to co-host with Falklands hero Simon Weston a Christmas Day special broadcast from HMS *Belfast*, *Christmas with the Royal Navy*, presenting a series of live link-ups with sailors and their families. I was embarking on the initial stages of a new series called *Turner Round the World*, in which I'd get to travel the globe at breakneck speed, and the holiday programme *Wish You Were Here* had invited me to do a celebrity spot from Brazil.

With so many demands on my time and so many other projects in the pipeline, I finally decided that enough was enough as far as *GMTV* was concerned. I'd been with the programme for two and a half years, and a contract for another two was on the table, but I opted not to renew it. Pete and I discussed the matter at length and he and Peter McHugh flew out to Majorca, where I was doing another 'Fun in the Sun' series, to sort out the terms of severance. Dear Peter McHugh was fantastic about it. 'I'm very sorry that you're leaving, Anthea,' he told me. 'But I wish you the best of luck and I want you to know that you'll always be welcome back at *GMTV*.'

The situation with Eamonn didn't improve once I announced I was leaving; in fact, if anything it got worse. He was full of Irish charm when he wanted to be, but the next moment he could be like a bear with a sore head. I never knew where I stood with him. In December 1996, four days before my last show, Peter McHugh and Michael Metcalf hosted a lavish dinner for me at the Belvedere hotel in Holland Park. They drew up a guest list of my friends at *GMTV*, not forgetting the cameramen and lighting staff, make-up artists and secretaries who worked so hard behind the scenes, so that I was surrounded by friends and 'family'. Not out of any malice, but because I thought he'd probably find the evening uncomfortable, I didn't myself specifically invite Eamonn, although I told my bosses that he'd be welcome if he wanted to come. 'It's your night,' they reminded me. 'You don't have to ask him if you don't want to.' In any event, he wasn't asked. So, in Eamonn's absence, and with Pete at my side, I was given the most marvellous send-off.

On Christmas Eve, my final day at *GMTV*, the team put together a fantastic farewell party for me in which Eamonn was asked to host a spoof *This is Your Life*-style presentation featuring highlights of my career. The whole thing was broadcast live that morning. It came complete with a video tribute from David Cassidy, who said, 'I wish I could be there to celebrate with you,' which really made my day. There was a surprise visit from Brian the Bear (wearing my *Blue Peter* badge), and Bonnie the *Blue Peter* dog, who leaped up on to the settee next to me and licked my face.

'You knew this would make me cry,' I said to Eamonn, wiping my eyes, 'and, once I start, that's it, I can't stop.' But there was more.

I was forced to relive some of my worst moments on *Blue Peter* with Tim Vincent (with whom I had to make a scale model of the *GMTV* set out of cardboard and glue), and given an astral reading from Mystic Meg, who predicted a bright future. The poor viewers even had to endure my *GMTV* debut tape, in which I could be seen complaining about how uncomfortable the settee was, fidgeting, fluffing my lines and generally looking terrified. 'I can't tell you how nervous I was that day. I was shaking,' I told Eamonn. 'It was only you who got me through that.'

Just as I had done at *Blue Peter* and Signal Radio, I wept openly at the kindness of my colleagues and drank the champagne they poured for me. Lorraine and Penny Smith were there to drink a toast, the *Sun* presented me with a bouquet from their readers and *GMTV* had a cake made with little icing figures of me and Eamonn on the settee and a plaque reading: 'She came, she spoke, she conquered.'

But, once the show was over and the credits were rolling,

Eamonn – who'd done a sterling job hosting the show and who had privately presented me with a tiny little alarm clock – was accidentally filmed leaving the set, apparently without so much as a backwards glance. We didn't know it then, but one eagle-eyed newsdesk had spotted his hasty exit and sent a reporter after him to catch him off guard at home in Ireland.

Pete and I had already been north to see our families and catch up with all the news. We'd had a quiet time with our respective relatives, sitting on the floor opening our presents and pretending it was Christmas Day. We played our usual game, How to Host a Murder, a whodunit that had become something of a tradition in the Turner household. Wendy – fresh from playing Goldilocks in pantomime in Reading – was on particularly good form that year in the role of wanton woman.

Pete and I arrived home at 11.30pm on the night of Saturday 28 December. It was our first Christmas in the new house, and I'd gone to a great deal of trouble to make it look festive, even if we weren't going to be there much to enjoy it. I'd set aside time in my diary weeks beforehand, invited my mum down to help me, bought two Christmas trees – one for the hall and one for the lounge – and adorned the stairs and windowsills with holly and ivy and branches of pine. There were bowls of apples, oranges, nuts and satsumas; candles, poinsettias and chocolates for any visiting children. The remaining presents were all wrapped up and ready under the tree. The whole house looked like some sort of film set when we walked in.

The telephone rang just as I walked into my bedroom with my suitcase. It was Sue Carroll, a journalist from the *Sun*.

'Hello, Anthea. I wondered if you had any comment on the article in tomorrow's *Sunday Mirror*?'

'What article?' I put my handbag down and sat down on the bed to slip off my shoes.

There was a pause. 'Hasn't anyone spoken to you yet?'

'No,' I replied. There was something about her tone that bothered me.

'Oh . . . ah . . .' She was clearly embarrassed now. 'I'm afraid you're not going to like it. Eamonn's done a real number on you.'

'Eamonn?' For a moment I couldn't think who she meant. Then I twigged. 'Eamonn Holmes? Are you sure?'

Sue was in no doubt whatsoever. 'Certain,' she said, adding: 'and it's really awful. The headline reads: "Why I Hate 'Princess' Anthea" – and that's just for starters.'

Having listened to all that she had to say in stunned silence, I cut the conversation off as quickly as I could without being rude. Pete had come into the room by now, and he could tell from my face that something was wrong. When I told him what it was, he slumped down on the bed next to me.

I didn't know what to do. Pete, however, jumped in the car and drove to Charing Cross Station to buy an early copy of the paper so that we could see what the piece said. Before he left he kept telling me that it might not be as bad as all that, but when he got back and we both sat down at the kitchen table and read every word, we were aghast.

Eamonn, the experienced colleague for whom I'd always had so much respect, had completely annihilated me. He said he loathed me; he called me 'horrid' and said that working with me had been 'unbearable'. He dubbed me 'Princess Tippy Toes' and 'Tiny Tears' and said I was a pain in the arse from start to finish. I was, apparently, a prima donna, obsessed with my looks and devoid of a sense of humour. He claimed that working with me was like partnering a twelve-year-old. I was a 'nightmare' about lighting, and terribly precious about how I looked on television. Finally, he claimed that the show's bosses had got rid of me by bowing to his ultimatum to choose between us. 'I was the only one with any power or clout to voice the concerns,' he said. 'I was a bit of a hero.'

There was, as there usually is, some small element of truth to what he said, but the rest was pure fiction. Yes, I did ask for the lighting to be improved, but that was for everyone, not just for me. The lighting director and I used to laugh and joke about it; all television presenters have to get on well with their lighting directors or they can be finished. But I'd never insisted on anything, I had merely asked firmly, but in the nicest possible way.

It was well known that Eamonn and I were never each other's number one fans, and as I have recounted, towards the end of my time at *GMTV* I felt he looked on me with contempt and thought I wasn't good enough for the job. But whatever I might or might not have been, when I left *GMTV*, the viewing figures were the highest they'd ever been. Maybe it was because people liked to watch the spark between the two of us, I don't know, but there was clearly something that worked.

There was never any question that Eamonn was the professional journalist and excellent at dealing with the heavyweights. I still think that he is one of the best live presenters on British television. But this wasn't a quantum physics programme and that's where I came in. I am strictly middle-of-the-road, light-entertainment, family viewing. That's me. People can sneer, but that is the sphere in which I feel most comfortable. And the vast majority of people who watch *GMTV* simply want to have a general idea of what's going on, to know what the weather's going to be like and to have a smile brought to their faces as they start their day.

I never fought Eamonn for an interview with a senior politician. From that point of view he had someone at his side who was a complete pushover. I was more than happy to do the jobs he didn't want. If he felt I wasn't up to scratch because I wasn't a proper journalist, then I don't think he really understood the programme or its target audience.

Whatever he thought, I now felt sick to the stomach. I was worried that anyone who read the article would assume there was no smoke without fire. Up until then I'd enjoyed a pretty good track record within the industry and people had seemed to like working with me. The only other person who had ever done anything like this to me before was Bruno Brookes. It was the ultimate betrayal.

Pete was furious. I think he was ready to consider murder. He knew that Eamonn's diatribe would damage me because invariably it is the bad articles people remember, not the countless good ones. The public want juicy stories; they would want to believe that this was what I was really like, the kind of person who threw tantrums behind the scenes.

The phone didn't stop ringing for days. Everyone wanted me to give my reply. The temptation was enormous but in the end I decided to keep silent, and, as it had with Bruno, the tactic worked. Columnist after columnist laid into Eamonn for his indiscretion. Philip Hodson wrote an open letter to Eamonn in *OK!* magazine in which he said he had 'a yo-yo waistline, a broken marriage, an increased risk of having a heart attack and a series of jealous squabbles with a woman you consider beneath your contempt. You're on the attack because you crave recognition, like some desperate and ambitious beginner.' Even Lynda Lee-Potter, who admitted to her 'endless criticism' of me, called him a 'venomous Irishman' with a 'gigantic and fragile ego'. She said I won the battle between us 'hands down' because of my hard work and common sense. The *Sun* ran an entire page on the story, headlined 'You Rat, Eamonn'. They interviewed people I had worked with at *GMTV* and declared that I was 'loved by everyone', from the girl who opened my mail to the managing director. Peter McHugh went on record as describing me as 'one of the most genuine people in the business'. Report after report claimed that Eamonn had been carpeted by *GMTV* for his comments, and within a few days he was forced to issue a retraction, maintaining that his relationship with me was 'cordial'. That interview became an albatross around his neck.

In the new year Eamonn and I were scheduled to work together hosting a big television charity snooker event in Birmingham which had been organised months before. There was no getting out of it, and I don't suppose Eamonn was looking forward to it any more than I was. Fortunately, the powers-that-be were aware of the delicacy of the situation and kept us apart for much of the recording, allowing us to do our respective pieces to camera separately, even though we had to speak to each other over a microphone link during the televised event.

'Over to you, Eamonn,' I said, as cheerily as I could.

'Back to you, Anthea,' he replied, just as breezily, when his piece was over. It was all highly professional.

In the long term I have forgiven him. I cannot find it within myself to hate him. We've seen each other professionally three times since and he has never made any attempt to apologise to me. I have always been cordial towards him. I should think he is probably totally embarrassed and fed up with people mentioning the article as if it were the only thing he has ever done in his life.

There was an epilogue, of sorts, however. Some time later, Eamonn was kind enough to refuse to talk about me in a live Channel 4 television interview with Chris Evans, who was trying to prise some information out of him. 'I think Anthea's going through quite enough right now,' he told Chris firmly. I was eternally grateful for his discretion. One day, we might even sit down and get everything off our chests and learn how to be friends. I do hope so. After all, thanks to him, I've been able to sign off most of my letters with my new pet name: Princess Tippy Toes.

7

The Danger Zone

The first thing I did when I left *GMTV* was to take a couple of weeks off. I felt I'd earned it. It was wonderful doing exactly what I wanted to do without the dreadful tyranny of those early-morning alarm calls. I spent much of my time planning a garden with my friend and designer Sue, trying to create the 'Secret Garden' of my favourite book. A seed company had very kindly named a beautiful pink-and-white sweet pea after me, so my mum was busy propagating seedlings to fill our garden with heavily scented 'Anthea Turners'. What a thought.

When I wasn't out digging in the flowerbeds in my wellies, I'd be lolling around inside the house in my pyjamas, eating biscuits and indulging myself. Switching on the television, I'd watch Eamonn and my replacement Fiona Phillips, feeling very strange to be on the other side of the screen. Turning off the TV one morning, I went up to my dressing room and rummaged through all my clothes. Laying them out in two huge piles, one for the charity shop and one from which Wendy and my girlfriends might like to help themselves, I cleared out all my *GMTV* outfits, the uniforms of a breakfast-television presenter. I was on a mission, clearing out the rubbish of the previous year. It felt very therapeutic, like a sort of cleansing. I knew I'd never go back. It was as if something in my mind said, 'That's it, *GMTV* is finished. Now it's time to tidy up my life.'

I only wished things could have been that simple with my marriage. I had the increasingly worrying feeling that Pete and I were letting something very special slip through our fingers. In the words of the Whitney Houston song, I would always love Pete, but it was no longer enough.

That New Year's Eve, we threw a huge party at Ormonde House. I did all the catering and the champagne flowed freely. All the usual suspects were there, and among our friends and Pete's clients were several people from *GMTV*, including Peter McHugh, Michael Metcalf, Liam Hamilton, Ross Kelly and Helen McMurray. Still in the throes of the fall-out from Eamonn Holmes' *Sunday Mirror* article, I was grateful for such open support. We had a big clock reflected in the grounds to enable us to watch the seconds ticking by towards midnight. It was a lovely, magical night, the last we were ever to have in that house. The place looked perfect, I was free of *GMTV* and the new year held some inviting prospects work-wise.

'Happy New Year, AT,' Pete said, kissing my cheek as the clock struck midnight. 'Let's hope it's as good as the last.'

Squeezing his hand, I kissed him back. 'No, Pete,' I said, smiling sadly. 'Let's hope it's even better.'

My new year-long contract with Carlton would see me presenting a series of shows, including *Pet Power* and *Turner Round the World*. I knew it would be sink or swim now that I'd gone solo. No longer would I have the banner of *GMTV* or *Blue Peter* to hide behind. The critics would be waiting in the wings, daggers drawn. As far as my career was concerned, 1997 was going to be the pivotal year of my life. It could also, I knew, prove to be pivotal personally.

I was thirty-six years old and if Pete and I were going to decide to have a family, then I knew I had to start thinking seriously about making the leap. Reporters had been asking me the question and speculating on our behalf for years. 'I'd like to think that one day it will happen,' was my stock answer, when all I really wanted to say was: 'It's none of your bloody business.' The problems that parenthood presented were manifold. The way things had been between Pete and me over the previous few years, with our separate bedrooms and crazy schedules, it would have taken divine intervention to have

made me pregnant. But, aside from that rather fundamental logistical problem, I had also been diagnosed as suffering from
endometriosis, chronic inflammation of the pelvis, which often
causes infertility.

I'd had it now for nearly ten years, suffering monthly bouts of
severe pain and discomfort, which nothing I tried did much to help.
I'd lost count of the times I'd had to rely on a handful of painkillers
just to get me through a show. If my biological clock was going to
start pushing me towards motherhood and my plumbing wasn't up
to it, then Pete and I might have to consider IVF, which was a path
I wasn't sure I wanted to go down. All that I'd read about it – the hor-
mones I'd have to take and their side-effects, the collection of the
eggs, the clinical bonding of the sperm and egg, and the fact that
there were no guarantees at the end of it – made me feel it wasn't for
me. Pete was very noncommittal. 'It's up to you, AT,' he'd say. 'You're
the one who'll have to go through it all.'

As always, my parents were hugely supportive. 'If it's meant to be,
it's meant to be,' my mum said when she next came down to stay.
'Whatever you decide, you know Daddy and I will be here for you.'
I've never stopped marvelling at their seemingly limitless capacity to
see the bright side of everything and to accept fate unquestioningly.
They had been a rock to me throughout my entire life, and here they
were, grey-haired and pushing past middle age, still the most decent,
sensible people I knew and never once complaining about not having
any grandchildren. I threw my arms around my mum's neck and
hugged her until it hurt.

As it turned out, my new baby was not what most people
expected. It was the MG sports car I'd always wanted, a lovely British
racing green MGF 1.8i VVC, which I christened Pumpkin II. It was
just like the car my parents had first had when I was a tot. Dad loved
that car, a 1938 MGB TB, and I vowed that one day I'd find it and
buy it back so that I could rekindle some of my happiest memories,
sitting in the same seat my dad sat in when he drove us to Tenby or
around the Potteries.

Just because I was away from the daily grind of *GMTV*, it didn't
mean that the press left me alone. Analysing the reasons why I'd left,

they began, rather alarmingly, to speculate on the state of my marriage to Pete. Rumours were going around the industry that our relationship was a sham; that it was merely an arrangement of convenience between a television wannabe and a would-be Svengali. People were saying they couldn't believe we'd lasted so long under such extreme working conditions. I heard some horrific tittle-tattle and each word cut me to the core. It was as if people were willing my marriage to fail and urging me to fall flat on my face.

It wasn't the first time that the intense media scrutiny to which I had long been subjected had switched to my personal life. There had been that report on my wedding day about Ruth being buried in the same churchyard, and of course Bruno's cruel article. But this latest focus seemed to me to have a new malevolence about it. It was as if the reporters writing the articles somehow knew how unhappy I was. For the first time in my life, I began to become a little paranoid about who I spoke to and where. I knew of those in the business who trusted no one, not even their closest friends, let alone their cleaning ladies, nannies or gardeners. I never wanted to become that suspicious of people around me, yet I found myself being guarded on the telephone and trying never to say anything which might be misconstrued.

Happily, on the work front, things were on an even keel. *Pet Power*, which was first broadcast on 14 January, received good reviews and had viewers weeping into their mugs of tea with its heartwarming tales, even if one wag suggested in a newspaper that I had only taken it on because I thought, with my dyslexia, that the name of the show was *Pete Powell*. It was a great format, a good medium for me and made for great viewing. Mind you, they say never work with children and animals, yet for most of my career I'd worked with nothing else. I've lost count of the times I've been dragged across the studio floor by an overexuberant hound, or nearly slipped in something that would most definitely have ruined my best pair of Manolo Blahnik shoes.

One of the most important lessons I learned on *Pet Power* was that whenever a bird-owner tells you that their bird will not fly away when you open the cage door, do not believe them. That budgie or parrot will take one look at all the lights and gantries in the gods of the studio and that's it, it'll be off. We had macaws stuck up on the rigging for hours, pooping on the people below and picking at the electrical wires. Then there are the dogs which suddenly decide to try to make love to your leg, the puppies that wee everywhere, the rodents that bite and the cats that scratch. Maybe because of the participants' unpredictable behaviour, the ratings were good and held up against some pretty stiff competition from the BBC, or so I'm told. The only reason that *Pet Power* was eventually dropped was because there was a change of personnel at the network centre and the new broom wanted to make his own mark on the programming.

To celebrate the success of the show and our seventh wedding anniversary, Pete and I flew to the Maldives for a fortnight, and had a lovely, relaxing time. Poor Pete was at the furthest end of the exhaustion scale and really needed the break. The time away from work gave us both a chance to unwind and enjoy each other's company again, something we hadn't done for almost a year. It was like Montego Bay and our honeymoon in Grenada all over again. I'd forgotten how good we were together and so, I think, had Pete.

Yet in many ways, that pleasure served only to sadden me because I knew that it would not last. Unless we radically changed the way we lived and managed our careers, the minute the holiday was over, we'd revert straight back to the bad old days of never having enough time for each other. The awareness that the idyll of the Maldives and Montego Bay could only ever be a temporary state of affairs during a rare respite from work was even harder to cope with now that I had such serious concerns about our future.

Pete sensed the tragi-comedy of our situation as well. He gave me an anniversary card which read: 'Seventh heaven. Let nothing come between us. We've got more than anyone – trust, love, support and each other. All my love on our Paradise Island. 31.1.97'

Turner Round the World was my next broadcast, and it didn't go too badly at all. It was essentially a travel game show in which contestants had to guess where in the world I or one of my celebrity guests was from various clues, avoiding red herrings. The prize was a pair of round-the-world air tickets. The show meant a punishing new schedule for me. I travelled from Amsterdam to Singapore and Australia to Ireland in a matter of days. It was a real case of 'if it's Tuesday, it must be New York'. The programme drew an average 6.1 million viewers, which was not to be sneezed at, but sadly not enough to warrant a second series.

Halfway through the first series, in March 1997, Pete and I, plus twelve friends, went on a week-long skiing trip to Le Clusaz in the French Alps. We were having a great time, enjoying the warm sunshine and the excellent snow, when, as I hurtled down a red run some 2,000 feet up, my skis slipped on some pack ice and I fell, badly hurting my knee. I heard and felt something twang inside my leg before waves of excruciating pain overcame me. Pete, who was skiing in front of me, heard me cry out and came hurrying back to help, but it soon became obvious that I would need to be stretchered down the mountainside. Easing me on to a ski-carrier, the ski-instructors and paramedics shepherded me gently down the slope and put me into an ambulance. I thought I'd broken my leg, but in many ways, it was worse. I'd done a Gazza: torn a cruciate ligament in the middle of my left knee and ruptured two on either side of it. That taught me to try to keep up with the boys.

I had some initial treatment at a French cottage hospital, but then Pete and I had to fly home early so that I could have surgery and begin the six months of physiotherapy I'd need. I was determined that the injury wouldn't affect my work, and it didn't. I went into the Wellington Hospital for surgery, taking Brian the Bear with me, and stayed there for four days. After a week's convalescence at home (during which my leg turned every shade of purple and yellow in the spectrum), I was soon back on the road, filming in Ireland for *Turner Round the World*. We were just outside Waterford, doing a 'Guess Where This Is?' film incorporating all the usual confusing clues to throw the contestants off the scent. I was at a polo match, speaking to the Spanish wife of the owner of a polo stud in the hope that viewers would think we were in South America. 'Fancy a match?' the colonel running the tournament asked me on camera. How could I refuse? But with a polo stick in one hand and my mind on where the camera was and how I could say my piece without riding out of view, I wasn't concentrating properly. When the whistle blew, the ponies raced off like Ferraris. I was frightened to death.

Chasing the ball across the field, I turned the horse towards the camera, as I'd agreed, so that I could be filmed but it took one look at the film crew, with their reflector, microphone and shiny equipment, and panicked. Rearing, it started trying to buck me off.

'Hold on!' the colonel shouted, galloping across to my rescue. But it was too late. I had no control. Falling awkwardly to the ground, trying to save my knee and still clutching on to my stick, I landed on my hand, which twisted round the stick. I felt my little finger snap like a twig.

At Waterford Hospital the doctors gave me two choices: 'You can have a general anaesthetic and have your finger reset properly, or you can have a local and we'll do it for you now.' Knowing that I had to catch a plane that night to my next destination, I opted for the second. The local anaesthetic barely touched the pain. I was in agony. With my hand bandaged up and the swelling travelling all the way up my arm, I looked like the walking wounded. Three days later, when filming ended, feeling awful, I went into Queen Charlotte's Hospital for a long-arranged laparoscopy, a procedure designed to investigate and to try to ease endometriosis. The doctors must have thought I'd walked in straight off the set of *Casualty*. It clearly wasn't going to be my year. I barely had time to recover from all that before I was out filming again. This time, there were very few shots of me moving much at all and my right hand was always firmly stuffed in my pocket.

At the same time, I was working for Carlton on the pilot of a new programme called *Change Your Life Forever*, of which I was to be the presenter. The concept was daring and brave, but so phenomenally complicated that it would never have made it to a series. The idea was that contestants could, if selected, swap their lives for a dream lifestyle in another part of the world for a year. More than 3,500 people applied to take part in the show, although not all of their wish-lists were realistic. One woman wanted to become a princess and live in a bubble for the rest of her life, and another wanted to have every conceivable part of her body pierced.

In the end the applicants were whittled down to six finalists, among them a sheet-metal worker who wanted to run a tea shop on a Greek island, a keen fisherman who dreamed of catching a blue marlin in Bermuda, a chap who longed to become Red Adair and put out oil-rig fires, a seaman who wanted to travel the world coaching kids at football and a woman whose ambition was to become a wine expert. The contestants were interviewed by a celebrity panel. The winner was a window-cleaner from Ayrshire called Nicky Mastrangioli whose heart's desire was to be a gamekeeper in an African national park.

In April, I travelled to Brazil for *Wish You Were Here*. The crew were fantastic and we had a brilliant time touring that extraordinary country. The *News of the World* sent a photographer, Dave Hogan, to snap the key moments. He filmed me meeting the great train robber Ronnie Biggs in Rio de Janeiro, whitewater rafting at the stunning Iguassa Falls, fishing for piranha, trekking through a jungle full of tarantulas, baiting an alligator and keeping my cool when a screeching toucan defecated down the front of my top. I managed to carry on speaking to camera despite the disgusting goo dripping down my cleavage. The lads all applauded when I'd finished.

All this and I was getting paid for it, too. Better off financially than I'd ever been in my life, I was able to spend some money on the people I cared about. Mum, Wendy and I had finally persuaded Dad to give up his ten-year battle to keep Turner & Sons going. He was nearing retirement age anyway, and he had ended up with high blood pressure from the stress of it all. My mother was incredibly worried about him. They had had so much anxiety in their lives, what with Ruth and everything else, that I would have done anything I could to cushion it. They'd ploughed their own money into the company to keep it going, and there had been at one time a possibility that they might have to sell their home, so I bought it for them. With a little help from me, the company was closed down with every member of staff paid off and not a single debt left behind. It was just another sad statistic in the catalogue of small businesses that have gone to the wall in the face of insurmountable competition from the out-of-town giants – a tragic end to the family firm, but at least Dad was able to do the honourable thing in the end. So many companies nowadays are impersonal and have no heart in them. That was never the case with Turner & Sons.

My parents had reached a point in their lives when they should have been slowing down. I was able to buy them that time and take away their financial worries. Dad was a man who'd worked hard all his life, brought up his family well, dealt with everything and then, through no fault of his own, teetered on the verge of losing everything. It is heartbreaking for people like him, and he felt very bad about it all. 'I'm only paying you back for all the money and time and love you've invested in me over the years,' I'd tell him.

A patron of nearly sixty charities, I also took great delight in continuing to give my time to those less fortunate than me, widening my portfolio to include several more children's and animal charities. I wanted to share my good fortune wherever possible, still not quite believing that it was mine for keeps.

But I had no need to worry about where the next cheque was coming from because, within a few months, I was approached by Marcus Plantain, the controller of the ITV network centre, to take over from the retiring Judith Chalmers as the chief presenter of *Wish You Were Here*, television's leading travel programme. I thought back to when I'd first met Judith at her sister's leaving party in the days of BBC Radio Stoke, and how wonderful and glamorous I'd imagined her life to be. I remember looking up to her and thinking, 'Here she is, a celebrity, and I'm just struggling along.' Now here I was stepping into her shoes.

'We loved the Brazilian film you did for us,' Paul Corley, the head of factual programming, told me at a meeting Pete and I had with him at his office in Gray's Inn Road. 'It was looking at that which made us realise you're a natural to take over from Judith.'

Kim Robson and Doug Hammond, both senior producers at *Wish You Were Here*, were also there and talked me through what doing the programme would mean. My biggest concern was how much time I'd be spending away from home and from Pete. 'It's a lot of travelling and a lot of hard work,' Kim warned me with a smile. 'Don't be fooled by what you see on the television. One idyllic beach looks much the same as the next after a while.' I could tell she was talking from experience.

Filming was to start in August 1997, for twenty-one separate programmes in each year-long series. I was offered a two-year contract. 'It's a dream job, AT,' Pete promised me. 'It's the flagship of ITV. It'll be a fantastic showcase for you and an incredible opportunity to see the world.' He knew I wasn't a great fan of travelling for long periods of time, having been terribly homesick in Argentina and elsewhere, but he assured me that this time the trips would be much shorter. Most of all, the job seemed safe and high-profile. Taking Pete's advice, as always, I signed on the dotted line.

The prospect of spending up to six months a year away from him did nothing to soothe my growing anxieties about my marriage, however, especially as Pete seemed emotionally more distant than ever. His company was doing so well that it had become the target of a hostile takeover bid and he and Russ might as well have set up their beds at the office for all the time they spent at home. Pete was troubled by a lot of things in his life: by his business, by his loyalty to friends and family and by how much pressure we continued to pile on to ourselves and on to each other. He didn't know how to get me off the treadmill, or even if that was what I really wanted. The prospect of me without a career bothered him even more than the stresses of me with one, because he knew that if I left television I'd crash. He would also have felt he had let me down. Either way, he was deeply compromised.

Meanwhile we'd become more like brother and sister than husband and wife. Even when my gruelling hours at *GMTV* came to an end, I rarely returned to the marital bedroom. We were both exhausted by our self-inflicted work regimes and too busy to find the time to try to save our marriage. Any thoughts either of us might have had about starting a family were scuppered not only by our situation but by my new job. *Wish You Were Here* laid that idea permanently to rest.

I was thirty-seven years old, ostensibly one of the most successful women in British television, but secretly desperately lonely and deeply unhappy. I blamed myself entirely and assumed that our lack of a sex life was all my fault. I thought I must have been unattractive to him. I'm a very old-fashioned girl and all I wanted was passion and a little bit of romance. I began to think, 'Maybe this is it. Maybe this is what married couples become after a few years.'

But I'd see other couples touching and kissing and I really envied them. Pete and I weren't like that at all. We were just good friends. Increasingly, this wasn't enough. I remember looking at the photographs in my wedding album and trying to rekindle the feelings I'd had on that fabulous day in Longsdon seven years earlier. I still loved him and wanted our marriage to work, but I didn't know how to fix it.

Pete had also never truly settled into Ormonde House. He missed his old home in Ibis Lane, which had been his anchor for many years before I came into his life. I worried that he sometimes felt he was a guest in my house, rather than a partner in ours. And as I had become more and more of a household name the limelight he'd always hated intensified. He resisted having to go to all the showbiz events to which we were invited and yet he now had a wife who was expected to attend with her husband.

He was terribly tired all the time, we both were; permanently knackered, which inhibited us both physically. We thought we were superhuman and could handle everything and it would all be OK, but it wasn't. While I was looking for passion and intimacy, he was struggling with the business and feeling like he needed space. I sometimes think he secretly enjoyed his independence and the freedom he had within our relationship. Either way, we were out of control and on a collision course.

Nor did we seem able to talk about it. When Pete was under pressure, it was far easier for him to put on his manager's hat and dish out sound, unemotional advice, forcing us both to remain professional, than it was for him to put his arms round me and give me a hug. After a while, it got to the point that he didn't know how to do it any more, and I no longer asked. We both freely admit that we had blood on our hands. We wrongly assumed that the strong bond of friendship between us could sustain our marriage. But there is much more to a relationship than just friendship. We were both guilty of

Peter Powell and David Cassidy during Pete's days at Radio Luxembourg.

Peter Powell, Phillip Schofield, Russ Lindsay and Paul Worsley at Phillip's wedding to Stephanie.

Kissing goodbye to *Wish You Were Here* during my last assignment on a cowboy ranch. SCOPE FEATURES

Eamonn Holmes presenting my *This Is Your Life*-style farewell from *GMTV*.

Larking about on a *Daily Mail* fashion shoot at Epsom Racecourse.

Wendy and I return to Tenby for ice creams, Caldey cake and a trip down memory lane.

Being stretchered to hospital after my skiing accident, my black run days over.

The controversial picture of me posing with just Ben the python for
Tatler magazine. ANTOINE VERGLAS INC.

Sweet revenge: dressed as Shane MacGowan for a *Hale and Pace* spoof of *Stars in Their Eyes*. PRESS ASSOCIATION

Meeting my heart-throb at last. David Cassidy and me on the settee on *GMTV*. GMTV

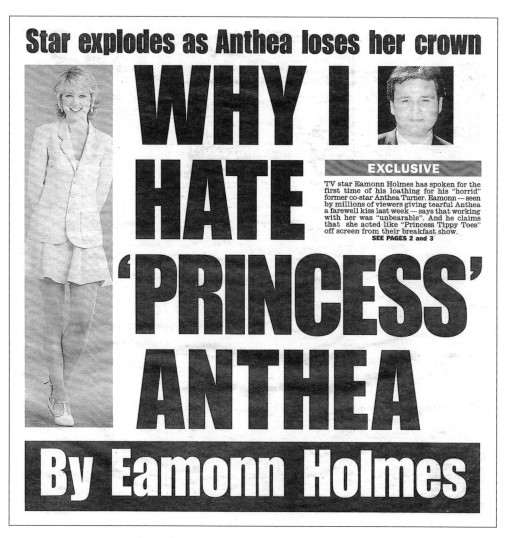

Eamonn's attack on me in the *Sunday Mirror*, December 1996.

ANTHINNER TURNER

Star's shock weight loss

LOTTERY golden girl Anthea Turner shocked passers-by when she stepped out yesterday — because there is a Lott LESS of her to see.

Anthea, 37, has shed nearly a stone since leaving her husband at New Year — and pals blame "emotional turmoil."

Bubbly blonde Anthea wore a stylish, loose-fitting suit as she launched BBC1's new National Lottery Big Ticket Show yesterday.

Stunning

But she could not hide the fact that she looks worryingly frail.

Just two months ago Anthea was pictured looking stunning on a Caribbean beach while filming for TV's Wish You Were Here?

And friends say she will not be happy at losing so much weight.

One said: "Anthea has never been one of those anorexic types who wants to look stick-thin. She

By **SAM CARLISLE**, Woman's Editor
and **SIR LENNY LOTTERY**

prides herself on eating healthily. The reason she has lost weight is because of the emotional turmoil she's going through."

Anthea left hubby and manager Peter Powell for dad-of-three Grant Bovey, 34. She has stayed friends with Peter, 46, but admits she feels tormented at hurting him.

Her friend added: "Things are very hard for her but she is determined to get through this."

Yesterday Anthea blushed as Big Ticket co-host Patrick Kielty confessed he has a crush on her.

Patrick, 26, said: "I used to watch her on Top of the Pops and really fancied her. I still do."

The BBC hopes its new 50-minute show will boost plunging ratings when it replaces National Lottery Live from Saturday.

A studio guest gets the chance to win £100,000 and a separate draw offers up to £50,000. The show ends with the main Lottery draw.

10 WEEKS AGO
Stunning . . . Anthea in Caribbean

Worry . . Anthea reveals thin frame at launch with Patrick Kielty yesterday   Pictures: **JAYNE RUSSELL**

One of the many
articles to appear
about my weight.

One of the many publicity shots taken of me when I was nominated to
present the *National Lottery Live* programme in in November 1995.
REX FEATURES

Della Bovey with Kerry Ross at the Michael Flatley party in London,
wearing the dress for which she will always be remembered. REX FEATURES

With Noel Edmonds on the first *National Lottery Live* show. REX FEATURES

Meeting the Queen at the Royal Variety Performance, 1995.
PRESS ASSOCIATION

My sister Wendy with Mum, Dad and our old horse Caramac
in the paddock at the back of their home in Norton. REX FEATURES

The crew and me on safari in Africa for *Wish You Were Here*.

Talking to the local children in Kenya for *Wish You Were Here*.

On assignment with the *Wish You Were Here* crew in Namibia.

My Showbusiness
Personality of the Year
award. Not bad for a goofy,
dyslexic kid from Norton-
in-the-Moors.

With hairdresser Nicky Clarke during one of *GMTV*'s 'Fun in the Sun'
episodes in Spain.

Grant and Della reunited for *OK!* magazine. SCOPE FEATURES

Grant and his 'top totty' on the karaoke machine at a Valentine's party we held at our local pub. SCOPE FEATURES

The *News of the World* piece which told the world that Grant and I were still in love. JOHN FROST HISTORICAL NEWSPAPER SERVICE

A recent shot of my new husband and I, happily married.

having doubts and of brushing them under the carpet. We were equally culpable for thinking that somehow, when the madness stopped, everything would be fine. I just hoped and prayed that I would wake up one day and feel again the feelings I had lost. Most of all, I needed to feel that I wanted to make love to this man I'd vowed to spend the rest of my life with, but I didn't and, somewhere down the line, he clearly didn't either.

I began to fear that maybe I had a sexual problem. Women did go off sex, I knew – I'd read all about it in various women's magazines. I'd more or less convinced myself that that was what had happened to me.

Despite all my angst, then, later and even now, I can honestly say that I do not regret one single day of my marriage to Pete. We have both enriched each other's lives and if I had my time over, I'd marry him again. But the aching in my heart at that stage of my life, when I was about to embark on a whole new series that would send me abroad for months, was almost palpable. Yet like Pete, if ever I have a problem, I always put it to one side and concentrate on my work in the hope that the problem will have disappeared by the time I've finished. And Dr Television has been wonderful for me in that respect over the years. So once again I just threw myself into my work.

In June 1997 I flew to France for a Littlewoods fashion shoot, feeling glad to be able to get away. The Littlewoods team are a great bunch, always good fun to be with, and they took me out of myself. As usual, the setting was sumptuous and the pace manageable. I must have changed clothes a hundred times and had thousands of photographs taken, but the gang made it feel more like play than work. It was a welcome respite, because my schedule for July, my last month of 'freedom' before I started working for *Wish You Were Here*, was as hectic as ever. In the space of three weeks, I had five work-related dinners to go to, six meetings, two presentations, one radio commercial to make, four photocalls, two hair appointments, a *Top Gear* piece to film about my new car, a lunch with Camelot, the lottery people, three charity events to attend and an end-of-series party to host at Ormonde House for the people who'd worked with me on *Turner Round the World*.

In the middle of all this mayhem, Pete and I were invited to a big
summer party-cum-football-tournament at Grant Bovey's recently
renovated country house in Sussex. Everyone from Pete's company
was invited, plus spouses and partners. We very nearly didn't go, we
were both so tired. We changed our minds at the last minute, partly
because Russ was going, along with Paul Worsley and a gang from
James Grant, and it seemed like a good opportunity to catch up
with them before I disappeared for months on end.

I hadn't seen Grant and Della for some time. They'd moved from
London into a nine-bedroomed house in Fittleworth, West Sussex
where they had started their family. Pete couldn't believe the distance
Grant was commuting to London every day. We'd once gone down
there for Sunday lunch with John and Cathy Comerford and their
baby, Milo. Russ and Caron had also been there with their baby,
Gabriel, and I remember feeling completely and utterly out of it,
because the entire conversation revolved around kids and nannies. It
was incredibly hot in the house and I felt stifled. I thought I might
faint. I felt like an alien because I didn't have children and I couldn't
wait to escape.

Since they'd moved I'd seen Della very occasionally, an omission I
sometimes felt guilty about. To rectify it I had taken her to lunch at
San Lorenzo with Stephanie Schofield one day and another time I
had gone down to see her most recent baby. From time to time we'd
seen Grant on his own or with other people when he was in town.
He'd sometimes stayed overnight with us, or with Russ and Caron,
when it wasn't worth his while travelling all that way home. But I
hadn't seen him since we'd all met up in Blackpool the previous year.
I gathered from Pete and Russ that things weren't quite going as well
for him as he'd hoped. He'd taken on a great deal with the Sussex
house, which needed to be completely rebuilt and had turned into
something of a money pit.

There was a lively social atmosphere at the party, which was essentially a PR exercise for his company, Watershed Pictures. Grant was
very good at organising this sort of do. It started in the afternoon and
ended with a dinner and disco in the evening, which was to include
the presentation of the trophies for the football tournament. James

Grant had entered a team though it didn't include Pete. 'I'm too old and too tired,' he protested. So Russ and Paul and the others did their bit while the rest of us sat in a marquee drinking Pimm's and cheering them on.

The sit-down black-tie dinner after the tournament was very glitzy. I wore one of my favourite dresses, a lavender figure-hugging Amanda Wakeley full-length dress. When we all consulted the seating plan to find where we were sitting, I discovered that Grant had put me on the top table, right next to him. I found my place and sat down. He smiled at me and said: 'You knew I'd do that, didn't you?' I just laughed and we carried on with the dinner. Pete and Della were on the same table, too, along with various friends and colleagues. The trophies were duly handed out. Watershed had won one, which I was asked to present to Grant. I did so with the customary kiss, and then the tables were cleared and everyone started dancing.

I don't know why, but I was in a very happy mood that night. It's not very often I go to a party and let my hair down, but I love dancing, and it was a particularly good disco which played all the old songs Ruth and I had sung along to when we watched *Top of the Pops* as kids. The hits by Abba, Queen and Blondie really brought back some memories. It seemed like only yesterday that I'd been dancing Pan's People routines for Mum and Dad in Norton, or listening to Blondie in my little Mini en route to the AA in Hanley. Where had all the years gone? Now I was approaching forty and wondering what had happened to my dreams of marrying Donny Osmond and producing five children with the gleaming white Osmond teeth.

I've never been much of a drinker, but that evening I drank more than usual. The mood seemed right for it: the champagne was flowing, the candles were lit and I was surrounded by friends. Grant was very attentive and I felt flattered and more than a little excited. It had been a long time since anyone had flirted with me and I was enjoying the novelty. The two of us basically picked up pretty much where we'd left off in Blackpool, chatting and laughing together. He was telling me his life story, which, like Pete's and mine, had a humble beginning.

Grant was the son of a cinema projectionist and union official, born in a suburb of Nottingham just forty miles from where I grew up. He was the youngest of three children. His father bought a plot of land and, brick by brick, built the house they were to live in. His mother, a machinist, instilled in Grant an entrepreneurial spirit and endorsed a schoolboy scheme to sell fashion items to friends for cash. Leaving school at seventeen, he became a market trader selling ladies' clothing. He opened a shop, bought a house and, by his early twenties, was employing twenty-five people, but his empire collapsed due to excessive overheads and he lost everything.

He moved down to London to find work. After a four-week spell as a double-glazing salesman and then a stint in a record shop, he got a job with a company called Braveworld, which sold video rights. Within six months he had worked his way up through the ranks and had been appointed sales director of the multimillion-pound firm, travelling the world attending film festivals and living the high life. He started dating Della on his first Christmas home and they continued this long-distance relationship for three years.

In 1988 Grant had a brush with stardom when he released a single called 'Don't Turn Your Back' under the name of Michael Grant. It reached number 99 in the charts and he was signed up with a record company. But when his music career failed to take off, he left Braveworld and set up a similar company called Watershed Pictures, a much smaller operation which made films specifically for the video market. Della moved to London and found a job as a sales representative for a dental firm, but the relationship foundered and she returned home. Three months later, Grant – who'd always wanted children – was nearing thirty and seeing many of his friends getting married. He went to Derby to see Della and to ask her to come back. She agreed, but only if he proposed. They were married a year later.

Grant's business went from strength to strength. His biggest clients were the Football Association, from whom he bought all moving-picture image rights, excluding live transmissions, and Nigel Mansell, who had been like a brother to him. His house, Catercross, was set in twenty acres and had all the trappings of wealth, but Pete and Russ had told me privately that they thought Grant had rather overstretched himself financially. 'I want the lifestyle, Anthea,' he told me frankly. 'I always have. Some of the risks I've taken to get it would frighten most people to death. I think Pete sometimes thinks I'm a bit of a chancer.'

I laughed and said: 'Not so much a chancer, just someone who likes to live dangerously.'

Looking back on that night, I realise now that I didn't police myself properly at all. Grant and I spent a massive amount of time with each other, laughing our socks off. Della was busy playing hostess, and Pete, who hates dancing with a passion, was used to leaving me to my own devices on the dancefloor. I danced with lots of other people as well – there were plenty of furtive taps on my shoulder and requests for a dance – but somehow Grant and I seemed to keep ending up with each other.

Halfway through the evening, as we were dancing to a slow number, we talked about how long we'd known each other and when we had first met. It was in 1989, before either of us were married. I'd walked into Pete's office in Hammersmith and Grant had been sitting there with his briefcase, waiting to see Russ about a possible video shoot with Phillip Schofield. I remembered stopping in my tracks, quite taken aback by the handsome, blond-haired, hazel-eyed boy before me. Now here we were dancing cheek to cheek.

'You should have asked me out eight years ago when we first met,' I said suddenly, not having thought about the remark at all before voicing it.

Grant stopped and stared at me. The intensity in his eyes made me pull away slightly. I wished I hadn't spoken. When we'd finished our dance, I wandered over to find Pete, who was deep in conversation with a client, and stuck closely to his side for the rest of the night.

The party ended in the early hours. Pete and I were staying the night and would be leaving early the next morning as we had tickets for the Men's Final at Wimbledon. Pete went to bed first and fell asleep almost immediately. I followed him up at about 4am, put on my pyjamas and padded downstairs, barefoot, to make myself a cup of coffee and a piece of toast – I've always been a great believer in late-night 'blotting paper'. I found Grant in the kitchen, drinking wine with his brother, Paul. Various other guests were scattered around the floor of the living room in sleeping bags. I busied myself with the kettle and toaster, half listening to the general conversation, from which I gathered that there'd been some sort of argument between Della and her sister, and that Della had gone to bed. The next time I looked round, I realised I was alone in the kitchen with Grant. Once again, he was staring at me with that strange look in his eyes.

I sensed that suddenly I was in a mighty dangerous situation. Intoxicated by the evening, it wouldn't have taken much for either of us to have made a move. Feigning a yawn, I stretched and said, 'Gosh, I'm tired. Well, goodnight, Grant. I'm off to bed.' I gave him a quick peck on the cheek and fled in about forty seconds flat. I remember climbing into bed next to Pete, feeling butterflies in my stomach and thinking: 'Phew, close call.'

The following morning we got up, thanked Grant and Della for a fantastic party and set off. I didn't give the evening another thought. On the way into town, weaving our way through the Sunday-morning traffic, Pete and I chatted about how much fun we'd had.

'You had a great time, didn't you?' he said, his hands gripping the steering wheel of his Porsche.

I nodded and giggled. 'Yes, I did. I can't remember the last time I danced so much. I think Grant's the first person I've met who likes dancing as much as I do.'

Pete looked thoughtful. 'You should have married someone like Grant Bovey, you know. He's much more your type.'

I felt as if someone had walked over my grave. Rattled, I spun round to face Pete. 'What do you mean?' I asked.

He shrugged his shoulders and concentrated on driving, leaving me feeling decidedly uneasy. For some reason, I suddenly remembered that psychic from Stoke who'd foretold a strange future for me. I shot a sideways glance at Pete and wondered why on earth he'd said what he did.

Three weeks later, on Monday 28 July, Grant phoned Pete at work to ask if he could stay the night with us because he had an early-morning appointment in town. Pete rang to tell me what they'd arranged. A couple of hours later, he called again to say that he'd been summoned to an unexpected meeting and wasn't going to be home until late. 'Why don't you take Grant out for dinner and I'll try to catch up with you later?' he suggested.

I remember putting the phone down and panicking a little, thinking, 'This could be awkward.' But a little part of me was excited, too, and I was surprised to find myself making a special effort that night with my clothes, hair and make-up.

When the doorbell rang, I nearly jumped out of my skin. I was as nervous as a kitten, as if I was going out on a date. 'Don't be ridiculous,' I told myself crossly. 'Pull yourself together.' I let Grant in, fixed him a drink and told him, as casually as I could, that Pete couldn't join us, but that he'd suggested I took him to Sonny's, a local restaurant in Barnes.

'Great,' Grant said, with a smile. 'Is that anywhere near Cathy and John's house? I haven't seen them for a while and I thought maybe we could drop in and see them en route.'

We arrived unannounced at the home of our mutual friends and had a lovely time sitting out in their garden, drinking wine. It was just the type of evening I'd once imagined Pete and me having as a married couple. We were enjoying ourselves so much that I decided to cancel the restaurant booking and buy everyone a Chinese takeaway instead. Sitting out under the stars, we naturally fell into 'coupledom' – John and Cathy on one side of the table and Grant and me on the other. It all felt very easy, and Grant and I were very comfortable with each other. Everyone was talking, having fun, telling jokes. It was so much more relaxing than any evening I'd spent with Pete in recent memory.

Grant was getting braver by the glass, and halfway through the evening, he leaned across to John and said something like: 'Well, you know, I've always really fancied Anthea.'

I remember pricking up my ears and thinking that he had crossed a line by saying openly what he felt privately. I was a little surprised, even though we were both being slightly flirtatious with each other. There was certainly still a little frisson there.

When it was time to say goodbye, I drove Grant back to Ormonde House and we sat at the kitchen table drinking coffee. Pete still wasn't home and, on past form, I didn't expect him until much later. I was trying to keep the conversation light, but I began to sense danger again. Suddenly I became aware that I was doing all the talking while Grant was just staring at me. He looked deeply troubled. Something clearly wasn't right, but I didn't know if I should intrude.

'What's wrong, Grant? I asked.

He remained silent.

'Are things OK with work?' I asked as gently as I could.

He nodded, but kept his eyes locked on mine.

'There's a problem with you and Della, isn't there?' I said, still picking up the vibe that something was very awry.

'No more than usual,' Grant sighed with an air of resignation. 'We don't even talk to each other about the things that matter any more.'

He paused, then added quietly: 'But that's not my problem, Anthea.'

I've always tried to solve other people's dilemmas, even if I was never very good at dealing with my own. Relieved that my intuition was right, that something else was the matter, I adopted my most caring look, touched his knee and asked earnestly: 'What is it, Grant?'

'It's you,' he said.

'What do you mean?'

'It's you.'

I stared at him wordlessly, trying to take in what he was saying.

He spelled it out for me. 'You know I've always had a bit of a thing about you. And now I don't know what to do about it.'

I was frightened half to death. Eventually I managed to compose myself and gave a nervous little laugh. 'Well – er – there isn't anything you can do about it,' I said. 'After all, we're both married.'

Grant shrugged his shoulders and looked down. Trying to avoid any sort of scene, I began to point out the reasons why it wouldn't be a very sensible idea for us to consider embarking on any sort of relationship. I finished my speech by blurting out: 'It's a nice idea, Grant, and in another life, maybe. But there'd be too many dead bodies.'

He sat back in his chair. 'Yeah, yeah,' he said slowly, 'you're probably right. That wouldn't be good, would it?'

We talked for quite a while. In a manner which now seems almost laughable, we discussed, in quite clinical terms, our mutual attraction to and respect for each other. I was so rattled that once I'd started talking, I couldn't stop. 'I mean, it's not that we couldn't be great together, I think we both feel that, but it's just not on, is it?' I concluded.

Eventually I managed to change the subject and we chatted about other things for a while, but my heart was thumping so hard in my chest that I wondered if he could hear it. As the clock struck one, I led him upstairs, showed him his room, made up his bed while he stood there watching me and then went to my own room, shutting the door firmly behind me.

I hardly slept a wink all night. The events of the evening were spinning round and round in my mind. The danger was so close I could almost smell it. I felt excited and flattered all at once, because although I'm in the public eye and get hundreds of letters from fans, I knew it took a brave man to approach me directly. Or someone who knew me very well. I knew he'd been serious, deadly serious. I'd seen it in his eyes. And that only made me tremble even more.

Pete eventually came home very late and climbed into my bed because Grant was in his. I pretended to be asleep. He rolled over and I listened to his breathing slowing down as he nodded off. I only wished sleep would come to me as easily. I must have dropped off eventually, because the next thing I knew, it was morning and I was alone in bed. I went downstairs in my pyjamas to find Pete and Grant in the kitchen, both dressed and ready for work. I said goodbye rather shyly. Nothing more was said.

The events of that evening disturbed me more than I could say. I tried to reason it all out in my mind. I decided that there had been an intoxicating atmosphere about the evening and that Grant must have got carried away. In the cold light of day, he was probably seriously regretting the whole episode. I'd analysed it all to death overnight and worried about how it might affect our friendship, and his business relationship with Pete. 'What if he can't bear to be in the same room with me after this?' I asked myself. 'Won't Pete smell a rat?' Having given the matter considerable thought, I decided to ring him to make sure everything was all right. I thought that if I took this full-frontal approach it would prevent any bad feeling developing between us in the future. The last thing I wanted was any awkwardness that might be misconstrued.

Sitting in my car outside the Wellington Hospital, where I was due for a check-up on my knee, I called Grant on his mobile. 'Hi, Grant, it's Anthea. Are you all right?'

'I'm fine,' he said breezily, as if nothing at all had happened.

'Er – oh,' I stammered. 'You're not too upset?'

'Upset about what?' he asked. My face began to redden.

'Well – er – about my refusal of your kind offer,' I said, losing confidence by the second. 'I mean, I was hugely flattered, and it was very sweet of you, but I don't want you to feel at all bad about anything that happened last night.' I was approaching the problem with almost matronly concern.

'I don't,' said Grant matter-of-factly. 'I'm very comfortable with it. We've agreed that we are both very attracted to each other, but that it would be better if we just remained friends. Right?'

I could feel the blood burning my cheeks.

Grant filled the uneasy silence. 'Thanks again for a lovely evening,' he added almost casually. 'We really should do that more often. I can't remember the last time I enjoyed myself so much. Why don't we meet up some time?'

I laughed aloud at the suggestion. 'Er, I don't think that would be a very good idea.' I was backtracking, big-time.

There was silence, and then he said: 'OK, I understand.' Another awkward pause filled the airwaves. Suddenly, he said: 'How would it be, then, if I just called you every now and again, for a chat, just like we're doing now? There couldn't possibly be any harm in that, could there?' He made it sound so reasonable, so innocent, but I knew we were playing with fire. Despite all my misgivings, I told him that he could. 'I'd like that,' I added, and I meant it.

I guess in my heart of hearts I was enjoying the tingling feeling in my stomach that Grant gave me, even talking on the telephone. I thought I'd become immune to all that stuff, but now someone I knew very well and liked very much was suggesting that we fulfil a need in each other in some way with the odd telephone call. As he'd said, where was the harm in that?

Grant called the next day. We didn't talk about anything special, just about mutual friends; about something funny he'd heard on the radio and how his car needed a service. The day after that he rang again, and the following day, I called him. Over the next few weeks we started speaking to each other every day. I found myself actually anticipating his calls, and if he hadn't rung me, I'd phone him instead. Sometimes I'd be in London, but mostly I was away, filming with *Wish You Were Here* in Magaluf, on a Mediterranean cruise and in Biarritz.

The television-presenting itself was relatively straightforward. The format of the programme was very formulaic and had hardly changed in twenty-five years. With only five to six minutes air time for each film, there was no scope for proper interviews or any pieces to camera that taxed me in any way. But the job was incredibly demanding from a logistical point of view. As soon as I arrived somewhere with the crew, we had to rush all over the island or resort or cruise ship or whatever it was to capture key areas and events on film without ever having enough time to get into the subject properly.

The really arduous part, however, was the travelling and the distances involved. I was living out of a suitcase for weeks on end, hurrying to catch flights, trains, boats or buses, and no sooner had I got home, unpacked and done the washing than I'd have to repack for the next assignment. For the entire time I was doing *Wish You Were Here*, I could never settle. It's a job for a young person with no home life, not for a thirty-something woman running away from her problems and struggling with her marriage and her mixed-up emotions. I'd end up alone in my hotel room at night aching for companionship. When I phoned Pete to talk to him about my day, he was often busy and we couldn't speak for long. Grant, on the other hand, always seemed to be available.

We talked about absolutely nothing at all: the weather, what we were doing, what we'd eaten for dinner, where he was in which

London traffic jam. We had the most remarkable ability to talk for hours on end about nothing in particular and yet say so much between the lines. Waiting excitedly for him to ring, I felt like a teenager again. Gradually, imperceptibly, our relationship shifted as we grew closer through our conversations. We became bolder, confiding in each other about personal matters, about areas of our lives about which we were unhappy. I found that I could speak to Grant about the most intimate subjects. I could really open up to him in a way I'd forgotten how to with Pete. After all the years of loneliness and separation, I clung to my new friendship like a limpet. 'It's OK for us to talk like this, isn't it, Grant?' I'd ask him, constantly seeking reassurance. 'I mean, we're not doing anything wrong, are we?' We even began to fantasise, half-jokingly, about what life might be like if we had done something about each other all those years before.

The trouble was, the more we got on, the more it made us realise how desperately empty both our marriages were. We'd touched a nerve in each other. Up to then, we'd both been muddling along, accepting our lot in life and hoping that one day things might improve. Then, suddenly, we were thrown into a situation where we were allowed a taste of the intensity and vibrancy that a relationship could have, and it made our home lives seem even less tolerable. Like the *Titanic* and the iceberg, we were moving inexorably closer together and neither of us had the strength, or the will, to pull away.

One weekday morning towards the end of August, Grant rang me from his car while I was filming for *Wish You Were Here* at Littlecote Manor in Berkshire.

'I really need to see you,' he said. There was an imploring tone to his voice I hadn't heard before. 'Could we possibly get together before you fly off again?'

I hesitated, my stomach doing a triple flip.

He tried a different tack. 'You remember that voiceover you kindly said you'd do for the CD-ROM for my new company, Sports Check? Well, I've got all the equipment now, and I really need to get it done soon. What do you say?'

I was due to fly to Corfu the following Tuesday night and Pete was

leaving for a week's sailing in Majorca the Saturday before. I knew
what I'd be walking into but I couldn't seem to stop myself. I stalled
Grant as best I could, but I didn't block him completely. I was missing something in my life, something I needed desperately as a
woman. I tried not to analyse it too much. Having previously been
convinced that I had some sort of medical problem, I was now feeling emotions which I'd thought were dead. Something was lighting
my fire, I was experiencing physical sensations I hadn't felt in years,
and I liked what I felt.

Perhaps because I didn't firmly pull the shutters down, Grant rang
again and pressed me further for a meeting. 'It won't take long,' he
promised. 'I'll just pop in before you go off to the airport and we'll
do the voiceover. Then I'll be out of your hair.'

Somewhat reluctantly I relented, and invited him over for tea at
4pm on the Tuesday. I had reasoned it all out in my mind. By meeting him so late, just a few hours before I was to leave for my flight,
scheduled to take off just before midnight, I hoped there'd be no time
for anything other than the voiceover. We both knew that the
encounter would be pivotal. Either something would happen or it
wouldn't. But I also saw it as a major test of my resolve.

I did what I always did when I was travelling. I took a shower and
put on my best bib and tucker. But I was paying extra attention to
my perfume and make-up that evening. I remember wishing I had
something more special to wear than my comfy white Hanro knickers. Grant arrived early, at a few minutes to four, by which time I was
dressed and packed and ready for my driver, who was due to pick me
up at 9.30pm. I noticed that Grant's hair was still damp from a
recent shower and that he smelled nice.

I did the voiceover for him, which only took about ten minutes,
and then we moved into the kitchen. 'Tea?' I asked, reaching for the
kettle and placing it firmly on the Aga. With my back to the stove,
clinging to the towel rail, I made small talk. We chatted about all
sorts of harmless, general matters for about three quarters of an hour.
Then we sat down at the kitchen table facing each other. My legs
were firmly crossed. It was almost comical, in retrospect, like something out of a sit-com. We both knew why the meeting had been

arranged, and yet we both seemed paralysed. Finally, I heard myself say: 'Grant, why exactly are you here?'

I began to feel light-headed with anticipation as we sat there, inches apart, the electricity sparking between us. Something was definitely about to happen. My skin was covered in goose bumps and for a moment I held my breath and closed my eyes.

Before I could open them, Grant had leaned forward and kissed me. From the second our lips met, I knew that I was lost. Grant was rekindling feelings I'd thought I'd forgotten. He knew I wanted him as much as he wanted me. Once more, in repetition of the events of a decade earlier, I found myself vulnerable, afraid and in the arms of someone other than my partner.

Locked in that embrace and afraid to let go of each other, we moved up a floor from the kitchen into the living room, where Grant gently undressed me, strewing my clothes across the carpet. Fearing we'd be seen from outside, we climbed another floor, more of our clothes littering the stairs, and finally into the bedroom, where I made love for the first time in ages. With every new flight of stairs our fate had been sealed. We'd forgotten there was anyone else in the world.

What happened in the hour that followed was a golden time that will stay with me for ever. I shall feed on its memory into my old age. I'd practically convinced myself that sex didn't matter in my life. Now I was euphoric at the realisation that it did, and that I was in the hands of an experienced man. I felt fabulous – loved and wanted and needed all at once. It was the first time in years that a man had made me feel like that.

As I lay in Grant's arms afterwards, in the bed that should have been shared by Pete and me, I knew that I'd broken the silver thread of marriage. It was not something I'd done lightly, or without reason, but now that I had crossed the line I knew there was no going back.

Corfu passed in a blur. Staggered by what I had done, happy and frightened and sad all at once, I wanted to stay on that magical Ionian island for ever and never have to return to face the music. Coming down to breakfast on the Sunday morning, I was approached by some of the guests in the hotel who had befriended me in the previous days. 'Miss Turner?' asked an anxious middle-aged man, clutching his wife's hand. Behind him stood several worried-looking guests. 'Could you help us, please?'

'If I can,' I said.

'There have been some terrible rumours flying around the hotel. People are saying that Princess Diana is dead. Do you know anything about it?'

Shaking my head and thinking how ridiculous this sounded, I brushed them off and promised to investigate. It was eight in the morning Corfu time, two hours ahead of London, and I wondered who I could call. Grant would be home in Sussex and Pete was on a boat off the coast of Spain. Remembering the twenty-four-hour news room at GMTV, I dialled my old work number.

'I'm sorry to trouble you,' I said to a female reporter coming to the end of a night shift, 'but it's Anthea Turner. I know this sounds ridiculous, but I'm in Corfu and I've been asked to check out some preposterous story that Princess Diana is dead. I didn't know who else to call this early, and then I thought of you.'

'I'm afraid it's true,' said the reporter, clearly shaken. She talked me through the tragic events of the previous night in Paris. I could hardly believe what I was hearing. I slumped back on to the bed in my hotel room. Like so many others, I felt personally bereaved. Princess Diana was not someone I knew or had even met, but we all felt we knew her, and loved her, and to hear that she had died at the age of thirty-six, a year younger than me, seemed so terribly shocking.

I tried to compose myself before retracing my steps down to the hotel lobby and the waiting guests. 'I'm terribly sorry,' I said, my voice faltering, 'but the rumours are true. Princess Diana died early this morning. She was killed with her boyfriend Dodi Fayed in a car crash in Paris.' The gentle British holidaymakers in front of me burst into tears. I felt terrible to have to be the one to break the news to them, so I stayed with them for a while, offering what comfort I could.

Thankfully I had a day off so I was able to go and lie by the hotel pool, where I tried to absorb what had happened. Amid my own personal trauma, I found myself enormously affected by the Princess's death. It was that day, and the loss of that woman, that finally made me reassess my own life. It made me realise that I wasn't immortal either, and it struck me that you really do have to live every day as if it were your last. It was a curious time. I needed to take stock and I saw that I needed to change my perspective. I remember thinking: 'Life can just be taken away like that, so easily, just like it was with Ruth. I have to seize the day. I shouldn't waste time having an unhappy life or an unhappy marriage. Not after this.' I returned from Corfu a different woman. I felt that from then on, I had to put my emotional needs at the top, rather than at the bottom, of my list of priorities. Grant was the one who fulfilled those needs, and I wasn't going to resist seeing him any more.

But that was easier said than done. September was another frantic month, and in the space of four weeks I travelled to Moscow, Donegal and Turkey with *Wish You Were Here*, spending twenty days out of the country. Of the ten days I had in the UK, eight were taken up with meetings, charity gigs, business lunches and physiotherapy sessions for my knee. I was able to see Grant only twice, once on the eve of my nine-day trip to Russia, when we met incognito at the Conrad Hotel at Chelsea Harbour, and then at a polo match Pete and I attended in Sussex, an event I wished I'd never gone to. That was when the guilt really started to kick in. The sight of Della with her children, and of Pete chatting animatedly to our friends, made me feel physically sick. I retreated behind my sunglasses and told Pete I had a headache and wanted to go home.

I was always deeply uncomfortable with the subterfuge required for Grant and me to meet each other. It's not something I'm at all proud of. In some ways, I'd preferred our relationship when it was just telephone talk. Now, not only was there a risk that we'd be caught, but the way we had to sneak around made me realise how sordid and immoral it was. I felt very ill at ease having convinced myself that it was something much purer than that.

To cope with the complicated emotions raging in my heart, I went into hyper-professional mode, organising my diary even more in the manner of a super-efficient secretary. Everything was colour-coded, with notes of what I was going to be doing each day and which outfit I planned to wear for it, all written neatly in the margins. I confined all my future 'meetings' with Grant to a set period, logging them in my diary as if they were just another business lunch. Grant watched me enter our next 'appointment' in my Filofax, slipping the letters GB in between the hairdresser and the acupuncturist.

'What are you doing?' he asked incredulously.

'Just logging you into my diary,' I said, sitting on the edge of the bed as he lay under the covers beside me. 'Now, I'm sorry, but I've got to go. I'm late for my next appointment.' I'd leave the room as quickly as I'd arrived, no doubt leaving Grant wondering what sort of unfeeling monster he'd become involved with.

At least at work I did not have a chance to agonise about what on earth I was playing at, although the Russian trip was very strange, and gave me far too much time to dwell on things. Cruising down the Volga from Leningrad to Moscow, lying awake in my cabin, my head was filled with all sorts of weird and frightening images that haunted my dreams, too. Faces loomed at me in the darkness – Ruth, Grant, Della, Pete, Princess Diana – and paranoia gripped my heart. I was hugely grateful to get back on dry land.

In November I was asked back to present the National Lottery's third birthday programme, a half-hour special devised as an attempt to revive the show's flagging viewing figures. It was to be a precursor to me returning to the programme full-time for a while. Pete and the BBC had been in negotiation for some time about this possibility, and I was happy to go back. There had been no fewer than eleven different presenters since I'd left, but nothing had halted the slide in ratings. According to some at the Beeb, I was, in the minds of the public, part and parcel of the lottery, and it was hoped that my return might do the trick.

At about the same time, I brought out my first fitness video for Virgin Vision, called *Body Basics*, one of several which collectively went on to sell over a million copies. With television shows, videos and children's books ensuring that the name 'Anthea Turner' remained a hot property, the requests for newspaper and magazine interviews showed no signs of waning. My picture still appeared regularly in everything from the *Sunday Telegraph* colour magazine and the 'Life' section of the *Express* to the news pages of the *Sentinel* in Stoke-on-Trent.

More and more frequently, these features included Wendy as well, as the press latched on to the new angle of profiling two sisters in television and publishing together. She moved into a house a hundred yards down the road from Ormonde House and we became even closer. According to one reporter, we 'finished each other's sentences' and broke into 'hysterical, girly giggles at the slightest provocation'. Close as we were, though, I couldn't bring myself to tell Wendy about Grant. I couldn't tell anyone. I longed to drive to Stoke, sit down with my mum and dad and pour out my heart to them, as I had often done, but I couldn't. They were incredibly understanding and perceptive and, like many of my friends, they'd realised that my marriage was in trouble, but how would they react to this? They loved Peter. I loved Peter, for goodness' sake. What was I doing?

The only outward sign of the angst I was going through was that once again, as some of the journalists who interviewed me pointed out, I was 'wafer thin'. As always, during times of stress, I'd forgotten to eat. I was at the very peak of my career, rivalled only, according to one paper, by Princess Diana as the blonde most little girls had wanted to be. My fitness videos and Littlewoods clothing range sold phenomenally, my most devoted female fans were still copying what I was wearing, and I had all the trappings of fame and fortune to show for such popularity. And here I was risking it all.

Grant and I kept in touch via our mobile phones. Wherever I was, we still rang each other every day, talking for hours. As I travelled the globe with *Wish You Were Here*, I ran up thousands of pounds' worth of phone bills. The programmes in that series still represent to me the various painful stages of our affair. I was on the road to self-destruction and I couldn't seem to get off it. In October I was away for another twenty days, in Turkey, France and the southern American states of Miami and Texas. I was, by now, totally screwed up. I didn't want to go away, I just wanted all the madness to stop so that I could think. As I packed my bag for the umpteenth time, Pete sensed my distress, but instead of holding me and telling me it would be all right if I postponed or even cancelled the trip, he put on his manager's hat. 'You've got to pull yourself together, AT,' he said, holding my face in his hands. 'You can't back out of this now.'

It was the type of thing his father would have said to him. 'Oh, stop bleating, stand up straight and get on with it.' But that particular night it didn't help me. I cried tears of really deep anguish. Pete had never heard me cry like that before and he began to fear that we really were in trouble. Half of him was trying to hold on to the brand, Anthea Turner, the television presenter, while the other half was wondering where his marriage was going. In the end, I felt he chose to stick to what he knew best – the professional side of our relationship.

My few spare days at home that month were earmarked for a launch in a Hanley bookshop with Wendy for our new *Underneath the Underground* book, an interview for *TV Listings* magazine, three trade shows, a reunion of old girls from St Dominic's and a lunch with Carole Malone of the *Sunday Mirror* for her 'My Favourite Restaurant' series. Somehow, I managed to find the time to see Grant for a couple of afternoons in between, at London hotels, usually. I would arrive through one side door in dark glasses, he'd use another, and we'd leave separately and at different times. 'Don't follow me out for at least half an hour,' I'd hiss as I left him. In our paranoia we trusted no one and feared everyone, from the maid to the bellhop. We knew that any one of them could have made several years' salary overnight just by picking up a telephone and calling one of the tabloids.

I cannot explain or justify my actions to my fans or to my fiercest critics. I was beyond any control. When Grant and I were alone, it made sense. We revelled in our new-found happiness, falling deeper and deeper in love. The physical side of our relationship never became any less intense. It was as if all the years of lost passion had been stored up and recovered through this one man. I longed for the passion we enjoyed when we were together and tortured myself with the angst we endured whenever we were apart. Mostly, I just agonised over what I was doing and fretted my life away. Pete was so busy, he didn't even seem to notice.

Grant, too, was going through hell. He found himself falling for me and yet he was constantly trying to fight it. To him this had started off as a fling, an 'experiment' to test how we really felt after being so drawn to each other. Now that it had developed into this living entity which ruled our lives and crowded every waking moment, he felt asphyxiated by the position into which he had manoeuvred himself.

By my return from Istanbul, however, Grant and I were getting bolder. We decided to risk having lunch together in public, at Brown's Hotel in Mayfair. We persuaded ourselves that if anyone saw us, it would be fine. We were just two people having a meal together. I often had lunch with strangers, so it was no big deal. We wouldn't exactly be snogging at the table, and if Pete or Della ever found out, we had a very plausible excuse lined up. During the lunch, we admitted to each other that what we had treated as an uncomplicated affair that would run its course had dramatically changed into something else for us both.

'I've broken the golden rule, Grant,' I burst out over coffee. 'I've fallen in love with the person I'm having an affair with.'

Taking my hand in his, Grant said: 'I know you have, Anth.' He kissed my hand. 'And, the trouble is, I feel the same way, too. I'm totally torn. You're the love of my life, and yet I have my children to think of. I'll be honest with you, Anthea, I'm absolutely terrified of the consequences of what we're doing.'

We made the lunch last as long as possible and we were the last to leave the restaurant. I needed to go to Swaine, Adeney, Brigg to collect some horseriding gear for a trip to the south of France, so Grant came along. We tried our best to be inconspicuous, but there was a tremendous electricity between us whenever we were together, and it was even stronger after the confessions of our lunchtime meeting. High on our newly declared love for each other, we flirted openly together in the shop and in the street outside. I felt truly happy. As we parted company, I longed to reach out and hold him, but I knew I couldn't. Instead, waving to him through my taxi window, I called to him, 'See you next month.'

The following day I had lunch with Carole Malone at Brian

Turner's restaurant in Walton Street. I'd spoken to Grant at length on the mobile beforehand and had promised to call him when I got out. Carole was someone I had come to know as a friend and whom I liked and trusted very much. Halfway through the interview, she said: 'Oh, there was something I was meaning to ask you, Anthea. A photograph came into our picture desk yesterday, a picture of you and some bloke in Bond Street with a Swaine Adeney bag. They wanted to know who he was and asked me if he was your brother.'

I looked up and met Carole's steady gaze. She'd known me for years, ever since I worked on *GMTV*, and she knew damn well that I didn't have a brother. Still watching me carefully, she added quietly: 'I didn't delude them about the identity of your "brother", so the pictures aren't being used.' She paused and studied my expression. By this time I was beetroot red and had almost choked on my rocket salad. Turning off her cassette-recorder, she leaned forward, looked me straight in the eye and said: 'Anthea, what the fuck have you been up to?'

I wish to God I'd just bluffed it and dismissed her with something like, 'Oh, that's my cousin, Tim,' or even told a half-truth and said, 'Oh, that's just Grant Bovey, he's an old friend of Pete's and mine. We were all out together and Pete had to go off.' But I didn't. She knew there was more to it than that. I've never been a very good actress and this time I completely lost it.

As my mascara threatened to run, I told Carole, 'OK, I was with someone I shouldn't have been with, but nothing's happened, nothing's going on. Honestly.'

She looked dubious. Squeezing her hand and pleading with her, I asked her: 'Please, Carole, for the sake of our friendship, do me a favour. Forget we ever had this conversation, would you?' She gazed at me in silence for a few minutes and, seeing my pain, nodded her assent. Picking up her fork, she got on with her meal. God bless her, she was true to her promise and as far as I know she never breathed a word.

I couldn't eat another morsel. I couldn't wait to get out. I felt as if I was going to throw up. I had no idea whether Carole would be able to keep her promise. In any event, the photographer could have sent the picture to any number of other papers. I rushed away from the restaurant as fast as I could and rang Grant on my mobile. He was clearly shocked; it frightened the life out of him that we'd been photographed on the street without our knowledge. He began to get an inkling for the first time of just how big the story would be if it got out, and that scared him even more.

'It's OK,' I told him, hoping it was. 'I think it's sorted. I don't think anything is going to happen.' We talked for ages and decided to see this as a warning shot across our bows. We knew that we must never be seen together in public again.

Off on my travels again, I still talked to Grant every day. To try to maintain the fragile emotional link between us, we came up with an idea that I should use a key word, suggested by him, in each of my travel presentations. 'Today's word is "moon",' he'd say. 'Use that and think of me.' It became a game, a secret between us that no one else knew about. Struggling to make up a sentence into which I could seamlessly incorporate his key word for that day, I'd smile inwardly to myself and send him my love across the miles.

We were falling deeper and deeper in love with each other, and yet seeing each other was becoming harder and harder. We were in an impossible situation, and I knew in my heart that one day the story was going to blow. When it did the repercussions would be horrendous all round. Yet still I was unable to give this man up.

I knew that it was going to take something momentous to make me come clean, but in the meantime we were both finding it all more and more difficult to live with. In many ways it was even harder for Grant because he had to go home to Della every night and share her bed. Inevitably, after a while it became clear to her that he was not reacting in the same way, and she started to suspect that something was going on. She accused him of having an affair. His relationship with Della hadn't been right for some time, but now it was appreciably worse.

Yet crazily, Grant and I began discussing the possibility of being together permanently one day. It started out as a fantasy 'what if' topic that was almost completely out of bounds as a regular subject for discussion. I persuaded myself that, although Pete would be devastated at the break-up of our marriage, it probably wouldn't come as such a huge shock to him after the way things had been between us. For Grant his children were always the biggest hurdle: he knew it would be a terrible wrench to leave them, and he simply couldn't countenance it.

'This isn't going to work,' he'd tell me. 'We're going to have to try to pull away from each other.'

'I know, I know,' I'd respond, gripping his hand tighter. 'Let's set time limits on how often we see each other. I'm away filming for most of next month anyway, so let's just say we won't see each other at all in November.'

We'd agreed to each self-imposed limit and kiss each other good-bye. But within weeks, we'd be missing each other too much, and at the first available opportunity, we'd break every ban and rush into each other's arms.

Desperate for some independent advice, I decided to confide in Russ, Pete's partner. I went to see him alone one night at his home. He was clearly shocked at what I had to tell him and counselled extreme caution. I couldn't help but feel I'd let him down. I'd placed him in a particularly difficult situation because of his close friendships with both Pete and Grant, but he was still kind enough to treat me as an ally.

'You're playing with fire, Anthea, you know that,' he told me. 'Don't do anything rash, for God's sake. This isn't just about you and Pete, or about Grant and Della and the kids This is your whole career we're talking about. Please try to break away from Grant and with a bit of luck it'll all blow over.'

I listened to his sound advice, but I knew in my heart of hearts that he was asking the impossible. It felt to both Grant and me that the gunpowder had already been mixed. All someone had to do now was throw in a match.

8

The Show Must Go On

By 5 November, Guy Fawkes' Night, Pete began to sense that something really was seriously wrong. For the first time, he decided to accompany me on one of my foreign assignments. The week-long 'break' that followed, in Kuala Lumpur, Malaysia with *Wish You Were Here*, was one of the most painful trips of my life. We were thrown together for the first time in ages and all the while I was praying he wouldn't suspect anything. Things were starting to come to a head and I was finding it very difficult to keep it all together. It was like walking on broken glass. It was obvious that Pete had started to notice a difference in me.

'Are you all right, AT?' he kept asking as I did my best to avoid being left alone with him.

'Fine,' I'd lie. 'Just tired, that's all.' For the first time in all the years we'd been together, I suddenly found myself uncomfortable in his company. I so desperately wanted to break down and tell him everything, to confide in him as I always had, to ask his advice about what I should do, but this was not a subject for discussion with my husband. It all felt very strange and incredibly stressful. At the same time, I was trying to do my job and missing Grant. How I got through that week without cracking, I'll never know. I will never willingly return to Kuala Lumpur – even the name gives me the heeby-jeebies now.

Pete knew our marriage was now in deep trouble, he just didn't know why. He, too, found himself very uncomfortable in the presence of someone with whom he'd always previously been completely at ease. He feared he'd left things too late. A series of deep 'life chats' followed, in which we both opened our hearts to each other about our respective problems, although I always fell short of telling Pete that I had fallen in love with someone else. We agreed that we'd drifted apart, we unearthed lots of difficulties in our marriage which we should have aired long before but hadn't. I knew it was too late: now there was someone else involved from whom I was unable to disentangle myself. I was in love with Grant. I kept testing it, thinking maybe it was just an infatuation, but it kept coming back to me as real love.

I couldn't seem to let go of him and yet at the same time I did so want to try to make things work with Pete. I wondered whether, now that we had talked everything else through, I might cross a threshold and my physical and emotional feelings for him might flood back. He was so kind to me, so gentle with his questions, and his love for me was evident. But no matter how hard I tried, I couldn't rekindle what I had once felt for him. I so much wanted to, because I could see it all crumbling away, but I couldn't help myself. I just couldn't fight any more.

In December I was away again, for two weeks in all, in Mustique in the Caribbean and Tenerife in the Canary Islands. Dotted in between were interviews with Mavis Nicholson, a photo session, three charity gigs, an appearance on *This Morning* with Richard and Judy, interviews with two tabloid newspapers and a slot on *Noel Edmonds' House Party*. I managed to see Grant only twice that month, once at a hotel in Birmingham when I went up there to open a wildlife exhibition, and once in Nottingham, where I went for a book signing for the latest edition in the *Underneath the Underground* series.

Wendy came with me on that last trip and, as with Pete, I longed to tell her what was happening, to seek her counsel and her understanding. But I couldn't; I just didn't have the nerve. I knew what she'd say. She'd worked for Grant and would most certainly have

disapproved. To begin with I hadn't told anyone because I hadn't
imagined for one minute that it would develop in the way it had. I'd
fully expected the affair to serve its purpose, re-spark my feelings for
Pete and to be over before anyone else needed to know. How foolish
can one be? By the time 1997 drew to a close, I still couldn't tell
anyone. Now, though, it was because once the secret was out, I knew
I'd be forced to choose between Pete and Grant.

My final engagements that year were on 23 December, after which
Pete promised me three days off at home. 'It'll be just what we need,
AT,' he said. 'Time alone at home together, so that we can sort everything out.' I reflected on how little he must suspect if he thought
three days at home could solve all our problems. However, no sooner
had I finished work than Pete's widowed mother, Margaret – an
invalid with Parkinson's disease and arthritis – had a fall and he had
to dash up to Stourbridge to see her. 'Never mind,' he told me on the
phone. 'We'll catch up properly on New Year's Eve. I promise.' Pete
had been planning a New Year's Eve party for some time, trying to
replicate the last great one we'd had at Ormonde House. I was dead
against it, in light of how I was feeling. So much had happened in a
year, so much had changed. I couldn't imagine standing at the
bottom of the staircase meeting and greeting guests and pretending
to be the contented wife with all these complex emotions raging in
my heart.

So when Carlton Television asked me to present their live New
Year's Eve television party from Edinburgh, I jumped at the chance.
But although this meant that the Ormonde House party would have
to be abandoned, Pete then arranged for about a dozen friends to
come with us to Edinburgh for a private celebration after the show.
I was dreading it.

I went through all the motions, but as I put the finishing touches
to the Christmas tree and decorated the house with holly and ivy, my
heart simply wasn't in it. Holding Olive, the black kitten Wendy had
brought home for me after filming an episode of *Pet Rescue*, I looked
around our home. It was perfect, a shrine to my organisational skills,
with everything colour-co-ordinated and stencilled. I even had
home-made mince pies cooling by the Aga. And yet I could have

wept. For only the second time in my life since Ruth's death, I was dreading Christmas. It all seemed so phoney: the gift-wrapped presents under the tree, the cards chosen for their meaningful words, the festive cheer. I wasn't sure I could go through with it. I knew the time was approaching when I could no longer spare Pete from the truth.

We travelled up to visit our respective families on Christmas Day, but it wasn't easy. 'Is everything all right, Lil?' Dad asked me, catching me sitting alone in my room halfway through the day. I'd had Sue van der Ree come up and redecorate my childhood bedroom, stencilling and painting it in the pastel colours I loved, but it still held so many memories. There was the spot where David Cassidy's poster had been hung, and over there was where Peter Powell's picture had been carefully placed. The old toys Ruth and I had played with and fought over and loved were congregated in a corner. Mum had kept all the paraphernalia of our childhood; not even Ruth's things had been thrown away.

'I'm OK, Dad,' I nodded, my eyes sunken from lack of sleep. 'I'm just not feeling very good. I think I may have overdone it a little. I'll just lie down for a few minutes and then I'll be fine.' He smiled and left the room, closing the door gently behind him.

By the time Pete and I arrived back home the day after Boxing Day, we had come to the edge. The atmosphere between us could have been cut by a knife. Hardly a word had been spoken in the car since Birmingham. I sank heavily on to a chair at the kitchen table and rested my head on my hands. The poor man didn't know which way to turn. And on top of all this, he had his own problems. His business was still threatened by the predatory takeover; his mother had not yet recovered from her fall and now he feared that his marriage was falling apart. At his gentle instigation, we'd brought just about every skeleton out of the closet, dusted it off and put it back again. We'd spoken of his commitment phobia at the start of our relationship, of how I'd rushed headlong into his arms to escape a life of unhappiness with Bruno. We'd analysed where we'd gone wrong and how much our respective selfishness over our careers had been to blame. We knew that our biggest crime was not having addressed the problems sooner.

'We could try for a family now, if you like,' he'd suggested tenta-
tively, thinking, I suppose that motherhood might bring me back to
him.

I knew, of course, that wouldn't solve a thing. 'No, Pete,' I said
gently. 'It was never right before, and it's certainly not right now.'

He could see that none of his suggestions were having any effect
on my obvious despair and he had tried to work out what else could
be the matter. Now, for the first time, it suddenly dawned on him.
Reaching out and taking my hand across the kitchen table that night,
he peered into my pinched features and asked quietly: 'There's someone else, isn't there?'

My bones turned to ice. My first reaction was to shake my head
violently and deny it. But then, looking into his eyes, I could no
longer maintain the deceit. I'd woven a tangled web of lies around
myself since August, and at last Pete was seeing right through it.
Before I could stop myself, the tears were falling and splashing the
table. 'Yes,' I told him. An overwhelming relief at admitting it
engulfed me.

His face ashen, he stared at me for a few seconds, slowly taking it in.
'Who?' he asked eventually.

I swallowed hard. 'Grant . . . Grant Bovey.'

There was an awful, echoing silence. Clearly the news had come as
a body blow to Pete. But he didn't get angry. He just slumped forward, held his head in his hands and wept. Instead of shouting at me
or pushing me away, his response was to want to hold me, to physically cling to me and not to let me go. He didn't want to believe it.
He wanted me to be lying. The umbilical cord between us had been
cut, leaving him gasping for oxygen in the harsh world outside.

It was only then that he realised he was about to lose his wife. He,
of all people, knew I wouldn't embark on an affair just for kicks. After
all, the last time I'd gone through an experience like this, Pete had
been the 'other man', and I'd ended up marrying him. Everything fell
into place for him now: my weight loss, my distracted manner, the
lack of communication between us. The way I'd pulled away from
him when he'd tried to comfort me. It was an exact echo of the
events of 1988.

My biggest mistake was being stupid enough ever to believe I could experiment with having an affair and leave it at that. I am just not that sort of person. With me a relationship is all or nothing. Grant and I shared equal responsibility for what had happened, but in spite of our conversations on the matter I don't think either of us had truly appreciated just how much pain we would inflict on those nearest and dearest to us.

Pete was highly emotional and desperately upset. We talked and talked that night. I couldn't believe what I was doing to this gentle man who had only ever been kind to me. What made it worse was that it was not me he felt betrayed by, but Grant, someone he had considered a close friend. They have not spoken a word to each other since. Part of me wished that Pete would rant and rave, hurl something at me or throw me out of the house, to make me feel some of the pain he was patently suffering. But instead this big-hearted man was still trying to protect me, still trying to dry my tears and hush my sobs. After he'd calmed down a little himself, he said he needed some time to think and he was going to go to his office for the night. As he left the house, he turned and said softly: 'You'd better phone Grant and tell him I know, but for God's sake don't tell anyone else.' Even on that dreadful night, he was keeping my best interests as a client at the forefront of his mind.

Pete's impeccable behaviour did nothing to ease my troubled soul. Trembling from head to toe, eventually I managed to get hold of Grant on his mobile and told him what had happened. He was clearly shocked and didn't know what to do for the best. He, too, had had a miserable Christmas with his family and was planning to escape to his sister's house in Nottingham for a day and a night, ostensibly to drop off some presents. I was in a terrible mess, crying my eyes out down the phone. 'I never wanted to hurt Pete,' I told Grant. 'Seeing him like that will haunt me for the rest of my life.'

Grant listened to my sobs and said he would come and see me as soon as he could the following day en route to Nottingham. I don't know how I managed to get through the next twenty-four hours, but somehow I did. Pete stayed away and when Grant finally got to me, he found me on the settee in a soggy heap. In the time it had taken him to escape from Sussex, I'd completely cracked. All the tension and stress of the previous few months piled in on me all at once and I felt as if I was going to implode. He held me and tried to comfort me, but I was beyond help. I had spent those long hours alone agonising over what I'd done and what I could do to put it right. When I was finally able to string a few words together, I told Grant that I couldn't take any more.

'What do you want to do?' he asked, more than a little fearfully.

My eyes red-rimmed, I took a deep breath. 'I can't believe I'm causing this much distress. I don't think I can go through with it and do this to Pete. It's too much.'

He stared at me, blinking, the colour draining from his face. We both knew that I was more or less telling him that it was over.

'I owe it to Pete to try again, Grant,' I went on. 'It was terrible watching him crumple like that. He doesn't deserve this. Please understand, I have to give him another chance.'

Grant studied his hands in silence for a moment. Then, pulling away from me slightly, his eyes glistening, he said: 'I'll give you three months. For three months we won't be in touch.'

I must have looked shocked at his suggestion. The thought of not seeing him or hearing from him for that length of time was almost more painful than the thought of hurting Pete. We had tried to break away from each other like this several times before, and we'd never managed to go longer than a few days without one of us picking up the phone.

Grant was thinking out loud for us both, reasoning it all out. 'You're not ready to jump,' he said, lifting my chin with his hands and staring into my puffy face. 'You need time to sort yourself out. We both do.' Put like that, it sounded so wise. I told him I thought he was right, and reluctantly agreed. Hugging me goodbye, he said he would be in touch in twelve weeks' time, in March 1998, and we'd see how we felt then. 'If we still feel the same, then we'll think again,' he said as he buried his face in my hair. Pushing me away for a moment and holding me firmly by the shoulders, he added: 'But if you feel by then that you might still be able to save your marriage to Pete, I'll walk away from you for ever, OK?'

He left the house and I watched him drive away in his Jaguar. Slumping on to the settee, I felt completely numb. There were no tears left to cry; my pain threshold had been reached and crossed. I lay in a semi-comatose state, my mind drifting from one agonising choice to the other. Should I stay with Pete and try again or make a clean break to be with the man I loved? Pete and I had no children to involve, and we both knew that our marriage was all but over. So what was the point in trying to rekindle a fire which had gone out long before? On the other hand, being with Grant had horrendous implications. He had three small children, an element of the equation that had never really entered our heads until we'd been foolish enough to fall in love.

Every option open to me was constantly overshadowed by the fact that, quite apart from all the private grief we would be causing, since I was one of the most famous women in the country, any decision I took would be subject to intense public scrutiny. I could almost predict the headlines as the newspapers jumped on me, the blonde television presenter with the 'brilliant' career and the 'perfect' marriage, and Grant, the unknown businessman who would be portrayed as a fortune-hunter and groupie. And yet the prospect of carrying on pretending that things were fine with Pete, of living my life without the man I loved, seemed unbearable, too. I would have given up all the money and the fame and the celebrity just to be able to run away with him and live happily ever after.

When the telephone rang an hour later, it was Grant. 'The three months doesn't start until tomorrow,' he said. There was a pause. 'I just wanted to make sure you were OK.'

I told him that I was, which was a lie, and signed off with: 'See you in March.' It seemed like for ever and a day.

On 30 December, Pete and I flew up to Edinburgh to prepare for the special New Year's Eve broadcast I was co-hosting with Phillip Schofield. It was a case of plastic smiles. The Carlton Television *Hogmanay Extravaganza* was to be a live ninety-minute broadcast from a specially built studio in Princes Street Gardens. It would feature stage acts, street entertainers and prerecorded messages from stars such as Elton John and Cilla Black. An estimated 10 million viewers were expected to tune in to watch me and Phillip sparkle.

Missing Grant, desperately trying to get on with Pete, preparing myself for the arrival of the gang of friends who were oblivious of our personal problems and were flying up to help us celebrate, I felt sick and tired of it all. Celebrate? I could barely put one foot in front of the other. This was a really big gig, and it would undoubtedly be one of the toughest nights of my life as I battled to keep my smile fixed and my eyes bright when inside I felt like howling. Needing to talk to someone, anyone, I had finally broken the news to my mum. As ever, hard as it must have been for her, she was very supportive. 'I knew things weren't right, Anthea,' she said, sadly. 'I knew something was missing. I'm so sorry it's turned out like this.'

I threw myself into my New Year's Eve gig in a big way. I had to – it was going to take 100 per cent concentration. Peter McHugh from *GMTV* had agreed to fly up from London to look after me, and there were loads of friends and 'family' around wishing me well.

Just half an hour before the show was due to go on air, I was sitting in front of the mirror in my caravan trying to psych myself up for the ordeal ahead. Peering at my reflection, I wondered what sort of self-destruct button I had pressed when I'd started up with Grant. What was the matter with me? I had it all, didn't I? The career, the husband, the wealth? I'd been incredibly lucky to get the breaks I had, and to have been given the opportunity to prove myself. Compared to most people's, my life was nothing short of idyllic. I had my health, I lived in a beautiful house with a man who adored me, and I'd never have to worry about money again. 'What more do you want?' I asked my reflection angrily.

My mobile telephone rang. I picked it up and pressed the answer button. 'Hello?'

'I can't stand it, Anth.' It was Grant, yelling to make himself heard above the hubbub in the West Sussex pub where he was seeing in the new year with Della and their friends. 'I know I'm not supposed to call, but I can't cope with not speaking to you. Not tonight. I miss you too much. This is killing me.'

My spirits soared. Much as I knew I shouldn't respond, and that only a week had passed since we'd vowed not to contact each other, I was elated. I think I'd always known that one of us would crack sooner or later, and the relief of hearing his voice engulfed me. The tears threatening to ruin my carefully applied make-up, I burst out: 'I'm so glad you called. I've been absolutely desperate. I've missed you more than words can say.'

We spoke for fifteen minutes or more and told each other how we truly felt. 'There has to be a way out of this,' he told me. 'I don't think I can give you up.' We both knew that by breaking our promises, we had effectively signed the death warrants of both our marriages. But by then it was already too late. Della and Pete must have known, in their heart of hearts, that their respective relationships had been dead in the water for some time. All that mattered now was finding a way to make it as painless as possible for everybody.

'I can't go on like this, Anth,' Grant said finally. 'I'm ready to jump.'

I held my breath. 'OK, then, jump,' I shouted.

There was silence.

Signing off, I said: 'Happy New Year.' I hoped he could still hear me. As the line went dead, I caught sight again of my face in the mirror. 'Whatever it may hold.'

Pete knew the moment I emerged from my caravan that night immaculately dressed and ready to face the cameras that something had happened. He said later that there was something about the way I walked, and the way my eyes were shining again, that gave me away. When he saw me hurrying into a corner to answer my mobile phone later that evening, he mistakenly assumed it was Grant calling – in fact it was my mum, to see how I was and to wish me a Happy New Year. But either way, the trust was gone. On the stroke of midnight, he deliberately slipped away into the crowds to avoid me.

The next call I took was the following morning as we were preparing to leave for London. I hadn't slept a wink all night and neither had Pete. Our performance at the party had been nothing short of Oscar-winning. No one would have suspected a thing. Later we'd shared the same bed, lying just a few inches apart, and yet we might as well have been on opposite sides of the world. In the morning I lay very still under the crisp cotton sheets as I felt Pete get up and listened to him shower and dress. I could breathe easily only when I heard him say that he was going down to settle the bill and I knew that in a few seconds I would be alone. But with disastrous timing, my telephone rang just at that moment. I jumped out of bed and grabbed it from the dressing table before Pete could pick it up. It was Grant.

'I've told Della,' he said.

I heard a sharp intake of breath and realised it was mine.

'I couldn't hide the truth from her any longer, not after last night,' he explained, struggling with his words. Then, quietly, he added: 'She's gone off in the car. She's absolutely distraught.' It was obvious that Grant was in tears and he was unable to say any more.

I knew from recent bitter experience how agonising it was to see the person with whom you have shared your life crumple at the news that you have inadvertently fallen in love with someone else. The memory of Pete's face that ghastly night a week before would haunt me for ever. The taste of my own guilt in the back of my throat, I offered Grant what crumbs of comfort I could and made him promise to keep in touch. Then I rang off and hurried to the window to study the scene below in the vain hope of blocking out the world.

So it was that at 9am on New Year's Day 1998, I found myself staring down on the near-deserted streets of Edinburgh as the last of the all-night revellers meandered blearily home, my eyes glistening as I tightened my grip around my phone, my ears still ringing from the news I'd just received. I hoped for a few minutes to compose myself before I had to face Pete, who had been standing the other side of the bedroom when I'd taken the call.

Suddenly I was aware of his presence by my side. He'd listened to my responses and he knew what it all meant. Forcing himself to put one foot in front of another, he had come over to where I was standing alone at the window, lost in thought. He was silent for a moment as his gaze followed mine to the street below. After several seconds, he said simply: 'It's over, isn't it?' His voice caught as he spoke.

I blinked hard and stared down ever more intently. 'Yes, Pete, it is,'

I said as softly as I could, not moving an inch. We both knew only too well that we were referring not only to the end of our eight-year marriage but to the end of the line for me as the 'golden girl' of British television. The charade was over. From now on, life would never be the same again. Anthea Turner, the squeaky-clean girl next door, had grown up with a vengeance. The disastrous mistakes I had made in my personal life were about to become common currency. It was the end of an era.

I turned to face Pete at last. I could hardly bear to look at his pained expression as he struggled to control his emotions. Right before my very eyes, Peter Powell, that sweetest and gentlest of men, was having his heart broken.

'Grant's told Della,' I said, my voice tremulous. 'I don't know what to do.'

'Does she know it's you?' Pete asked, evidently concerned for my public reputation as well as my private feelings.

I nodded.

With the courage and stoicism so typical of him from that day to this, he attempted a smile and shrugged his shoulders as nonchalantly as he could. In the few seconds since I had given him the news he dreaded most, he had mentally donned his manager's hat, setting aside his own feelings to help me through what he knew would become a trial by media. It could only be a matter of time before Della or one of her friends spilled the beans to the newspapers, and then the feeding frenzy would begin.

'Right then, AT,' he said, 'in that case, let's sort this out.'

Standing before me now was not Pete my husband and partner, the man I loved more than almost any other in the world and with whom I'd always thought I'd spend the rest of my life, but Peter Powell, my agent and manager, my best friend and closest confidant; the one person who would guide me through the next few terrible months and do his very best to protect me from harm. I knew I didn't deserve such loyalty.

Bewildered and confused, I flew back with Pete that afternoon to Heathrow and we drove home. Ormonde House, once my pride

and joy, now seemed like some sort of vast monument to material-
ism, an ostentatious symbol of how much we'd achieved on the
surface and how little we had progressed as human beings. Waiting
for us outside the ornate electronically operated wrought-iron gates
was Russ, his expression grim.

'Come on in, mate,' Peter said, grateful to see his best friend and
partner at such a critical time. He patted Russ warmly on the shoulder, but bowed his head quickly so that Russ couldn't see his eyes.

Safely locked away inside the house with the pair of them, I listened to them drawing up a plan of action with military precision
and suddenly felt very frightened. In the four months I'd been seeing
Grant, I don't honestly think that I had fully appreciated just how
serious an effect the affair could have on my career. I knew I was on
low moral ground, but foolishly I had believed that it would all blow
over and no one would ever know. Up until that moment it had all
felt so private and personal. In my naïveté, I had assumed it was my
business and nobody else's. But I was wrong. Very wrong.

I had one of the best-recognised faces in British public life. I'd
been seen as a role model for the women of the nineties for my
'scandal-free' existence. I even had a sweet pea named after me, for
goodness' sake. Now I'd stuck my head well and truly above the
parapet and Pete knew that I was about to be fired upon big-time.
He needed to get me to a safe place as quickly as possible; to warn my
parents and friends what was about to happen and to organise a
speedy damage-limitation exercise.

'We could only have hours, not days,' Russ warned. 'The press
pack could be on their way now for all we know.' The three of us
glanced nervously at the doors and windows. We all jumped when
the intercom buzzer at the gate sounded. Had it already begun? But
it was Mark Stephens, our solicitor, who, summoned by Pete, had
arrived breathlessly from east London to help draw up a press release
to tell the world all it needed to know without offending anyone
legally. Neither he nor Russ seemed able to look me in the eye for
very long.

I made everyone coffee and leaned against the Aga in our limed-
oak kitchen, cradling my mug. I felt as if I were on a runaway train,

hurtling towards certain doom. I had now set off an unstoppable chain reaction. I was in danger of losing my links with everything – my husband, home, friends and family, my management company and even my future in showbusiness. At the very peak of my career, I was giving up everything, and for what? For love?

Love. At the very thought of the word, an image of Grant flickered across my mind and I exhaled. The depth of passion I felt for him still overwhelmed me. The thought of being with him permanently, seeing him openly without subterfuge, warmed me. If I had my time all over again, I knew I wouldn't have done a thing differently. I loved Grant more than anything in the world, even more than my career. The whole thing was out of my hands. I had never even had a choice.

I was jolted from my reverie by my mobile phone. It was Grant again. He was, by now, beside himself. Della had come back and he had left the house. 'It was terrible, Anth,' he said. 'She went berserk. She's so upset.' He was heading for the Conrad Hotel in Chelsea Harbour in his Jaguar and he needed to see me urgently. Sheepishly, I relayed this information to Pete.

'You must go,' Pete said, standing suddenly to reinforce his suggestion. 'He'll be in a terrible state.' The three of us studied him in silent admiration for his largesse and compassion, not only for me, his wife, but also for Grant, his former friend and colleague. I hesitated for a few seconds and stared across at him uncertainly. But before I could say anything, he added softly, 'Well, go on then, AT. There's not much time.'

I jumped into my beloved green MG and sped across London, feeling sick to the stomach. I found Grant white-faced and shaking in his hotel bedroom, his head in his hands. He was aghast at what he had done. He, too, had a lot to lose, chiefly access to his three beloved children, Olivia, then five, Amelia, four, and Claudia, one. And on top of all that he was about to enter the glare of the media spotlight in a way which no one could ever have foreseen.

I ran to him and held him and did all I could to reassure him, although I felt in just as much need of reassurance myself. I'd never seen him so upset. He'd cried all the way from Sussex to London and had nearly driven off the road. All he kept saying, over and over again, was, 'What have we done? I might never see the children again.'

There was a knock on the door. Grant dried his eyes and tried to compose himself. It was Russ and Mark, who had come over on Pete's instruction to show Grant their draft press release. There followed half an hour of professional briskness and a general agreement on the wording. The statement was to be faxed to the Press Association the following evening at five o'clock, which would give the papers the shortest possible time to follow up the story that day.

The statement read: 'Anthea Turner is sad to make the painful announcement that she has separated from her husband, Peter Powell. The pressures of work and celebrity contributed to the breakdown and she bitterly regrets any hurt caused.' It went on to announce that Grant and Della had also separated and continued with statements from all of us (apart from Della) expressing our sadness. Of Pete and myself, I said: 'We began as lovers and somewhere along the way work became our abiding passion. The breakdown of a warm and loving marriage is too high a price to pay for apparent success. What has happened between Grant and me was born out of circumstances and our emotional response to it has been beyond the control of either of us.'

Pete's contribution confirmed that he was 'deeply saddened' by what had happened, but added: 'I want Anthea to have a happy and fulfilling life and in these circumstances I have to recognise that I must let her go. My thoughts are with Della and the children.'

Grant's read: 'The breakdown of my marriage has brought great sadness to my family. I am no different to any father. I love my children deeply and am most concerned that in these circumstances they are both settled and supported.'

The statement finalised, Russ and Mark stood up to leave, evidently relieved that the meeting was over. Picking up my coat and handbag, I made for the door as well, as if on automatic pilot. 'Bye,' I called out to Grant as I followed Mark and Russ, my eyes wide with fear. 'We'll talk on the phone, all the time, OK?'

Grant looked up, puzzled. 'Where on earth are you going?' he asked, a frown creasing his forehead.

'Home,' I said, as if that were the most natural place for me to be. It simply hadn't sunk in that my life had changed irrevocably and that 'home' as I had previously understood it no longer existed.

Seeing the look of abject horror on Grant's face, Russ and Mark beat a hasty retreat and left us alone. 'Home?' Grant said, standing suddenly. '*Home?* To Pete?'

'Well, er, yes,' I said. I thought that was the right thing to do. I had nothing with me but the clothes I was standing up in; the press release wasn't going out until the next day and I knew that Pete needed me, too. But Grant's eyes were blazing. 'Anthea,' he said, in a tone I'd never heard before. 'I've just left my wife and three children for you, I've just walked away from my whole life, and you're going *home to your husband*?'

Put like that, it sounded ridiculous, and I knew that he was right. He needed me more than anyone just now and I had to stay with him. Catching up with Russ in the corridor outside, I told him that I would be staying the night with Grant in the hotel. 'I mean, the world and his wife will know all about us tomorrow, so we might as well have tonight,' I explained. Russ nodded, and went back to Ormonde House to comfort and counsel his best friend.

Grant and I spent that last night of privacy talking and crying. We clung to each other like victims of a shipwreck, fearing the daybreak that would herald a new era. Neither of us knew when we would be able to see each other again, or what the next few days, weeks and months would hold. All we could be certain of was that it was not going to be a very happy start to the new year for any of us.

The next morning, I left Grant sitting on the edge of the bed in abject despair and went back to Twickenham to see Pete and gather together a few belongings. Pete looked terrible; he clearly hadn't slept, either, and his manner was on the verge of being brusque. 'Pack everything,' he called after me as I climbed the stairs wearily. 'You won't be coming back here for a while.'

I emptied my wardrobe and threw everything I needed into my largest suitcase, the one I'd packed a hundred times in years gone by. Stopping for a moment, I sank on to the bed and stared up at the ceiling, wishing for the umpteenth time that things had been different; that I could have resisted temptation and addressed my marriage problems sooner. 'I should have been a better person,' I told myself angrily. I was so accustomed to feeling guilty, to that sense of near-suffocation from the burden of it, that I'd forgotten what it was to live without it.

Pete and Russ had arranged for me to go into hiding at the Chiswick home of Paul Worsley and his girlfriend at the time, Philippa Forrester, the *Tomorrow's World* presenter. But later that night they decided it would be better if I left London altogether. So Pete went to Paul's instead and I drove to the Berkshire home of Phillip and Stephanie Schofield. I sat up talking to them that night, desperately trying to justify my actions. 'I had to follow my heart,' I told them both, downing endless cups of herbal tea and spurning all offers of food. 'I couldn't pretend any more.'

I rang my parents at their bungalow in Norton, afraid that they'd be deluged by reporters. 'Don't worry, Anthea,' Mum told me firmly. 'We've got three noisy dogs and nothing to say. Let them come.' They were clearly hurt and saddened but, as always, they offered me their unconditional love and support. 'Be brave, Lil,' Dad said. 'Mummy and I will be rooting for you.'

Grant was alone in his hotel, Pete was with Paul and Philippa and Russ was at his south London home with Caron, all of them bracing themselves for the onslaught. Around the country that night, in Sussex, Berkshire, London and Staffordshire, none of us slept. The press release had been delivered, and we all dreaded its repercussions in our own separate ways, but I don't think any of us could have anticipated how truly awful they would be.

The news had broken nationwide that night, 2 January, a few hours after James Grant issued the press release. I soon became a fugitive, hiding in friends' houses, fleeing from pursuing cars and besieged by reporters wherever I went. We'd expected a great deal of media interest, but the enormity of the coverage astounded us. Just about every television, radio and print journalist had something to say about the end of my marriage. We seemed to feature in everything from the *Staffordshire Sentinel* to the ITN news. Even the broadsheets reported the event on their front pages. As for some of the tabloids, they lost all reason and self-control. It was as if we were members of the royal family or something. Banner headlines screamed the news; billboards outside newsagents announced it and picture-researchers across the country unearthed every photograph ever taken of me, Pete, Grant and Della.

Mum and Dad were inundated, but the reporters arriving in Norton in their droves received very short shrift. My parents' bungalow is well off the road at the end of a long private drive. As if addressing naughty pupils, my mother scolded all comers for bothering them. 'Kindly go away,' she'd say before letting the dogs out. Nonetheless the press tried every trick in the book to make Mum and Dad say something. They often work on the theory that if they leave a long gap in a conversation the naïve punter, discomfited by the silence, will be tempted to fill it. But my parents stood their ground and remained resolutely silent. The reporters gave up in the end, having described my father as looking 'shocked and pale', which made us all laugh because Dad is the healthiest, ruddiest-looking man you could hope to meet.

Della fled to Derby with the children for a short time and Grant moved from hotel to hotel as he, too, was pursued. As well as being astonishingly intense, the media interest was far more prolonged than any of us had imagined it would be. Eventually there came a point when we all had to try to return to some level of normality. Pete and I needed to work out how we were going to organise the logistics of our lives for the foreseeable future. Somehow, in the middle of the mayhem, we managed to snatch a quiet twenty-four hours together at Phillip's house for what became an emotionally charged meeting. It was the first time I'd seen Pete in a week. It was an incredibly painful discussion for us both, though it was made much easier by the fact that we were in someone else's home and not our own, with all its memories.

'Do you still want to continue managing me, Pete?' I asked, afraid of his answer.

'Of course, AT,' he replied tersely. 'That never entered the equation. Besides, there's a lot of work to do and no one is better qualified than me to know what's best for you.' He also made it clear that there was no question of us not remaining on good terms. 'Whatever happens, however this ends, we'll always stay friends,' he added firmly.

I had a lot of film commitments and other engagements that I couldn't and wouldn't break. I was due to leave the country shortly for the Caribbean and South Africa with *Wish You Were Here*, and I had a Littlewoods shoot planned in Florida. While I was away, Peter would arrange everything. He would use Ormonde House when I wasn't there and sort out all the business matters. In the clinical way in which we had come to conduct the latter years of our marriage, we came to an amicable agreement about property and finances. I would buy him out of his share of our home, and we would divide our goods and chattels equally. We had the documents drawn up, signed and ratified without fuss: our legal bill came to a modest £127.50.

My schedule became my saving grace. I didn't miss a single appointment, despite the turmoil in my personal life. I had a meeting about *The Big Ticket*, a new National Lottery programme, in the middle of all of this, and the BBC backed me all the way. When asked by the press if he was going to fire me, Michael Leggo replied that if he were to sack one of his staff on moral grounds, he'd have very few people left working for him. I devoted my energy to work, the one thing I could rely on. I was going to be out of the country for three weeks of January, but in the meantime my every movement was closely followed by the tabloids.

Calling on the advice of friends I'd made in the industry, I learned a few tricks of the trade. 'Wear the same clothes each time you go out, something very plain,' a friendly photographer told me. 'It means that when they snap you, they'll end up with an unremarkable picture no different from the last one. If they keep getting boring shots, the picture desks will soon tire of you.' So I chose a black skirt, black jumper and jacket and left my hair loose and simple. Sure enough, for a couple of days I was photographed again and again in the same clothes, but after that the pictures stopped appearing in the papers.

In preparation for my next batch of foreign trips, I needed to go back to Ormonde House and retrieve some clothes I'd left behind in my earlier haste. 'Go in at four in the morning,' another friend advised. 'The "monkeys" will all be asleep and no one will spot you.' So it was that I found myself creeping into my own home at some ridiculous hour while the waiting photographers snoozed outside in their cars. None of them saw me sneak in, collect my clothes and some clean pairs of knickers and steal out again.

Hard as it was to leave Grant and Pete and my family to the furore, it felt good to get away, and to be surrounded by people I knew and loved. The crews I worked with were friends and more than kind. They knew what I was going through and they helped me to keep going. By removing myself from the most intense scrutiny, I was able to pause to draw breath and to try to banish the sense of surrealism that had taken control of my life. Even so, if anyone looks closely at the photographs from that particular Littlewoods shoot or those travel films, there's definitely something about my smile which isn't quite right.

Pete divided his time between his family in Stourbridge and Ormonde House until I got back. He was scared stiff of the potential repercussions of the affair on my career and did all he could to rally support from our friends, relatives and colleagues. 'AT's the one that needs our love right now,' he told them all, including his mum and my parents. 'Whatever's happened between us, she's the one suffering the most.' He didn't want anyone to think badly of me and was deeply protective of my character. The only thing that mattered to him was my welfare. It was two months down the line before he really clicked back into handling me professionally again. He knew that our friendship was more precious to us than our love by that stage. It was all that was left and he was determined that this, at least, should remain intact.

I spoke to Grant on the telephone every day, but we couldn't see each other for weeks because of my punishing schedule. He moved into the Badger's pub in West Sussex until mid-February. The little hotel switchboard had never had to deal with so many international calls. Thank God for Vodafone. Grant also spent a lot of time at his marital home, fending off reporters and trying to protect his and Della's children from the ever-present cameras. He became obsessed

about his privacy and suspicious of everyone who worked with him
or had any dealings with him, for fear they might shop him to the
press. 'No bastard's going to stitch me up again,' he'd tell me on the
telephone, angry that one of his wedding guests had sold the *News of
the World* photographs of his wedding to Della, including one blown-
up shot of me innocently kissing him on the cheek in the official
line-up. And someone else, one of the guests at the charity football
match and dinner where Grant and I had first been attracted to each
other, had sold a copy of the corporate video of that event, in which,
again, Grant and I could be seen fleetingly in the same shot.

Whenever we could be together everything that happened seemed
to have been for a purpose and we only ever talked of a long-term
future together. We were both equally determined to make it. 'We're
going through all this for a reason,' I kept reminding him. 'One day
we'll be able to look back on all this madness and see it in its true perspective.' But alone in our hotel rooms night after night on opposite
sides of the globe, we often had secret doubts. It was awful being so
far away and feeling so miserable. The Caribbean trip was particularly poignant for me because it included a bittersweet return to the
island of Grenada, my first visit there since my honeymoon with
Pete, and on the very date of my eighth wedding anniversary. Sitting
on the beach, my sunglasses hiding my eyes, I couldn't help but
recall that idyllic time and wish things could have worked out differently. 'Let's come back here for our tenth wedding anniversary,'
Pete had said. We'd nearly made it. Eight years had passed, most of
them happy. But my solo return to the place that had meant so
much to us was sometimes more than I could bear.

To make matters worse, a photographer and reporter from one of
the national newspapers followed me out to Grenada to try to catch
me off guard. I was furious at first – it felt like a terrible violation at
that dreadful time – but I ended up actually feeling sorry for them.
I don't suppose either of them wanted to be on this particular job.
They'd been sent out by their editor at great expense and felt duty-
bound to go back with something. I didn't speak to the reporter
about anything much at all, so she went back empty-handed and
wrote a piece she could have just as easily written from her desk in

London. The photographer had to be satisfied with a picture of me sitting on the side of a boat looking wistfully out to sea.

On my return, Grant and I were able to manage the odd night together, but ironically, considering the affair was now public knowledge, only by using increasingly bizarre subterfuge. We met at Helen Parker's house in Twickenham or took refuge in the home of another friend, Terry Shand, who has a large estate in West Sussex. We'd arrive on the doorstep like a couple of waifs seeking sanctuary. The press were always hot on our heels but they couldn't get near us. They'd get as far as the electric gates of Phillip Schofield's house or Terry's estate and there they had to stay. We could write a blueprint for other couples in the same situation on how to sneak a person past waiting cameras. We became reluctant experts on which makes of car had boots suited to concealing someone, what sort of clothes to wear and how to behave. The photographers would be lined up, waiting for me to run their gauntlet, and I would drive past at speed with Grant curled up under a coat in the footwell of my MG. I don't think they thought a man of five feet ten inches could possibly fold himself into such a small space. It felt all wrong, though, so different from how we'd hoped and imagined things would be one day.

Poor Della didn't know what had hit her. She'd never had any reason to be on the sharp end of the media before and it terrified her at first. Her life had been completely turned upside down. Not only had she discovered that her husband was having an affair, she'd had a hundred camera lenses pointed at her, at her home and at her children, day in, day out, as she dropped the kids off at school, went to the supermarket, picked the kids up again. Each photographer wanted the definitive shot of her breaking down or looking gaunt or generally awful so that they could rub all our noses in it even more. I wouldn't have wished that on my worst enemy, and Della had certainly never done anything to deserve such treatment.

But everything changed with the arrival on the scene of Kerry Ross, the flamboyant wife of television presenter Paul, who thrust herself into Della's life. Kerry ran a nursery in Petworth, West Sussex, attended by Grant and Della's children. The two women had not previously been close friends but now Kerry, painfully aware of the pitfalls of marriage (since her husband Paul had a well-publicised affair) became Della's personal adviser.

With Kerry's encouragement, Della was transformed from victim to challenger, embarking on various ploys to attract media coverage in the hope of winning Grant back. She lost weight, had a complete make-over and posed for *Hello!* magazine, none of which actions she would even have countenanced without such outside advice. Kerry cleverly managed to get herself into a lot of photographs and newspaper articles as well. Grant hardly recognised the shy dental nurse he had married. He suspected that none of this was of Della's own making. Being famous for being famous is a road littered with casualties. If she took that path, I knew that her life would never be the same again, but sadly, I was hardly in a position to warn Della of the consequences.

Predictably, Della's orchestrated arrival on the stage played straight into the media's hands, filling the gap that Grant and I had consistently refused to fill. Just when we were hoping all the fuss was dying down, the feeding frenzy suddenly intensified again. The press know a good story when they see one, and the prospect of a spurned wife campaigning to get her husband back by transforming herself into a media icon was simply too good to ignore. An entire rainforest must have been destroyed to produce the column inches now focusing on us all. As for Kerry once she'd had her fun, she was able to take a back seat, leaving Della alone and exposed and the rest of us reeling from the aftershock.

Not surprisingly, Pete in particular found the media intrusion unbearable. It sickened him to open a paper each morning and read about the latest episode in the living soap opera that featured his wife, his former friend and his friend's estranged wife. 'This is personal,' he'd complain. 'This is about the break-up of my marriage. Can't they see how painful this is?' He stopped buying the newspapers there and then and has never bought one since.

February kept me away from much of the worst of it. I went on safari in Tanzania, to the spice island of Zanzibar and to the Caribbean islands of St Kitts and Nevis. I was away for nearly three weeks. The trips were amazing – fantastic scenery, extraordinary wildlife, a feast for the eyes wherever you looked. But my eyes were permanently red-rimmed and my heart was constantly heavy. Nothing I saw lifted my spirits. I wanted to run home a hundred times. I couldn't bear the idea of being so far removed from everything and everyone I loved. Grant needed me; I needed to see him, Pete, my parents and Wendy to make sure that they were all OK.

But I had too many commitments, as Pete was at pains to point out. 'You're going to fulfil every contractual obligation you've ever made,' he told me, 'and, what's more, you're going to do it with a smile.' Listening to the silence at my end of the line as the echo of his own voice trailed away, he added softly: 'Besides, you really don't want to be here right now. It'd only make matters worse.'

Only in St Kitts was I able to smile, briefly, when Grant Fed-Exed me a Valentine's card, present and letter, making his intention to spend the rest of his life with me very clear. 'Dear Anthea,' he wrote. 'The last few months have changed me beyond measure. I never understood how the feelings I have for you were possible, until now. My commitment to you is total. I will love you for ever. Grant.'

On my return I made a decision. 'We can't keep hiding like this,' I told Grant on our first night together in a month. 'It's not right. Let's face the music and get it over with. I want you to move in with me.' Happy to be able to leave his hotel at last, he packed his suitcase and came to Ormonde House. A few nights later, a photographer snapped us having a quiet meal together at a local restaurant. I wasn't prepared for it and was more than a little taken aback when the flashgun started popping, but I knew of old that the only thing to do was to smile and wait for it to end. So, gritting our teeth, that's exactly what we did.

Of course that photograph was plastered all over the papers the next day, which did little to help matters. The last thing I wanted was to flaunt our togetherness under the noses of Della and Pete, and I'm sure that picture must have really hurt them both. But Pete put me straight. 'The sooner you get over all this nonsense and back to normal coverage the better,' he said. 'And the only way that'll happen is if the press see you and Grant together openly and regularly.' Once again, I could only marvel at his sense of fair play.

On the night of 28 February, two days before I was due to fly off
to Queensland, Australia for two weeks, Grant and I decided that the
time had come to make our first formal public appearance together.
The venue was to be the *Lord of the Dance* party at the Wembley
Arena, held in honour of the dancer Michael Flatley and arranged by
my old friend Helen Parker. 'There'll be dozens of celebrities there,'
Helen assured me, 'I'm sure you and Grant won't attract that much
attention.' So off we went to the party, in some trepidation. I chose
my outfit carefully – a tight-fitting Ozbeke leopard-print trouser
suit which I hoped gave the message Pete was suggesting: that I was
being up-front about Grant and me, and was happy to be seen at his
side.

We watched the show first, which was fantastic. I love dancing,
and I'm a big Michael Flatley fan. My feet tapping in time to the
music, I almost forgot about the ordeal ahead. It felt like a normal
night out with friends. The party was to be held in the conference
centre at the stadium nearby. Unfortunately, Helen's belief that we
would be relatively unnoticed among so many other famous people –
Bob Geldof, Simon and Yasmin Le Bon, Pauline Quirke, Phil
Collins – proved sadly misplaced. As we stepped into the lobby, side
by side, we were met by a wall of press photographers. The flashlights
blinded us. I don't think Grant realised what was going on. He wandered ahead without me as the photographers all called out his name.
'Grant! Grant!' they yelled. 'Go and stand with Anthea.' Looking like
a rabbit caught in the headlights, he turned towards me in sheer
panic, unsure of what to do. Holding out my hand to him, I invited
him to come back and face the barrage with me. You could feel the
heat from those flashbulbs. It was like Oscars night and Princess
Di's first appearance after her divorce all rolled into one. We were
both so dazzled that we couldn't see properly for several minutes
afterwards.

Even inside the flashbulbs popped every time we came within a
few feet of each other. At first I wanted to run, but the performer in
me made me stop and smile every time. Grant clung to my side,
afraid to stray too far in case he was ambushed on his own. That
night was the first time he really began to understand what being

famous could be like. He also realised that his own life would never be the same again.

Michael Flatley was incredibly sweet. He didn't seem to mind at all that we were stealing so much of his limelight. He gave me a cuddle, posed for photographs with me, and said under his breath, 'Don't let the bastards grind you down.' I was with Michael on one side of the room, posing for some official snaps that Helen's photographer was taking, when Grant came hurrying over. 'Do you want the good news or the bad news?' he said.

My heart missed a beat. 'The bad,' I said, thinking, 'What now?'

'Della's here,' Grant told me, and his expression as he spoke her name was one of physical pain.

'What?' I asked, aghast, unable to believe what he was telling me. Grant had, I knew, told Della where we'd be in case she needed to get hold of him, but I'd never dreamed for one moment she'd turn up.

Without a moment's hesitation, Grant and Helen announced simultaneously: 'You're leaving,' and started to bundle me towards the door. I was in complete agreement because I knew it would be a media frenzy, which I suspected was exactly what Kerry wanted.

'I'll get your coat,' said Grant, 'Let's go now.' We slipped away before anyone noticed. I never even set eyes on Della; in fact I wouldn't have known she was there unless Grant had told me. Quite apart from the fact that I'm short-sighted and hadn't worn my contact lenses because of the smoky atmosphere, the party was crowded and I'd been busy posing with Michael. It was about 11.30pm when we left Della to the dancefloor and the photographers and the bubbly. Grant and I had to be up early the next morning anyway for a charity event, so we drove home, opened our own bottle of champagne and ate beans on toast.

The following day, the papers went wild. The headlines included: 'Revenge of Anthea Love Rival', 'Della v. Anthea', and 'Wronged Wife's PR Fightback Leaves Her Star Rival Rattled'. Della, they reported, had danced the night away to Gloria Gaynor's 'I Will Survive'. They have used the photograph of Della beaming out at them in that red dress, champagne flute in hand, ever since. According to numerous articles Della and Kerry had decided to 'play us at our own game', and indeed they went on to make as much mileage as they could out of the situation.

I soon stopped clipping out newspaper stories for my scrapbook. They were far too painful. Della was receiving widespread support for 'fighting back' against me and, hats off to her, she certainly wasn't giving up easily. I can't help but admire her for that, although I know that she was pushed into much of it. What she and Kerry didn't quite realise was that this was never intended to be a game. Della, Grant, Pete and I were all caught up in the middle of an extremely distressing situation. It certainly wasn't something we had done for publicity. Where was the benefit of attracting even more media attention, especially on to Grant and Della's children? I know people might think that this is just sour grapes – that I would have much preferred Della to stay locked up at home while I swanned around town with her husband – but it was never like that. I had become famous as a byproduct of my job, not just because I was once married to a person who went out with somebody famous. She was damaging herself as much as us, and I genuinely felt for her.

What Della didn't realise was that you slam up against a brick wall when you get out there in the real media world. I'd learned that the hard way. Della had entered the ring without knowing the rules. When she was doing the *Hello!* piece, I told Grant: 'You've got to try to stop her. They'll make mincemeat of her.' I knew she'd come to regret it. She started to play the fame game and then found it too difficult to continue with. Fame is a double-edged sword, and to this day journalists arrive at her house, doorstepping her and phoning her up almost every time Grant and I make the headlines. It is an invasion of privacy I feel sure she would never have believed possible.

The same was true of Grant, who found his portrayal in the media deeply upsetting. The shame of what he'd done was already burned into his conscience for ever, as was mine, but to see himself depicted as the villain of the piece almost daily in the press was incredibly hurtful. 'Everyone hates me,' he'd moan. 'Nobody understands. They don't know what it was like; how we tried to break away.' If I'd been a secretary or a hairdresser, the breakdown of our respective marriages would never have come into the public domain and no one would ever have heard of Grant or Della Bovey. As it was, he was tormented by the fear of what all this publicity was doing to his children. He couldn't sleep, eat or relax. He adored his three girls and knew that, although he wouldn't have been doing them any favours by staying in an unhappy marriage, he'd still let them down very badly. I was becoming increasingly unnerved by his inconsolable sadness. The Della-and-Kerry publicity machine didn't help. By now it had gone into full swing, and the pressure was definitely getting to him. He was torn and I could feel his spirit ebbing away. It was something I couldn't fight, especially when I was still away filming so much trying to juggle this with all the other aspects of my life.

Stepping on to that plane to Australia was one of the hardest things I have ever done. I didn't want to go; I so wanted to stay with Grant, to help him fight his demons, but Pete had made my responsibilities perfectly clear. Nevertheless, the idea of leaving Grant alone in Ormonde House, a place in which, understandably, he felt uncomfortable, while I disappeared to the other side of the world for two weeks was unbearable. In these circumstances, Australia represented the lowest point of the entire debacle for me. The antics of Kerry Ross and Della at home were destabilising me, I was missing Grant and I felt very vulnerable being such a long way away. I suffered my worst-ever bout of homesickness there, and even now I can hardly look at that *Wish You Were Here* film without that same sick feeling creeping back. To cap it all, I was getting hate mail – long-winded, vitriolic letters in scrawly handwriting which accused me of being a home-breaker and a bitch. One woman, who has been writing to me ever since, repeatedly expresses the wish that any children I might one day bear be deformed. Fortunately, there were some lovely letters in my mailbag too: cards and notes from people who'd been in the same position and who offered me the benefit of their considerable experience.

Even when I returned from Australia, there was little time to spend with Grant. I had all sorts of filming commitments and charity gigs that I knew I couldn't miss. I'd also been signed up to co-host the new *National Lottery Big Ticket* programme with Patrick Kielty to promote the controversial new £2 scratchcards, which were widely criticised as encouraging gambling. And from that spring I'd be back on the *Lottery Live* programme for a while, under the deal Pete had negotiated long before all this had blown up. My days were spent in rehearsal, in between dubbing the soundtrack for the *Wish You Were Here* programmes. There was barely time to think or eat, let alone spend quality time with the man for whom I'd risked everything.

It was at this crucial time that Grant was summoned to the convent school his two elder daughters attended to be told by the staff that the break-up was affecting them. It was the realisation of Grant's worst fears. Della was away skiing in Switzerland with Kerry Ross and their children on a trip that was being covered by *Hello!* magazine. She had left Claudia, who was too young to go skiing, with the nanny. On the Saturday, the nanny's night off, Grant went to his old home to babysit. It was the first time he'd been back to Catercross since Della had kicked him out. Curled up with Claudia that night, he finally cracked.

I knew things weren't right. I'd had a churning feeling in my stomach for days, and I could almost smell Grant's fear. The physical effect it had on me was frightening. It only takes a couple of sleepless nights or the loss of a few pounds to make me look gaunt and hollow-eyed. For the launch of *The Big Ticket*, I'd worn a beautiful tailored Gucci trouser suit and smiled for the cameras, but the headlines the next day had nothing at all to do with the show and everything to do with how I looked. 'Anthinner Turner' screamed the *Sun*. 'Star's Shock Weight Loss,' its strapline ran, above a story about how 'worrying frail' I had become. Was it any wonder? It was like living in a goldfish bowl.

And yet I still had to perform in front of the cameras almost daily, turning on the Anthea smile for millions of viewers, no doubt including some who were rubbing their hands together in glee, waiting for me to break. Like them, I knew it was only a matter of time. For some extra moral support, the night Grant went to stay back at Catercross, I invited my old friend Jonathan Morris to join me as a guest on the third *Big Ticket* show. He took one look at me, shook his head and said: 'Look at those eyes! What has been going on?'

When I told him that Grant was away for the night, he offered to take me out on the town with some friends to try to cheer me up. 'Come on, what you need is a good bop,' he said. He took me to dinner and on to a nightclub to Soho, and we danced until I was ready to drop. Afterwards he brought me home. We sat up talking so late that he ended up staying overnight in the spare bedroom.

The next morning, Grant came back from Sussex early while Jonathan was still there. The two of them had never met, so they chatted over coffee before Jonathan made his excuses and left. As soon as he'd gone, I turned to face Grant. 'What's the matter?' I asked him, clenching my fists to stop my hands from trembling. He looked awful.

'Sit down, Anthea,' he said. 'I need to talk to you.' He started to speak of the children, about how much he missed them and how much he feared he was damaging them. He said things weren't working between us because of the way he was feeling and that he couldn't give me what I needed. 'This isn't an overnight decision,' he said. My mind was racing ahead of him. 'I've been thinking about it for a couple of weeks and it's simply no good us carrying on like this, because I'm falling apart. It's not good for either of us and you don't want me like this. I'm going to have to go back, for the sake of the kids.'

Biting on my hand to stop myself from screaming, I stared at him in utter disbelief. I knew he was unhappy. I knew how badly he missed his children, but I thought that was something that we could overcome together. I'd never believed he would walk out on me, not after all we'd been through. I started crying and I didn't stop for twenty-four hours. Grant was nearly as bad as me. We talked long and hard for nearly four hours and he kept assuring me I'd be fine. 'You'll soon find someone else and you'll be all right,' he kept repeating, as if that would solve all my problems.

'I don't want anyone else, Grant,' I wept. 'I've only ever wanted you.'

When it became clear that we were getting nowhere, he stood up and told me that his mind was made up. 'I'm going, Anthea. I have to. And I'm not coming back. I have to try to salvage what's left of my family. I've realised that I have a bigger responsibility to them right now. Please try to understand.'

I was crushed with grief as I watched him pack. I tried to warn him what the outcome would be, that he couldn't live his life for the sake of his children, that he'd only end up hurting them more. 'What do you think you can achieve by going back now?' I asked him 'You're only going to destroy Della, and the children, too.'

Although Grant was almost as upset as I was, strangely, he seemed relieved, too, that he had finally made the decision that had been tearing him apart for weeks. He had rationalised it all in his mind. 'Della and the kids will be better off with me at home, you'll be better off without me, career-wise, and I'll be better off if the children are happy.' It was like a mantra he'd clearly been repeating to himself for some time. He kept saying over and over again: 'I love you, Anthea. This isn't because I don't love you. But there are times when I have to put my children before you, and this is one of them.'

It was Sunday 5 April 1998. As I watched him go, I knew that his body was going back, but not his heart.

News at Ten made Grant's return to the marital home the top news item in the second half of their programme the following night, over and above a major breakthrough in the Northern Ireland peace negotiations. The next morning, the newspapers were full of it, too. Smiling and holding up a glass of champagne at a ski resort in Switzerland, Della appeared on the front page of the *Sun* under the banner headline: 'I've Won a Grant from the Lottery'. Other head-lines included 'Anthea Loses the Lott', and 'Anthea Lover Home to Wife'. The *Sun* ran a spoof 'Deirdre's Photo Casebook' of the affair, with sarcastic cartoon bubbles coming out of each of the key play-ers' mouths. All of which served only to plunge me into deeper despair.

The next few days, weeks and months were nothing short of hor-rific. Second only to Ruth's death, it was undoubtedly the worst time of my whole life. I felt as if I was in a living nightmare. My entire world had collapsed around me. I was beyond being heartbroken. My stomach was in knots, I couldn't eat and I lost even more weight. The nights were the worst. Behind closed doors, alone in bed, unable to sleep, I would toss and turn, mourning my lost love. I couldn't believe what was happening to me and I was frightened at feeling so out of control. I kept thinking that any minute now I would wake up and everything would be fine again. But it wasn't.

I lay there in my pyjamas all day, crying for Britain, watching television or listening to the radio. The first strains of the number one song 'My Heart Will Go On' by Celine Dion were enough to finish me off. I was an absolute wreck. Philippa Forrester moved in for a while, until Mum and Wendy took over to try to help me through it. But I was beyond even their comfort.

There were work commitments I couldn't escape, so once or twice in those first weeks I had to force myself to get to my feet, wash my hair, put on some make-up and dress smartly. Then, opening my front door, I had to face the world's press camped on my doorstep, their flashbulbs popping, the questions yelled from the gates. 'How do you feel, Anthea?' they'd call. 'Has Grant gone for good?' or 'Will you and Peter be getting back together?'

Fighting the urge to be physically sick, I'd get into my car, open the electronic gates and nudge the MG forward through the crowds of photographers, each one pressing his lens against my window hoping to get the definitive picture of a heartbroken television presenter. One picture which was widely used showed me dressed in black (that trick didn't work this time), driving off from my house. When he saw it, Chris Evans, the radio and television presenter and one-time self-professed enemy of mine, changed his mind about me overnight. He said I looked 'so sad', and even sent me a bouquet of flowers with a message which read: 'Keep your chin up, girl.'

Then, at whichever location, radio station or television studio I was doing my voiceover or presenting, I had to compose myself, summon every last reserve of courage within me and try to shine. It was one of the most difficult periods of my career, but I never missed a single appointment or let anyone down.

To try to get over my sadness, I needed to become angry. Friends helped by saying the right things and feeding me nuggets of gossip about Grant and Della which were enough to fire my fury. Among these was the news that Della and Kerry had been offered their own television slot as co-hosts of a trendy programme on Granada's satellite channel, along with Julia Carling. It failed after just a few episodes. Critics unkindly dubbed it *Wish I Was Her*.

Mostly, I was angry because I'd been betrayed. I'd believed Grant when he told me what he felt, and he had said the loveliest things when we were lying in bed together. I'd believed every word he had written to me in his letters when I was away. I'd believed what he'd said about the future we'd share together. I'd believed it all. Some people have called me naïve, but I'm just honest and I expect people to be honest with me. I'd never have turned my world upside down if I hadn't trusted Grant 100 per cent, if I hadn't thought he was going to be a part of my life for a very long time. This was the man I'd wanted to be with for ever, the man I'd wanted to have children with. It was just so incredibly sad.

Worse was to come. A month after Grant left me, Russ rang me at home. 'Anthea, I'm afraid I've got some bad news,' he said. 'Grant's done a deal with *OK!* magazine. They're on the front cover and all across a fourteen-page spread inside. I thought you should know.'

'Fourteen pages!' I exclaimed, sitting down, the wind taken right out of me. 'What on earth does it say?'

'Don't worry about it – and for God's sake, don't look at it,' he told me. 'It's not worth the paper it's written on.'

'Judas!' I cried. 'How could he do that? How could he humiliate me more than he has already?' Russ couldn't give me an answer.

I had no intention of looking at the *OK!* piece, but at Heathrow Airport a few days later, on my way to Sally Meen's hen party in Nice, I saw a copy on the news-stand and stood in front of it, transfixed. The temptation was just too strong. Picking it up, I flicked open the pages and what I saw inside made me feel physically sick. There were Grant, Della and their children, all 'happily' back together again. There were Della and Grant on a motorbike; Della and Grant in front of a roaring fire; Della and Grant canoodling with a cat. In the short article that accompanied the pictures, Grant made light of our affair, but added that he couldn't give Della any guarantees that he wouldn't stray again. 'Hopefully I won't,' he was quoted as saying. 'But I can't promise, because that's an impossible thing to do in a relationship. Having done what I have, there must be a slight temptation there, which I hope will never surface.'

Nothing will ever hurt me as badly again.

9

Annus Horribilis

I had no contact with Grant at all. I was sat upon by my close friends and family, all of whom forbade me to get in touch. Part of me was so angry after the *OK!* piece that I never wanted to see him or speak to him again. But another part, the soft spot deep within me, agonised over how he was and what he was feeling. Pete was in almost daily contact, to see how I was, and when Mum and Wendy moved out, Jonathan Morris moved into the spare bedroom for several weeks so that I'd always have someone to come home to. He was living in Sussex at the time, but he just dropped everything and came to help. The gossip columnists made a meal of him moving in, but by then I was past caring. The media were still camped outside my house day and night, the photographers' lenses trained almost permanently on the windows. I was followed at home and abroad, and pictured alone and always miserable.

I considered turning my back on showbusiness for ever and moving abroad, maybe to Ireland, or somewhere where people didn't know me and the press couldn't find me. I was so desperate that there was even a moment when I fleetingly thought about throwing myself off Twickenham Bridge. Pete, still a huge part of my life, did all he could to help. But there was nothing anyone could do. I had to accept the fact that 1998 was fast becoming my *annus horribilis*.

I did everything I could to shake myself out of the doldrums, but nothing seemed to work. I bought a four-year-old Andalusian stallion called Caramelo and rode almost every day, to try to blow away the cobwebs. I wrote a list of all the good things I had: a fabulous job, good pals and a marvellous family. To start with nothing had any effect on me at all, other than to remind me how empty my life was without Grant. But little by little I began to feel stronger and even had the odd good day where I hardly cried at all. Gradually I found myself progressing instead of standing still, especially when I was working hard, which, as always, really helped to take my mind off things.

My friends and family were wonderful and did their best to take me out and cheer me up. Jonathan, Helen Parker, Sue, Wendy and Philippa all played their part, along with numerous others like Diane-Louise Jordan and old friends from my *Blue Peter* days. I never failed to be surprised by the kindness the general public showed me, too. It was almost as if the public had warmed to me more since I'd had my heart broken. Market research commissioned by Pete and conducted by James Grant found that people thought me 'more human, more touchable', because of what had happened. I suppose every cloud has its silver lining.

One day, meeting friends for lunch in Chelsea, I noticed that Chris Evans was sitting at another table with a group of his friends. I had appreciated his flowers and his kind note, but remembering that he'd also once said he'd like to kick me in the face, I thought it best to ignore him. But he sent Jamie, one of his breakfast show crew, to my table inviting me to join him for coffee. This was going to be too good to miss, so I went over to his table and sat down. To my surprise, he was charming, charismatic and very funny. I never expected him to become a friend, and it was a shock when he did, but a lovely shock. He was the first person to make me laugh since Grant left, and I was truly grateful for his humour.

A few weeks later, on 12 May, Chris invited me to help him celebrate National Nurses' Day. He announced that he was going to be out and about dressed as a doctor and that everyone had to be nice to nurses that day. To make sure that he was nice to me, I decided to surprise him by dressing up in a thigh-high nurse's uniform. As it turned out it wasn't necessary, but he was suitably impressed. After appearing on his breakfast radio show and then on *This Morning* with Richard and Judy, and encouraged by Chris, I spent the day touring London pubs with him and fifty nurses, all brilliant girls, before rolling home way after midnight. An hour or so after I got home, there was a ring at the main gate. Answering it warily, I was surprised to find that it was Stuart Higgins, editor of the *Sun*. 'I thought you'd like to see the first editions,' he told me through the intercom. 'You're all over them.'

My photograph was, indeed, plastered over every newspaper, including across a double-page centre spread in the *Sun* under the headline 'Anthea's Night on the Chris'. The reports described me as looking well and happy and spoke of my 'recovery' after my 'heartache'. They were full of good wishes for my future and suggestions that Chris Evans and I might be an item. In Sussex, Grant read every word.

The following Monday morning, six weeks and one day after Grant left me, I was in my gym on the top floor of Ormonde House. Exercise has always been therapy for me: it clears my head. At about 10am the telephone rang. I was expecting to hear from Chris, who was due to call round later.

But it wasn't Chris. Instead a voice I knew only too well echoed across the ether and into my ear. 'You might want to put the phone down and if you do I'll completely understand, but I've just got to speak to you.' It was Grant.

I felt as if I was hearing someone who had come back from the dead. My knees gave way under me and I slumped to the floor, holding the phone away from me. I started to shake physically all over. I thought I was going to vomit. When I eventually brought the phone back to my ear, Grant was calling my name anxiously.

'Anthea? Anth, are you still there?' His voice was none too steady, either.

'Y-y-yes,' I stammered. 'I'm here.' I squeezed my eyes shut against the pounding in my head.

I can't recall the exact details of the conversation because it still gives me goose bumps to think of it, but Grant said he wanted to apologise for all the hurt he had caused me, especially with the *OK!* article. 'I wasn't thinking clearly,' he said. 'I went back for the children, but then they offered all this money and I thought it would just be tomorrow's chip paper. It's haunted me ever since. I'm so very, very sorry. It was never meant to come out like it did.'

I was extremely wary and very hostile. Part of me said: 'Tell him to go to hell, and that you never want to speak to him again.' But the trouble was I'd never stopped loving him. I'd never been able to get him out of my heart or my head.

He asked if we could meet, and it took me all my strength to refuse. 'No,' I told him, shaking my head. 'I can't. I won't. That's absolutely impossible.' Then a torrent of words spilled out of me, one rushing into the other, as I told him how I felt about everything he'd done to me. 'I've never been hurt by anyone as badly as you hurt me, Grant. You're not the man I thought you were, and I'll never give you another chance to make such a fool of me.' He knew I had a lot to get off my chest and he listened to my outburst in near silence, interjecting only to apologise over and over again.

'It's a nightmare at home,' he interrupted finally. 'Della and I barely speak to each other. Neither of us is making any effort. The utopia of family life I'd built up in my mind simply doesn't exist.' He was cracking. 'I can't get you out of my mind, however hard I try,' he pleaded, his voice breaking with emotion. 'There's no escape from you. I thought I could break away; I thought I could make my marriage work for the sake of the children, but I know now I can't. If you won't see me, couldn't we just talk every now and again? I'm at the end of my tether.'

I shook my head again. 'No, Grant, no. That would just be reopening old wounds.'

We talked for an hour and a half. Finally I conceded. 'You can call me if you like, as a friend,' I told him.

Signing off, I had a good cry and I thought long and hard about what he'd said. I could only begin to imagine what Della must have been going through. She'd got him back, or so she thought, but as I'd always suspected, he wasn't really back at all.

Chris Evans came over that afternoon and we lay in the garden sunbathing and chatting and he gave me some very sound advice, as well as a bit more confidence. 'What you need, Anthea,' he told me, 'is to believe in yourself a bit more. There must have been something inside you that made that gawky little kid from Norton into a star. You've got to find that strength now and draw on it. It'd be a shame to let it all go now for nothing.' I knew he was right and I welcomed his wise counsel. It was thanks to people like him and Sue Van Der Ree, the woman who'd been rooting for me since the days of Bruno Brookes, that I gradually found my way back.

Two days later I rang Grant. He was clearly surprised.

'Oh, er, Anthea, it's great to hear from you. Does this mean you'll agree to see me?'

'No, Grant,' I told him firmly. 'I'm not ready for that. Let's just talk. OK?'

The following day, he called me, and we talked some more. I could hear the desperation in his voice. I knew he was torn about his children and that he needed to come to some decision about his life. 'I don't love Della the way a husband should,' he told me. 'There's nothing between us any more. I'm utterly miserable at home. And yet the kids need me to be here for them. What should I do?'

I didn't offer him any advice; I wasn't in a position to do so. I was taking things very slowly, resisting him a lot of the way, wary and afraid of what might happen if I allowed him to creep back into my affections. I'm a great one for compartmentalising situations. I'd convinced myself that by chatting to each other we could help each other through; nothing more. Who was I kidding?

The next day, I rang Grant again. I wanted to see if he was feeling any better. I'd spent the previous night worrying about what he might do, he sounded in such a state. Once again he spent an hour agonising about his future and about what would be best for the children. 'Maybe if I made a clean break and left now, things wouldn't be so bad,' he said. 'Maybe the kids would understand. I'm sure Della wouldn't stop me seeing them. She's a good mother, Anthea. She wouldn't stop them seeing their father, would she?'

I told him I didn't know. He kept pressing for us to meet up and

I kept refusing. I knew that if we did something might happen that I would regret. Before long I realised we were getting back into it – talking to each other every day just like we had before. I didn't want it to happen. I kept trying to break the link, but I couldn't.

At the end of May it was my birthday, and I decided to hold a party at a hotel in Richmond as a thank you to everyone who'd been so kind to me and helped me through the previous few months. It was a lovely party, just what I needed to cheer me up. Pete came with a card which read: 'Dear AT, time to relax a little. Cross that bridge, build on your friends, take a deep breath, smile again, be positive, be strong, stay fresh and young at heart. Take care, happy birthday. Always here for you, Pete xx.' What a gent.

In June, he kindly invited me to Majorca for the launch of his new toy, a Sunseeker speedboat he called *Phoenix* because it represented his rise from the ashes. There was a gang of about fourteen of us, including Russ and Caron, and we had a great weekend, sunbathing, relaxing and generally unwinding. 'Thanks for coming, AT,' Pete told me, lying next to me on the sundeck one glorious afternoon. 'I wouldn't have wanted to launch her without you.' Reaching across, I ruffled his newly cropped hair affectionately. Unbeknown to us, the paparazzi were watching our every move. Their pictures of us appeared in the *Sunday Mirror* a few days later under the headline: 'Anthea's Back with Hubby. Has the Tide Turned for Their Love?' I didn't seem able to put a foot right.

When almost everyone else had gone home from that weekend and only Pete and I were left, sunbathing and relaxing, just like in the old days, I took the plunge and told him I'd been talking to Grant again. 'I didn't mean it to happen,' I said. 'But it just sort of did and now I don't know what to do.'

Pete was silent for a few minutes, considering what he should say. He'd been my mentor and adviser for so long that it didn't seem strange to either of us that I should turn to him once again, even about this. 'How do you feel about him, AT?' he said eventually, squinting into the sunshine to gauge my response.

'I still love him, Pete,' I said, staring into the middle distance.

'Then you must follow your heart,' Pete said softly. 'And if that is what you really want, you mustn't let what anyone thinks or says stand in your way. Because you only get one chance at love.' He paused before adding sadly: 'Believe me, I know.'

Later that month, Wendy and I undertook a bit of a pilgrimage for *Wish You Were Here*. We went back to Tenby, the scene of our happiest childhood holidays. For twelve years, for one week twice a year, in May and October, we'd driven across country to Carmarthen Bay. Neither of us had been back since 1973. Twenty-five years later, it was exactly as we remembered it. As our helicopter came in to land, circling Monument Hill, Wendy and I both had big lumps in our throats. The last time we'd been here, Ruth had still been alive. I could see her now, sitting on a blanket on the beach, collecting shells and watching as Wendy and I scrambled over the rocks. Mum and Dad would be sitting alongside her, brewing up tea on their little Primus stove, Mum calling out to us to be careful. 'Brian,' she'd say as I scampered to the top of the largest rock on the beach, 'don't let her – she'll fall off.'

We retraced our footsteps, visiting the sixth-floor flat we'd stayed in at 70 Croft Court, where I'd once threatened to throw Wendy over the balcony; the amusement arcade where we'd been given a few coins to play with as a treat; the fish-and-chip shop where we'd bought our supper; the tea rooms where we'd eaten Caldey cake. It was a bittersweet journey, rekindling memories of a happier and simpler time. When we tried to track down Charlie Burcher, a lovely old odd-job man who'd taken a shine to us girls and who we looked forward to seeing every year (even though he always smelled of oil), we discovered that he'd died two years after our last visit, aged sixty-eight. Finding his grave in the local cemetery, we stood by it in silence for a few minutes, bidding him a fond farewell.

I returned home to work and to the calls from Grant, still asking for a meeting. 'I have to see you, please,' he'd plead, but I would not agree. Instead I went off to France with *Wish You Were Here*, pony-trekking in Corbière. I stayed in a manky little hotel and one night, sitting in my room talking to him on the phone, I heard him sign off, almost casually, with: 'Goodbye, then. I love you.'

I heard him but pretended I hadn't. 'Sorry, it's a bad line, what did you say?' I asked.

'I love you Anthea,' he yelled.

I paused. A smile crept across my face and I marvelled at the way he still made me feel. Finally, I spoke. 'I love you too, Grant.'

A week later I was in Majorca, filming a new fitness video. Russ came along too, just for the hell of it, and we had a riot. 'How are you doing, AT?' he asked me one night, suddenly turning serious.

I considered his question for a moment before replying. 'Actually, you know, Russ, I'm doing all right,' I said. And – for the first time in ages – I meant it.

I came back to London just in time for the world premiere of *Dr Dolittle* at the Apollo Theatre, Hammersmith, in which Phillip Schofield was playing the lead role. Pete asked me to accompany him, and I was delighted to accept. It would be our first formal appearance together in public since the split and I was grateful for his decision to be seen to be supporting me. The evening was a fantastic success, made even more special for me by the presence earlier that day at a special tribute lunch of Julie Andrews, my childhood heroine. She was the voice of one of the key animals in the show. 'Remember me? Anthea? I interviewed you once on *GMTV*,' I asked her sheepishly.

With that radiant smile I knew so well, she took my hand and beamed at me. 'Anthea, of course, my dear. Liesl, wasn't it? How could I forget?'

Having seen the photographs of me and Peter together, smiling, in the newspapers the following day, Grant rang. Having denied him for so long, all the time desperate to see him, I finally caved in. I built it up in my mind as a test of how I would feel when I saw him. We agreed to meet on his return from Monaco on business and mine from my god-daughter's confirmation in east London. Grant was due to land at Gatwick at 9pm and had said he'd come straight to Ormonde House. All through the confirmation I felt like I had when I'd first known him. It was as if I was about to sit an exam. I couldn't relax. I sat in my pew in church, closed my eyes and said a silent prayer: 'Dear Lord, help me to make the right decision.' It was the first time I'd prayed to God since my Youth Fellowship days.

Grant rang when he landed and I set off from east London as he left the airport. We talked on our mobile telephones all the way, speeding towards each other. I arrived at Ormonde House about twenty minutes before him. I was as jumpy as hell. I hadn't told anyone; I hadn't dared. I knew what all my friends and family would say. I went upstairs and changed, all the time thinking: 'What *am* I doing?'

I unlocked the back gate to the garden, having told him to come in that way. The press would have a field day if they saw him coming in through the front door. I opened the back door, turned off most of the lights just in case anyone was watching the house and stood in the kitchen in the semi-darkness, leaning against the Aga, trembling.

When Grant appeared in the doorway a few minutes later and looked across at me in the dim light, I knew I was a goner. I'd wanted to feel nothing; I wanted him to have destroyed what I'd felt before by what he'd put me through, but he hadn't. There was no way I could truly hate this man.

It was a warm night and he stood there uncertainly for some time. The atmosphere was tense.

'Hello,' he said in the end.

'Hi.'

We stood awkwardly in silence for a few minutes longer.

'Do you want a cup of tea?' I asked. I put the kettle on, still hanging on to the Aga to stabilise myself.

I kept my distance, desperately aware that this could so easily become a rerun of that August night the previous year when we'd first got together. I genuinely didn't want that to happen. 'Don't let it, AT,' I told myself in my head. 'Just keep cool and keep calm.'

'What's that?' Grant asked, pointing at a piece of paper stuck to my fridge door with a magnet. It had the words 'Go Forth' scrawled in bold letters across it.

'Oh,' I said, blushing. 'Well, er, that's just something I wrote to make myself get up and face the world each morning.'

'It's been that hard, has it?' Grant asked, his expression one of concern.

Nodding, I busied myself with the milk and sugar.

We took our tea into the lounge and sat down. But the minute we did, Grant leaned over and kissed me. His hand came up and stroked my hair, his lips moved down my neck.

'I've missed you,' he said, and, before I knew it, we were locked in an embrace.

Grant and I ended up making love that night because it felt like the most natural thing to do. It was beautiful and marvellous and everything it always is with him.

When it was over, though, I lay back on my pillow, feeling cheap. Seeing my tears, he got up, dressed and went downstairs without a word. I followed him in my dressing gown and sat down at the kitchen table. 'I feel dreadful,' I said, my eyes filling up. 'I can't do this again, Grant. I can't just go back to the way we were before. It just won't work.'

Quietly, earnestly, Grant told me what was in his heart. He said he couldn't be without me. He said he'd spent the previous eight weeks feeling as if someone had died. 'I can't imagine you out of my life,' he said. 'Not now. Please. I know this isn't the right way to go about things, but I had to see you. Please, give me some time, Anthea. I just need time.'

Once again, my heart was battling with my head. I knew it wasn't right just to pick up where we had left off, but I loved him, and I couldn't bear to be without him, either. I couldn't just turn off the tap. It would have made a mockery of everything I'd ever felt about him. The right thing to have done would have been to have sent him away to sort everything out with Della, telling him to come back when he had. But I couldn't. We were both weak. You can only fight so hard in this life to make things happen. We couldn't fight this. We did try – we tried every trick in the book – but none of it worked, and there came a time when we had to say: 'Well, maybe we should just give in to it,' however painful that decision was.

Despite all my reservations and deep misgivings, we found ourselves back together again, secretly, just like before. Only this time it was even tougher. I couldn't tell a soul and the furtiveness was even more destructive. I hated the deceit but real life and real emotions kept forcing me to continue with it. I was speaking to Grant nearly every day and, whenever possible, about once a week, we'd try to arrange to meet. We used Ormonde House for some time and then the homes of a few close friends I eventually had to bring into the loop, having sworn them to total secrecy. We became ever more paranoid about being found out.

Although we were back together, I felt incredibly lonely. I wanted his love, but I was still too bruised. I had everything and yet I had nothing, and no one to talk to about the anxieties that continued to keep me awake night after night.

Grant undoubtedly had a great deal to sort out at home. I spoke to him daily, needing to know what was going on. I was tormented by the idea of him being with Della when I felt, quite unfairly, that he should have been with me. How he ended his marriage was a matter only he could sort out. All I could do was offer my advice, although of course it was loaded. He kept asking me to wait, but the waiting was killing me.

In August, Jane Proctor, then the editor of the highly successful society magazine *Tatler*, approached me and asked if I would give them an exclusive interview. The carrot was that I'd be dressed from head to toe in fabulous designer outfits and have my photograph taken by the fashion photographer Antoine Verglas.

'I just want to sound you out about something,' Jane said, over a lunch attended by Vivian Parry, the journalist who was to write the article, and Christine McCarthy, a mutual friend. 'We're planning on dressing you up in the guise of various legendary women, to show off the new, empowered you. You know, Cleopatra, Guinevere, Boadicea, that type of thing.'

I've never thought of myself as particularly strong or empowered, but I've always been a sucker for dressing up. 'Sounds great,' I said, enthusiastically. I remembered kitting myself out as Cleopatra once in one of my productions with Ruth and Wendy. We'd used Pat the dog's twisted rope lead as an asp.

'There's one woman we'd very much like you to dress up as, or rather dress you down as,' Jane added, enigmatically.

'Who's that?'

'Eve.'

I was silent for a moment. 'Do you mean you want me to wear a fig leaf?'

'No, no,' she reassured me. 'Well, not exactly. I mean it would all be incredibly tasteful, and you'd never actually be showing a thing.'

Shaking my head until my earrings hurt my ears, I told her: 'No, Jane, I don't think so.'

It was left like that, and I arrived at Antoine's studio in Holborn feeling unusually nervous. This was the first major exposure I'd allowed myself since everything that had happened with Grant and I was more than usually anxious that it should go well. I needn't have worried. Antoine was fabulous and instantly put me at ease. We started off with me as Guinevere, in a fabulous mediaeval grey chiffon dress by Versace, a fan blowing my hair and rippling the material of the dress. Then, after a quick change and a preening from my hairstylist and make-up artist, I swapped my outfit for a black catwalk jump-suit, complete with breastplate, for my role as Boadicea, before slipping into a gold sequinned dress by Helen David for Cleopatra.

'How about trying something a little more daring?' Antoine asked me in his seductive French accent.

'Like what?' I asked, laughing, thinking that it was a bit late in my career to start doing glamour poses.

'Like maybe Eve?' he suggested, smiling broadly. 'I know Jane spoke to you about it and I know you said no, but think about it – Eve, tempted by the snake to eat the forbidden fruit. Wouldn't it make a fabulous front cover?' He pointed to a nine-foot Indian python which had been secreted in a special cage in the corner of his studio.

I looked at the Frenchman and his snake incredulously. 'You're kidding, right?'

'No, I'm not,' he said. 'But I can promise you copy control. If you don't like any of the pictures, we won't use them. Deal?'

And so it was that this squeaky-clean former children's presenter ended up topless, but for a strategically placed arm and Ben the python curled over her shoulder, on the cover of the September issue of *Tatler*. The headline read: 'Naked Ambition: Anthea Turner Does the Full Monty (Plus Python) and Recounts her Post-Seduction Costs'. Well, I'd agreed to exposure, and exposure is what I got. I nearly died of it in the studio.

In another shot I was curled up face down on the floor, with an apple, my 'bare' buttocks exposed. In truth, I was wearing a G-string and the photo technicians airbrushed it out. But the photographs were beautiful and I was really pleased. I was thirty-eight and flaunting my body for all those women out there who were sick and tired of seeing skeletal teenage models. I did it because I was asked to and because I could. I have no regrets.

The newspapers went crazy. Headlines like: 'Sssensational,' 'Strip-Squeeze', 'Anthea's Snake-Over' and 'Forget Grant Bovey, he's Hiss-tory', accompanied my picture in just about every paper. If only they'd known.

Shortly after this, I flew to Namibia for *Wish You Were Here*. I was way out in the desert watching elephant, zebra, rhino and ostrich. It was mind-blowing. There were sand dunes to die for – vast, ridged, and the colour of terracotta. The crew and I climbed one, sat on the very edge and cracked open a bottle of champagne. It was breathtaking. We camped under the stars and flew over barren, mountainous terrain in a light aircraft. I was amazed by it all, even more so when I found I could get a mobile phone signal.

'I'm in the middle of a desert that's 80 million years old,' I told Grant. 'And thanks to new technology, I can talk to you as if you're just a few feet away.'

'Amazing isn't it?' he said. 'I love you, Anthea.'

Next I was off to Jersey to open an exhibition on behalf of the charity Well Being. A local photographer had taken lots of shots of celebrities, me included. I unveiled mine, a picture of me standing, laughing, by a huge terracotta pot. I took my mum with me to give her a bit of a break, and we stayed in a lovely hotel and had a really giggly, girly time together, acting like a pair of teenagers. Getting serious one night, though, I sat her down and started to talk to her about Grant.

'You're seeing him again, aren't you?' she interrupted. She'd always been able to see straight through me, ever since I was a little girl.

I nodded, 'Yes, Mum, I am.' In a way I was relieved to have the secret aired. 'I know what you're probably thinking, but you mustn't be too hard on him.'

'Well, how do you feel about him?' she asked, squeezing my hand.

'I love him, Mum,' I said, my eyes shining. 'I always have.'

'Well, just be careful,' she said. 'And remember, Daddy and I will always love you whoever you decide to be with.'

Hugging her tearfully, I wished there was some way I could let her know how much her friendship and non-judgemental counsel had meant to me over the years. She'd always been there for me, from my earliest days to the present, when I was going out with a married man in circumstances that had led to all my dirty linen being aired in public. I could only begin to imagine how that must have felt to the quiet couple who had only ever had cause to be proud of me before. Now all their friends and neighbours knew the minutest details of my disastrous personal life. And yet Mum was still backing me all the way. What a woman.

In September Pete and I were invited to Gloria Hunniford's wedding to Stephen Way at Hever Castle, where Russ and Caron had married seven years earlier. It was another glittering day. Among the guests were Cliff Richard, Phillip Schofield, Jim Davidson, Barbara Windsor, Frankie Vaughan, Esther Rantzen and her husband Desmond Wilcox, Janet Brown, Victor Spinetti and Su Pollard. The day was extra special for Gloria because her daughter-in-law Sandy (married to Caron's brother Paul), had given birth that morning to a baby boy. *Hello!* magazine was among those to cover the wedding, and, for their cover photograph, they chose a picture of the bride and groom flanked by me and Phillip Schofield.

For some reason, I felt especially emotional that day. It was the first wedding I'd been to since my own marriage had disintegrated and, standing next to Pete in the church, listening to Gloria recite her wedding vows, I nearly lost it completely.

'For better for worse, for richer for poorer, in sickness and in health . . .' My mind rewound and replayed the previous eight years: my Royal Tournament accident and Pete's gentle nursing; his proposal on that rainy day in Ireland; our glorious wedding day and honeymoon in Grenada; the fun times we'd had together, skiing and on holiday before all the madness began; his wisdom when it came to *Blue Peter* and *GMTV*. As the vicar pronounced Gloria and Stephen man and wife, I didn't dare look across at him, for fear of what either of us might do.

Seeing Grant a few days later, I told him what had happened and how I'd felt in church. 'I could tell Pete was finding it as hard as I was,' I recounted. 'I never meant to keep on hurting him like this.' What I was hoping Grant would say was that the time had come for him to make a break, leave Della and announce to the world that we were together again. At least then all the secrecy could stop, Pete could get on with his life and Grant and I could start anew. But no such offer was forthcoming, even though Grant and I had quietly started looking at houses in the country together in the hope that one day we could live together in peace. I told myself to be patient.

On 11 October, any hope we had of controlling the situation ourselves was blown out of the water by an article in the *News of the World* which revealed that we were in touch with each other on a regular basis. The newspaper had somehow acquired our mobile phone bills, gave a complete and accurate list of every phone call made between us, including the dates, times and duration. The report headed: 'Anthea's Secret Love Calls to Grant', trumpeted that we spoke to each other up to nine times a day and had been secretly ringing each other for two months.

Della asked Grant if the story was true. Still not ready to make the break, he denied it. A few weeks later she found in Grant's car the faxed details of a house he and I had looked at and she knew her marriage was finally over. She described this as the 'ultimate betrayal' and said she would never be able to trust him again. 'Something's broken, and no matter how hard we try, we just can't put it together again,' she said.

From that moment on, every painful detail of Grant's marital breakdown was covered almost daily in the newspapers. The press rounded on him mercilessly. He was variously called a 'Del Boy love rat', a 'cad', a 'flashy chancer', a 'love cheat' and a 'bounder'. They pitied me for my weakness and poor choice and advised me to drop him like a hot potato. Grant announced publicly that he was still in love with me; Della said that she no longer cared and it would be better to make a clean break. It was a horrible, undignified mess.

Five days after the *News of the World* article appeared, I was invited to attend *Blue Peter*'s fortieth birthday party at the Natural History Museum in London. I seriously wondered if I'd still be welcome and half expected a phone call from Lewis Bronze asking me to stay away. I knew that nothing so vulgar as what I was involved in should be allowed to taint the unsullied name of *Blue Peter*. But the call never came and I went along, pleased to be back in the bosom of those who'd given me the happiest days of my career in television. It was only when I'd walked away from that programme that things had really started to go pear-shaped for me: the early starts at *GMTV*, the increasing distance between me and Pete, meeting Grant and now the latest in what was fast turning into a new instalment of a very public soap opera.

I knew that the time was fast approaching when I was going to have to make a decision. I was either going to have to give Grant up completely and start anew, or I was going to have to push him to choose. He was still dithering, still torn about his children. Della was back and Grant had moved into the spare bedroom. They were communicating via terse notes.

Before flying off to the Himalayas, Australia and Chicago for *Wish You Were Here* that November, I gave him an ultimatum, for everyone's sake. 'Don't think I am going to wait for you for ever, Grant, because I won't,' I told him. 'I won't be your mistress, and if you don't make a decision soon and choose between Della and me, then I'm out of here.' The truth was I wanted him, but I knew the situation as it stood was wrong for all concerned. I felt terrible about that; and I knew that if I didn't make a stand now and end the pain for everybody, then no one else would. I set off on my assignment leaving him to think on what I'd said.

The Himalayas were extraordinary. We flew to Nepal and then went on an air trek up Mount Everest with Gorkha Airlines. Flying high above the clouds, watching our shadow chase us across the sheer rock face, light-headed from the altitude, I marvelled at the majestic sight below. 'What insignificant creatures human beings are,' I thought. 'With all our petty problems and concerns. We're less than ants on the planet compared to giants like this, and yet we think the world stops where we can't see it.' I felt humbled and at peace.

Returning to England, I went youth-hostelling in the Lake District with my dad and Uncle Bert to do a piece for the programme about how much it had changed since their day. We had the most gorgeous time, the three of us, walking and talking, hiking up fells and down dales, sitting up late into the night, chatting endlessly about life, and Ruth, Mum and Wendy, all that had happened in our lives and how we felt about things.

'Life's too short to take for granted, Lil,' Dad told me. 'You have to seize the opportunities you have and make the most of them. Up until now, you've done just that. Don't let your concerns about what other people think stop you from being happy.'

I decided there and then that if Grant walked away, I'd fight to get myself back into shape emotionally, and win my way back into the public's heart. I knew it would be tough, but I'd still have my parents, Pete, Wendy and my friends to keep me sane. If, on the other hand, Grant decided to come back to me properly, I vowed to do all I could to make our relationship a success. Never again would I put work first, or allow myself to be anything other than the wife I thought he deserved. Now all I had to do was wait and see which way he'd go.

Grant moved out of his marital home for the last time ten days before Christmas. He simply couldn't face another year of causing so much pain.

'If you'll have me, Anthea, I want to be with you,' he told me. 'I know you think I've been dithering, but believe me, I've never wanted anything else more in my life.'

He and I have been together ever since. Ormonde House, which had too many sad memories, was sold, and Grant and I moved temporarily into a cottage in Surrey. It was small and cosy and we loved it, curling up together by the fire at night, making joint plans and sharing dreams. Despite all the agony we'd caused and been through ourselves, it still felt so good whenever we were together that we knew we'd been right to follow our hearts.

Grant's children soon became a regular feature of our lives. They are lovely girls, a great credit to him and to Della. When they come to stay now, we all get on famously, although it was very awkward at first. I was terribly anxious about how they'd feel about Grant and me sleeping together. But I was seeing the situation through the eyes of an adult. To a child bed means sleep, not sex. Sex doesn't enter their heads. We decided to fudge the issue at first, so there was a lot of Grant sleeping with the girls in the big bed and me alone in one of their rooms. But when we moved from the cottage into our present house it was all a bit more defined. Amelia, aged six, gave the first floor the once-over and said: 'So, that's my room, and that's Claudia's, and that's Olivia's, and there is Daddy's bedroom. Where are you going to sleep, Anthea?'

I blustered and said, 'Oh, I don't know, where do you think I should sleep?'

She gave it some thought. 'I'd sleep with Daddy, if I were you.'

However my relationship with the girls develops, I hope that over the years as they grow up their memories will be of Grant and me as a solid influence in their young lives; more solid than if their mother and father had tried to stay together unhappily.

The time the girls spend with Grant is now of a much better quality than it was before; they have their own bedrooms and toys and clothes, so that they don't have to pack bags to visit. We clear the decks and cram the weekends with dressing up and games and outings, and they have a blast. It's very important when you take on a married man that you are also prepared to take on his children, and I have learned that the hard way. I still advise my friends to run in the opposite direction if they get an offer from a family man. You have to be 1,000 per cent committed. Other people's children are a lot to take on. It is not a labour of love, because they are not your flesh and blood. It has taken me a while to adjust to all this, and it doesn't come easily. But I have found myself falling for them. I know I can never take the place of their mother, and I wouldn't want to. I am more like a favourite auntie or a big sister.

Having gone from no children to three, it is privacy that I miss most acutely. I can't even go to the toilet without someone waiting at the door or walking in. There are little people everywhere, trying on every pair of shoes and all my lipsticks. It takes me straight back to those Friday afternoons long ago when Mum went to the hairdresser for a wash and set and I'd sneak into her bedroom and try out all her make-up.

Having spent so much time with the girls now, I am beginning to understand the incredible pull children can have on your heart-strings. For someone who is childless, that is quite a revelation. I had a blind faith that loving each other was all Grant and I needed. I'd fully expected to come before his daughters in all things, and in many ways I have. But he could never leave them completely. Just as Della never really got Grant back, I could never take him away from his children, and I wouldn't want to. Now that he is with me for good, and the children have become a much-anticipated and regular feature of our lives, I feel as confident as one can be that I will never lose him again.

People are always asking me when I'm going to start a family. I could say: 'I don't want children,' which has actually been true up until now, but then I would come across as a selfish, career-minded cow who would give up everything for the sake of fame and fortune. If, on the other hand, I were to say: 'Yes, I love children and one day I'd love one of my own,' they'd start clock-watching and asking me when, how, and could they be at the conception. The media are never satisfied. In the end I decided that it is sometimes better to tell the truth, which is that I like children, and they might one day be a possibility, but that actually I have a gynaecological problem which currently precludes that. The danger is that I'm then seen as a desperate person, racked with pain and angst because I can't bear a child. I can't win and I can't shake off the constant questions.

The truth is that if it happens, it happens. I'm not going to get myself all twisted and tied up in knots over it. I'm very happy with Grant and my maternal instincts have been allowed to come to the fore with his three girls. I'm not one of those people who feels my life will never be complete unless I have a child. I am a great fatalist. In the words of my mum, if it's meant to be, it will be.

Neither Grant nor I had ever had any idea how infamous we would become. We are now as well known for our relationship as I was for my job. It was a factor we simply hadn't bargained for and it continues to cause us anxiety. For a long time, we couldn't make a move without being followed. If we spent time with Grant's children, I was criticised for trying to take Della's place. If we didn't, I would have been accused of disliking them. It's a no-win situation.

We have inadvertently became a classic case study and the protagonists of a cautionary tale of what it's really like to live on Planet Fame. It was in any case never a place I originally set out to be. When I trod the boards at the Queen's Theatre, Burslem, singing 'I am Sixteen, Going on Seventeen', I would never have imagined in my wildest dreams (or nightmares) that things would have turned out this way. When Ruth and I sat flicking through *Jackie* magazine and reading about all the stars, neither of us ever actually believed that I would become one.

I get dozens of letters from kids and teenagers who want to get into television and I offer them what advice I can, but I know they're barking up the wrong tree if they say: 'I want to be rich and famous'. I never said that or even felt it. Wealth and fame are not an end in their own right, but a byproduct of a job or career. I was simply attracted to the media world because of Bruno and, later, the other people around me. It was and is a way to earn a living. Sure, it's exciting, it's living on the edge, it appeals to my Gemini nature. I definitely have the excitement chip in me, I love the element of danger and the media environment, and, of course, the rewards are good.

In the early stages of my career I only ever saw the good side of celebrity. I'd never have believed that people like Judith Chalmers or

Julie Andrews could go home and cry sometimes over what someone had written about them in the newspapers. I never truly understood that until I experienced the other side of the coin myself, when I joined *GMTV* and started on the National Lottery programme. The stakes were much higher then, and I learned the hard way.

Now, even if I were to walk away from showbusiness for ever, my rightful place in the media's eyes would always be on the gossip pages. That isn't all bad news, by any means. I still have a very good relationship with a lot of the press, some of whom I count as personal friends. Thanks to them, I'm invited to do fashion spreads and all sorts of other things most girls can only dream about. And apart from all the events and parties, there are many extras. Being famous means you can book a table at any restaurant, use the BBC car park and always get an appointment at Nicky Clarke's. Conversation is always easy with people because they feel they know you already.

And then there's the presents. I mean, who in their right mind wouldn't covet some of the gifts I've been given by people over the years – the county shields, the cut-glass vases, the fruit bowls, the toys. I've kept them all in a large box, and can tell you where each and every one of them came from. My two absolute favourites are a bronze replica of the air-traffic control tower at Luton Airport, which was presented to me in a lovely box with great pomp and ceremony when we did the Lottery show from the airport, and a solid silver brooch of the Stena Link 3 ferry, which I had the great privilege to launch. If the price I have to pay for such treasures is to stop and stand and smile for a few minutes, then it is a small one.

Among all the fun times there have been some instances of unintentional humour, too. Quite recently, at a party in a London nightclub, I nipped off to the Ladies' for a quick freshen-up. Emerging from the cubicle, I noticed several girls crowded around the washbasins. They seemed too busy to notice me, and with any luck, I thought, I might be able to whizz in and out without any of the usual: 'Oh, it's you, Anthea. Where's lover boy, then?' Squeezing between them, I managed to reach past one of them to wash my hands and splash my face under the cold tap. Seeing a hand-dryer on the wall, I turned it on, rubbing my hands together beneath it. My face was still a bit damp, too, so I twisted the nozzle upwards to dry it.

There was a sudden flurry of activity behind me. I turned to see that every face was looking at me, each one more indignant than the next. The reason why these girls had been so preoccupied at the basin was that they had been carefully chopping out dozens of lines of cocaine. When I had adjusted the blast of air from the hand-dryer, I had inadvertently dispatched several hundred pounds' worth of the drug into oblivion. So much for getting in and out unnoticed.

Another time Grant and I, staying in an obscure hotel up north, came out of our room to see a prominent member of the Della-and-Kerry entourage emerging sheepishly from their room with someone who clearly wasn't their spouse. Trying to suppress our giggles, we made the poor person squirm by insisting on chatting for a few moments and asking to be introduced. Callous as it may sound, it felt quite delicious.

And on another occasion, a taxi pulled up outside our house in Surrey and a blonde, middle-aged woman got out. Grant and I were in the kitchen having coffee and he sent one of the builders out to see who she was. 'She's asking for a Mr Grant,' the burly builder reported back, so Grant wandered out, mug in hand.

'Oh my God! My God!' the woman exclaimed delightedly as he strolled towards her. 'It really is you, isn't it?'

Puzzled, Grant smiled and glanced back at me, peering out of the window. 'Er, can I help you?' he asked.

'Can you help me?' she laughed incredulously. 'Look at you. You look fabulous. I caught the train to London from Essex, another train to Guildford and then I asked the taxi-driver to take me to Grant and Anthea's and here I am.'

'Yes, so it seems,' said Grant, frowning at the taxi-driver, 'but what do you want?'

'To see you,' the woman replied, 'and to collect my cheque.'

'I beg your pardon?' Grant asked her, wondering who on earth the woman was.

'You know, the one I wrote to you about a month ago?' the stranger continued, grabbing his arm and leading him towards the house. 'The £60,000 I need for my new flat in Essex?'

Stopping in his tracks, Grant turned to face her. 'I'm afraid there must have been some sort of mistake,' he told her. 'Who exactly do you think I am?'

She threw back her head and laughed. 'Oh, you're so funny. I know exactly who you are. I've seen every one of your films, Mr Grant. I particularly loved you in *Four Weddings and a Funeral*.'

Grant first found out he was being divorced by reading the front page of the *Sun* on Saturday 30 January 1999. Della had previously refused him a divorce to delay his freedom to marry me if he wanted to. She then named me as the co-respondent, an unusual move in these days of 'no blame' divorces, which prompted the headlines: 'Della's Revenge' and 'Della Names Anthea as Other Woman'.

The divorce battle was bitter and long. There were rows over money, over access to the children and over how much time I and Della's new boyfriend could spend with the girls. A settlement offer from Grant was rejected and Della threatened to drag him through the courts. It couldn't have been more of a contrast with the amicable agreement Pete and I had arrived at privately a year before, which had been rubber-stamped quietly in the courts.

Della had a particularly clever solicitor whose letters wound Grant up. In the end, he agreed to the settlement Della was seeking just to bring the whole matter to a close. Their final legal bill was £60,000, money he would much rather have given to his wife and children. In all, we estimate that being together has cost us personally well over £1 million. And, as usual, the biggest winners were the lawyers.

However bad anything thinks a divorce is going to be, it is usually ten times worse. And in our case, add to that the intense media attention and you can treble that again. Grant found out that his decree nisi had come through while driving into London, when a news bulletin on Capital Radio interrupted a Robbie Williams song to tell him that his marriage was over. He nearly went off the road. And not only was his marriage over, but his business life was a shambles. He had inadvertently become a circus act, a famous personality and a villain to boot. His misery was further compounded when some reporters posed as businessmen, offered him millions for some minimal work and secretly taped his responses in the hope of getting him to do or say something incriminating. It really shook Grant that people could go to such lengths of entrapment, and for what? After that he became quite paranoid. He was even reluctant to use a public toilet for fear that a reporter would follow him in and comment publicly on his physical attributes. Bizarre.

The articles about his business life were cleverly written, suggesting much but stating very little of substance. I'm the first to admit that Grant has sometimes sailed close to the wind, like a lot of entrepreneurs, but these pieces would never even have been written or worth writing had it not been for his connection with me. After spending £50,000 on legal advice with the intent to sue over claims in two of the articles, we decided not to waste any more money. We'd already lost too many days' work and several nights' sleep over them.

By and large, I try never to rise to the bait and take legal action, but I did threaten to sue the *News of the World* for a report which claimed I'd walked into Peter McHugh's GMTV office in tears complaining that the early mornings were ruining my looks and demanding plastic surgery. The article appeared under the headline 'Anthea to Have Face Op'. The whole idea was completely ludicrous and there wasn't even the tiniest grain of truth in it. *GMTV* was so careful with its budgets that Lorraine Kelly and I used to joke that if we snagged our tights on the coffee table we wouldn't get a new pair. You had to beg for a new lipstick. So the very suggestion that *GMTV* might pay for me to have a facelift was inconceivable and insulting. It was a vile story which upset me greatly, especially when I knew that some of the behind-the-scenes staff were working for peanuts, which

was why in that instance I decided to act. The newspaper compen-
sated me and I gave the money to charity.

My contract with *Wish You Were Here* was due to finish in June
1999. ITV already knew that I didn't like being away from home so
much, and Pete had made it plain to them that January that another
two years were not an option. It was never truly the job for me and
on top of that my stint with the programme had coincided with my
two most difficult years on the personal front. The films were good –
I didn't let down myself or anyone else on the job – but I became
increasingly homesick as I boarded plane after plane and stayed in
one hotel room after another. I knew that another two years of it
would have killed me and finished off my relationship with Grant.
Pete and I knew we had both gone wrong by spending too much
time apart, and I wasn't going to make the same mistake again. It was
time for a complete reappraisal. I was approaching forty, I wanted to
spend time with Grant and it was a perfect opportunity to take a
breather.

My last assignment for *Wish You Were Here* was the best of all – a
visit to a dude ranch in Texas. I pushed for it and the programme-
makers agreed as a way of saying thank you and wishing me well. It
was my dream to be a cowboy for a week, to help with the cattle
round-up and have a cook-up in the evenings. I even got to ride off
into the sunset. On my very last day of filming, I stood on a rock the
locals called the 'Church' and gazed across the valley to the Loma de
Blanca ranch far below. It was a spine-tingling moment, watching the
sun go down and realising that, for the first time in years, I had no
firm commitments and no contracts signed. There'd be nothing to
prove to anyone for a while. I could almost taste the freedom.

For the previous seven years, I'd worked virtually 365 days a year.
I'd given absolutely everything to my career. Along the way, I'd presented five of the biggest names in television: *Top of the Pops*, *Blue
Peter*, *GMTV*, *National Lottery Live* and *Wish You Were Here*. Most
people in the industry would be happy to have worked on just one of
them, and I've been lucky enough to have done the lot. But I didn't
want to get to sixty and find myself miserable and alone with only

my old videotapes for company. The looming fortieth birthday prompted me to think about what I really wanted out of my life, and right now, that's for Grant and me to be happy and together. I want to make this relationship work and I feel as if I've been given another chance at happiness. Which makes it all the more important for me to stop for a while and enjoy the part of my life that I've denied myself for so long.

Quite recently I came across an old Chinese proverb which runs: 'You have not lived as a woman unless you've been loved, hated, envied and talked about.' It made me laugh out loud to think I'd finally qualified for womanhood.

Epilogue

On 30 March 1999, Grant and I found ourselves in Mauritius, at a beautiful hotel overlooking the Indian Ocean. We ordered breakfast in our room and sat on the balcony, looking out at the view and feeling incredibly calm. It was Grant's birthday and I gave him his present – membership of a polo club he was desperate to join – along with his cards and presents from the girls, who'd entrusted them to me.

'Actually, Anthea, I've got something for you,' he said, getting to his feet and going into the bedroom to open his suitcase. He returned with a tiny bag with the word 'Tiffany' embossed on it.

Jumping up, I opened the bag and peered inside. Nestling at the bottom was a small leather box. Speechless, I looked up at Grant. Reaching in and retrieving the box, he suddenly dropped to one knee and held my hand. Tears welled in my eyes and in his. 'I love you more than anything else in the world, Anthea,' he said. 'I want to be with you for ever and a day. Will you marry me?'

Throwing my arms around him and kissing him over and over, I told him: 'Yes, yes.'

Two months later, on my fortieth birthday, Grant gave me another present. Blindfolding me and leading me outside, he whistled a signal to someone and I heard the sound of an engine firing up. Opening my eyes, I watched open-mouthed as a huge cardboard box in the driveway burst open and out flew my father's old 1938 MG, the one I'd vowed to track down. Grant and Dad had traced it through the MG Owners' Club, bought it back and had it restored, and now it was mine. It was the most thoughtful of gifts and I was overwhelmed with gratitude.

I know that I have changed beyond recognition. For much of my life I had everything and yet I had nothing. I was successful profession-ally, but deep down, I was unhappy. After a while, I began to accept my unhappiness, to believe that it was part and parcel of my success. 'Hey, you can't have everything,' I'd tell myself. Living with my man-ager, sharing my private life with the one person I'd always been trying to impress, didn't help. I became driven. I focused more on my professional life than on my private life, which always took second place. I turned into a control freak, evinced by everything from my colour-coded personal organiser to my fear of allowing myself to drink the occasional glass of wine in case I let the carefully packaged mask slip.

When the explosion came and my private and professional life was turned upside down it was in many ways a release. With time on my hands, and no one asking on a daily basis for a slice of me, I discov-ered how to relax, how to do things for me. I didn't have to get up at 6.30 every morning and work out in the gym, or stay in the office until late because I felt guilty if I didn't. I could lie in, read the papers, enjoy a good book, cook a meal or do anything I chose to. It gave me a whole new perspective and made me realise for the first time that there is more to life than professional success. I know now that I don't have to prove anything to anyone other than myself and those who have put their faith in me.

Of course, I still love my career; I still crave success and want to remain the woman I've become in television terms. I like to think that viewers relate to me because I'm like them: I live an average life, I love my job, I'm close to my family. I'm just normal, and that's how I come across. But the difference now is that if I never appeared on television again it wouldn't be the end of the world because of the happiness I have found with Grant. The new millennium saw us on a much firmer footing, having made a total commitment to each other for the rest of our lives. That decision is absolute and irrevocable as far as I'm concerned. We sleep together, wake together, eat together, go riding together and spend a lot of time laughing. We're often incredibly silly – Grant brings out the fun side in me. I can't ever remember laughing this often before. Pete and I had both a professional and a personal relationship and we did have a lot of fun, but not in the same way. It was much more serious. He was nine years older than me, and I think that was also a factor.

Grant can be a most wonderfully witty and charming person. He certainly bowls over everyone who meets him, including my parents and most of my friends. My mum and dad have grown terribly fond of him and have now embraced him as part of the family. People we meet who expect to dislike him tell me afterwards: 'Now we understand.' But in any event I honestly don't care what anyone else thinks any more; I'm past all that. I just feel incredibly lucky to have found my soulmate, someone I have no intention of letting go.

We've made some very important decisions about our lives and our careers which have had a tremendously calming effect on us both and on our relationship. By putting work on hold for a while, we were able to stand still while the rest of the world spun on without us. I would have stopped sooner – I was more than ready for a break from the merry-go-round – but Pete persuaded me to keep presenting *Wish You Were Here* until the very end, and I know that he was right to do so.

Pete and I still speak to each other regularly and I see him often for management meetings. We even travelled to Italy together recently for a friend's wedding. Our relationship has never really changed: it is still that of two dear friends who are incredibly fond of each other. I think it's a testament to our friendship that we've been able to remain so close, in spite of everything, and I still value his professional judgement above anyone else's. He remains my inspiration and my mentor in every way. On a personal level, I know that our break-up has been hugely damaging to him. I hurt him so much that he has never been able to consider remarrying, and hasn't even embarked on another serious relationship since. It tears me apart that Pete and Grant, the two men I love most in the world, can't be in the same room together, and although I know it is a great deal to ask, it is my fervent hope that one day this will be possible.

Pete and I still love each other very much and always will. We were just never meant to remain husband and wife, and he fully accepts that now. He keeps busy enough, and his life is full and rich. He is fantastically successful and has all the trappings that success brings: a wonderful home, a fast car, a beautiful office, a boat, and a ski lodge, to name but a few. He has some great friends, a kind and devoted family and is able to spend his spare time on his great passions, sailing and skiing.

Pete was right behind me in my decision to take a career break. He wanted nothing more than for me to be happy and to be able to lead a 'normal' life for a while. He agreed that I need some time and space to gain some distance from all that had happened. After an absence of a year, and with a new family show in the can, which I'm presenting with my sister Wendy, my hope is to return as an elder stateswoman of television, older and wiser, married to the man I love and – I pray – a different person in the eyes of the world. The offers I'm receiving now couldn't be more different from the type of television I did before. Producers and directors clearly regard me as a grown-up now. It looks like I'll be returning to the 'big girls' game', but this time it doesn't frighten me.

Grant, too, is entering a whole new phase. He claims I saved him from himself. He says he's learned a great deal from me about how to make the most of life. These are lessons I learned from my parents, who in turn learned them from Ruth. For many years Grant simply didn't enjoy his life; now he has completely restructured it and is no longer forced to feed the money-monster he'd created. He's involved with an exciting new internet company, for which he has raised millions of pounds in the City. Now, with the scandal behind us and the success of one of his other companies, he's suddenly considered a good investment again. He and Della are friendly once more, and are able to plan their children's future in a calm and relaxed way. She has a new home not far away with the children, who stay with us every other weekend, for one day during the week and half the school holidays. We've all had a chance to start anew, and the time has come to bury the past.

Mine has certainly been a remarkable life, the last ten years especially. It is astonishing that I have become who I am in such a short space of time. I did not join *Blue Peter* until 1992, and ten years ago nobody had even heard of me. Now women come up to me in the street and introduce me to their little Antheas, the daughters who have been named after me. But I have paid a price for that level of fame. It has not been an easy road, and in the last two years in particular, I went to hell and back for the crime of following my heart.

I've made some catastrophic mistakes and have done a lot of things I'm not proud of, but I have never deliberately inflicted pain on anyone. The fact that I unintentionally did just that to Pete and Della is something I will have to live with for the rest of my life. But I hope that, in time, they can both forgive me, and Grant, for what we did and accept that we did it out of frailty, not malice. I also hope that they will come to see that what we did was only the catalyst for the finale, not the reason our marriages fell apart in the first place. That sort of unhappiness goes back years.

I fell in love, that's my only defence. There are no winners and losers in the end. I don't consider that I won anything. It was never a game. This isn't *Blue Peter*, after all, it's the real world.

Grant and I were married during the last few days of August 2000, in a double ceremony that marked the most wonderful week of my life. With my parents and sister at my side, and Grant's children as flower girls, I walked down a red-carpeted aisle in a shimmering white wedding dress to meet the man I loved more than anything else in the world. It was the realisation of a dream. After all we'd been through in the previous two years, all the doubts and the pitfalls and the pain, we were pronounced man and wife as a gospel choir sang 'Hallelujah' and our friends and family threw rose petals at our feet. I shall never forget it as long as I live.

For months we had been inundated with requests from celebrity magazines to cover the wedding and we had agonised over whether or not to agree to any of them. We knew we'd be damned if we did and damned if we didn't, and that either way, we there would be the usual backlash. But on balance, and like so many others before us, we finally decided to accept the substantial amount of money on offer from *OK!* magazine. Instead of banking it and slipping away quietly to Venice or somewhere equally romantic, we decided to use it to pay for a reception of a lifetime for all our friends. Our one proviso was that a single wedding photograph be released to the media soon afterwards so that everyone could have a fair crack at the whip. We felt that was the decent thing to do.

When *OK!* offered to send us some free chocolate bars for the wedding, I thought it a bit strange, but it seemed a genuine enough gesture, and everyone knows how much I love chocolate, after all. Five hundred bars duly arrived at our Surrey home, and I asked the caterers to offer them to the wedding guests along with the coffee and other sweets I'd already arranged.

The wedding week was magical. First, Grant and I took our formal vows at Guildford Register Office with just two close friends at our side. We both cried so much we could hardly get the words out. Then we piled into a local pub for a celebratory meal. On the big day we had a second ceremony, followed by a fantastic party for 300 friends in the grounds of our new home. I spent the day in a happy bubble; not even the August rain could dampen my spirits. In front of all the people who mattered in our lives, Grant and I repeated our vows and promised to keep them. Again, I wept during the service, and so did he. It was such an emotionally charged day. We'd put a lot of effort into making it special for everyone and it really paid off. From the bower of pink roses under which we stood to the matching icing on the wedding cake, everything was just as I had dreamed it would be.

The *OK!* photographers covered every moment. Towards the end of the evening, just before we headed off to the dance floor, Grant and I were snapped eating two of the free chocolate bars. I should have been more alert; should have seen it coming. But it was my wedding day, I was in the company of friends and I just didn't think. With all good grace, we grinned inanely and posed for the cameras.

The party over, on the Sunday Grant and I flew off to the Ulusaba Game Reserve in South Africa for our honeymoon, looking forward to two glorious weeks of rest and relaxation. The *OK!* photographers accompanied us for the first day, as part of our agreement with the magazine, but after that we were to be left alone to enjoy our honeymoon. Meanwhile, as far as we were aware, a smiling photo of us on our wedding day was to be released to the press back home on the Monday morning.

The nightmare began with a long-distance telephone call early on the Tuesday from a close friend. 'Hi, Anthea,' he said. 'I'm afraid I've got some bad news . . .' It was worse than bad. It was disastrous. Completely without our knowledge or permission, and certainly without our blessing, the photograph chosen by *OK!* for release to the media, instead of the traditional wedding-day shot we'd expected, was the one of Grant and me posing with those chocolate bars at the reception. Worse still was the caption that *OK!* had insisted be used with it, which promoted the brand and announced that a bar was to be given away free with each copy of the magazine. The whole thing smacked of us selling our souls for sponsorship, which could not have been further from the truth. We'd never entered into any discussion or financial agreement with the chocolate company: our only link with them had been the box of confectionery they had sent for the reception. Indeed, the whole concept was absolutely abhorrent to us both. To say I was gutted would be a gross understatement. It just goes to show that even the most experienced of us can be lulled into a false sense of security and caught off guard.

My heart sank because I, of all people, knew what would follow – and sure enough, the papers didn't disappoint. The *Sun* ran the picture and story across its front page under the headline: 'SICKENER: ANTHEA'S WEDDING PHOTO IS SO, SO SAD'. The report read: 'This is the most sickening wedding photo ever, showing Anthea Turner and Grant Bovey plugging a new chocolate bar. The picture is the ONLY one released to newspapers by the greedy newlyweds.' The *Sun* went on to accuse us of 'such poor taste' and even quoted the agent Max Clifford as saying: 'It's sinking to new lows of tackiness.'

The other papers followed suit. Sue Carroll in the *Mirror* wrote, in an article headed 'Stomach Turner', 'I cringe at her greed for publicity and pity, her hunger for approbation of a union that's caused so much hurt.' Peter Oborne in the *Express* added: 'No one has yet discovered just how much [the company] paid the happy couple to advertise its latest chocolate bar in their wedding photo. But however much it was – and the sum was no doubt substantial – it was surely not worth it. In its squalid way, the Turner/Bovey wedding marks another low point in standards of taste and decency. As far as I am aware, it is the first time that a wedding celebration has actually been sponsored by a commercial organisation.' Even the *Daily Telegraph* reported the debacle, along with the accompanying picture.

For me at that point, the honeymoon felt as if it was over. The bubble had burst and what should have been the perfect end to the perfect week was in tatters. I couldn't even face leaving my room at the game reserve for a couple of days, my eyes were so puffy from crying. I've really been put through the mill by the media in my time, but I was more upset by what the media dubbed 'Flake Gate' than by almost anything else that had ever been written about me. It was all the more painful because I'd been duped into being complicit in my own downfall, and I couldn't believe I'd been so stupid as to walk into this one. I'd been so naïve, even after sixteen years in the business dodging the bullets. Even after Bruno and Eamonn and all the nasty tricks that had been played on me, I never saw it coming. And however much I told myself that the banner headlines would soon be tomorrow's chip paper, I couldn't help but feel cheated.

We released press statements, as did the magazine and the chocolate company, confirming our ignorance of the whole deal. I even did a live link with Lorraine Kelly on *GMTV* to explain what had happened. But nothing could get rid of the bad taste in my mouth. After realising how distressed I was, the magazine issued a public apology, but it was too late. However, I knew I couldn't let them win; I knew in my heart of hearts that one day, with my new husband by my side, I'd get over it and once again only have good memories of my wedding day, which is exactly what happened after a while. The letters and best wishes from those who attended our wedding helped enormously. They made me realise that it really was a very special day not only for Grant and me, but for everyone who was there, and I that I would feed on the memory of it for ever. And of course the fiasco which followed was soon forgotten by those who'd stirred it all up, and – in time – by Grant and myself. We even booked a second honeymoon to make up for the traumatic start to our first. Thanks to him, and to the love and support of our friends and family, I can now look at the photographs of my wedding day and smile.

They say that fools rush in where angels fear to tread, and that is certainly the case with me, in love, in my work and in most aspects of my life. From my earliest days – dealing with Ruth's death, my dis- astrous relationship with Bruno, my marriage, my time at *GMTV* and my divorce – I suppose I've always been led by my heart, not my head. Perhaps the greatest folly of this particular fool is to still believe in happy endings. But I do.